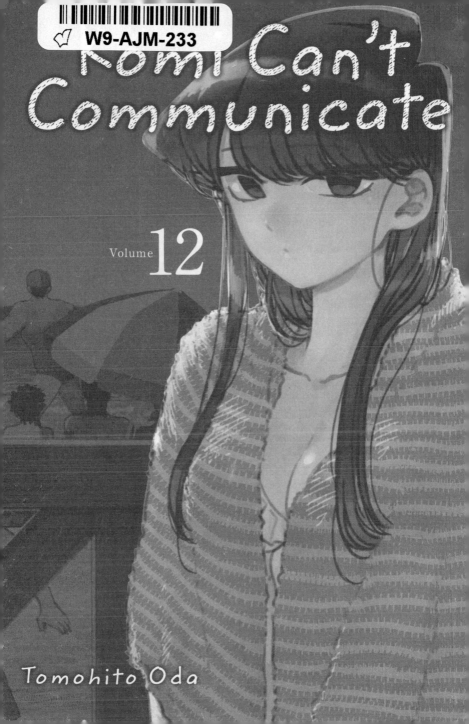

Komi Can't Communicate

Volume 12

Tomohito Oda

Contents

Komi Can't Communicate

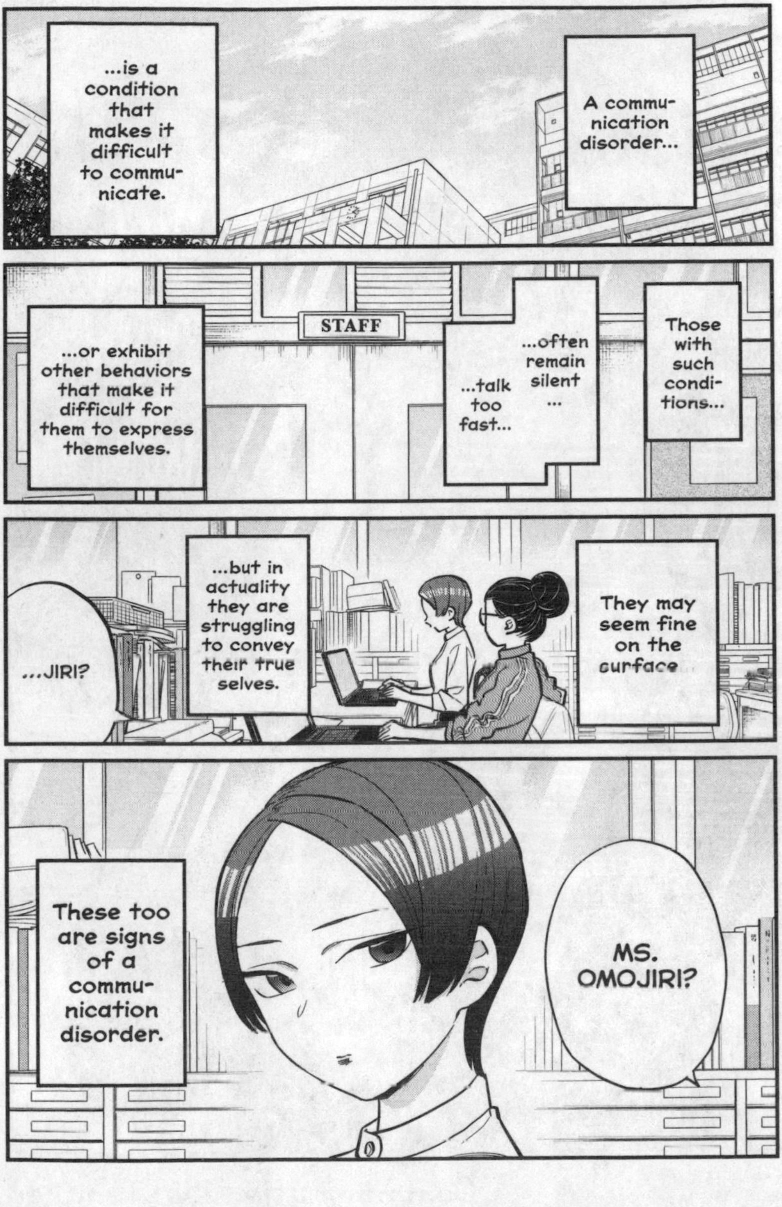
A communication disorder...
...is a condition that makes it difficult to communicate.
Those with such conditions...
...often remain silent...
...talk too fast...
STAFF
...or exhibit other behaviors that make it difficult for them to express themselves.
They may seem fine on the surface...
...but in actuality they are struggling to convey their true selves.
...JIRI?
MS. OMOJIRI?
These too are signs of a communication disorder.

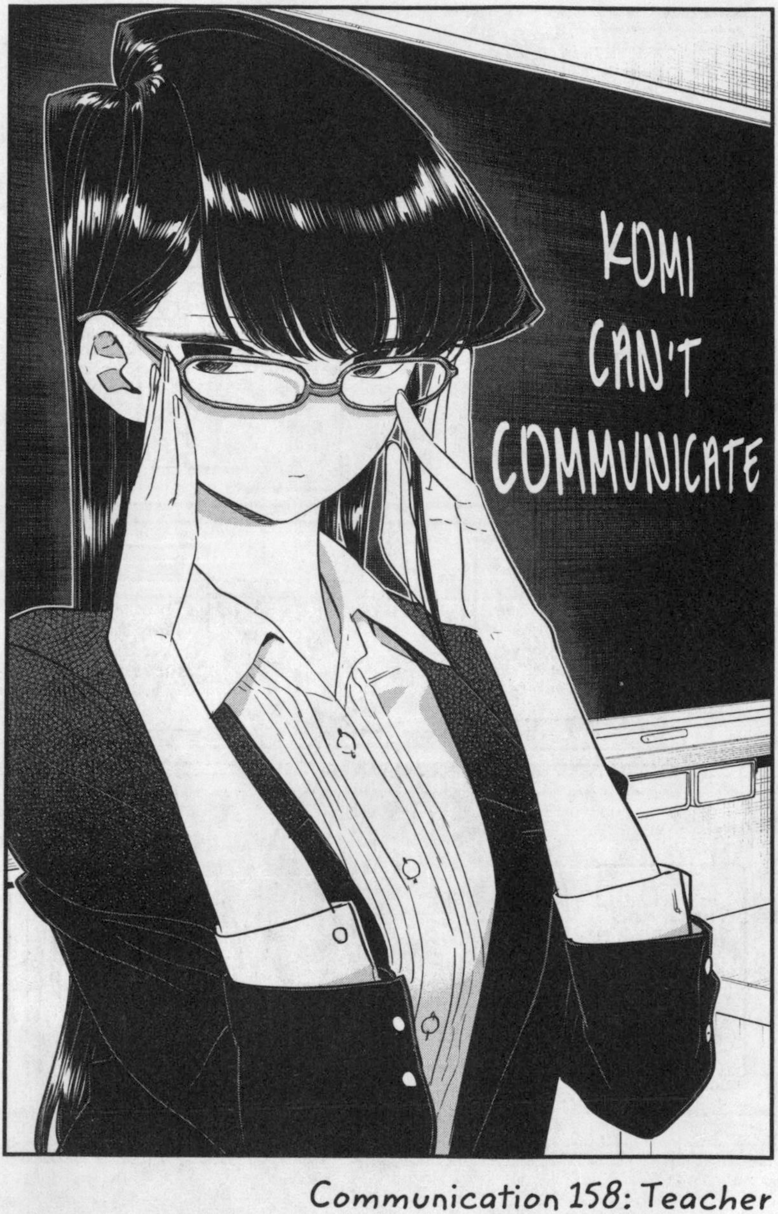
KOMI CAN'T COMMUNICATE

Communication 158: Teacher

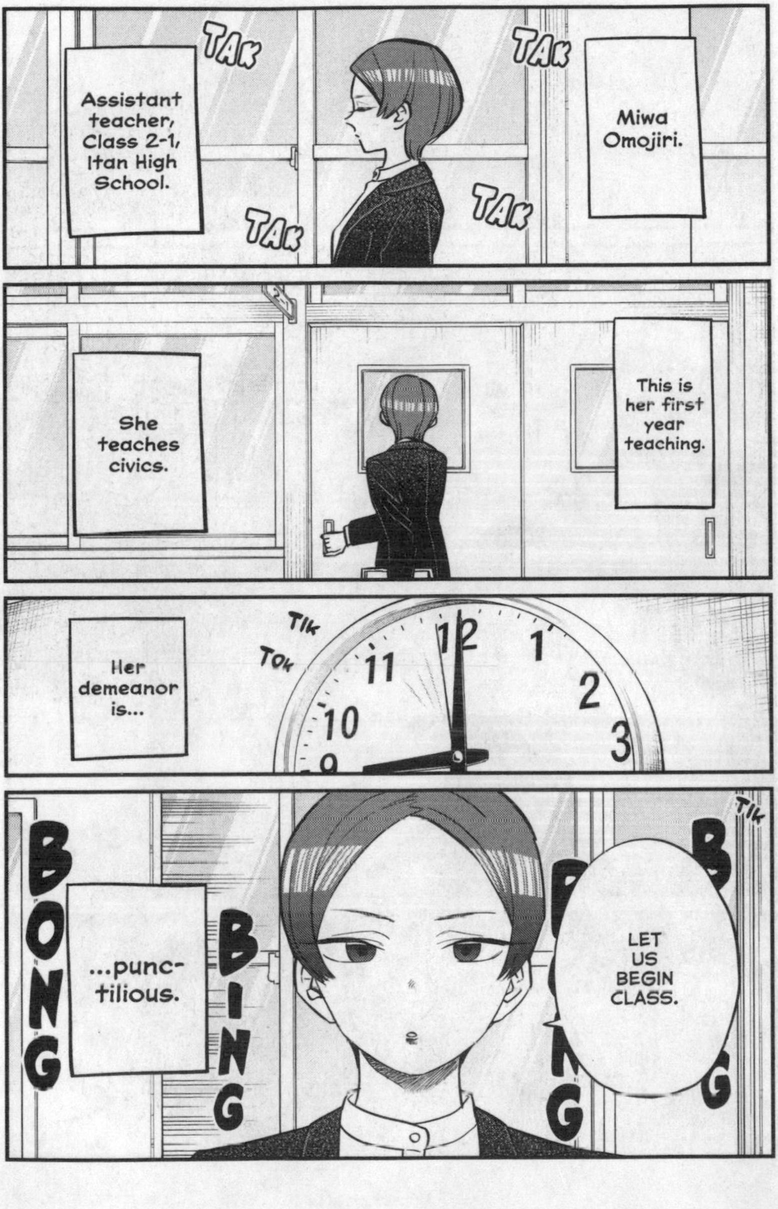
TAK
Miwa Omojiri.
TAK
TAK
Assistant teacher, Class 2-1, Itan High School.
TAK
This is her first year teaching.
She teaches civics.
TIK
TOK
Her demeanor is...
TIK
BONG
BING
LET US BEGIN CLASS.
BING
...punc-tilious.
BONG

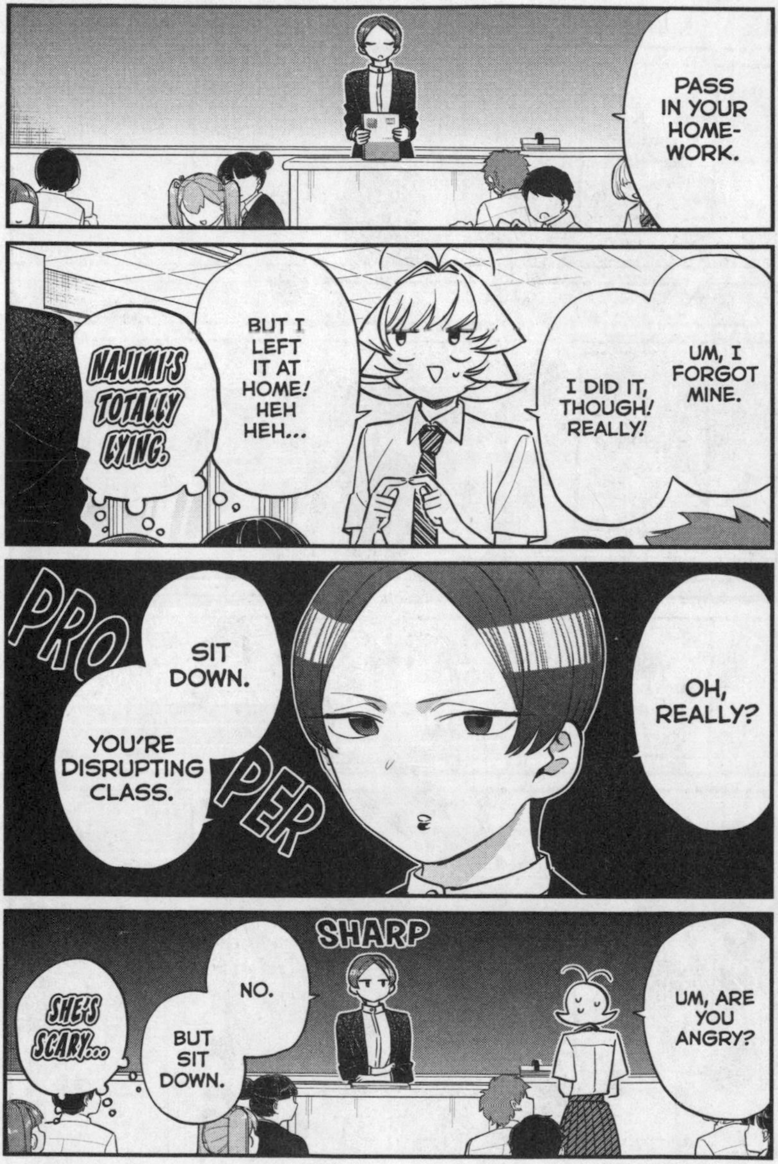
PASS IN YOUR HOME-WORK.
UM, I FORGOT MINE.
I DID IT, THOUGH! REALLY!
BUT I LEFT IT AT HOME! HEH HEH...
NAJIMI'S TOTALLY LYING.
OH, REALLY?
PROPER
SIT DOWN.
YOU'RE DISRUPTING CLASS.
UM, ARE YOU ANGRY?
SHARP
NO.
BUT SIT DOWN.
SHE'S SCARY...

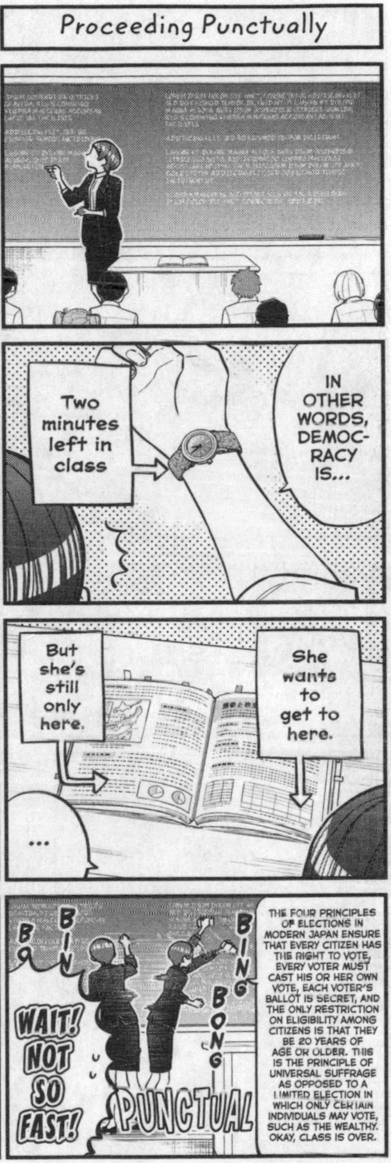
Proceeding Punctually
IN OTHER WORDS, DEMOCRACY IS...
Two minutes left in class
She wants to get to here.
But she's still only here.
...
THE FOUR PRINCIPLES OF ELECTIONS IN MODERN JAPAN ENSURE THAT EVERY CITIZEN HAS THE RIGHT TO VOTE, EVERY VOTER MUST CAST HIS OR HER OWN VOTE, EACH VOTER'S BALLOT IS SECRET, AND THE ONLY RESTRICTION ON ELIGIBILITY AMONG CITIZENS IS THAT THEY BE 20 YEARS OF AGE OR OLDER. THIS IS THE PRINCIPLE OF UNIVERSAL SUFFRAGE AS OPPOSED TO A LIMITED ELECTION IN WHICH ONLY CERTAIN INDIVIDUALS MAY VOTE, SUCH AS THE WEALTHY. OKAY, CLASS IS OVER.
BING BONG
BIN BA
WAIT! NOT SO FAST!
PUNCTUAL

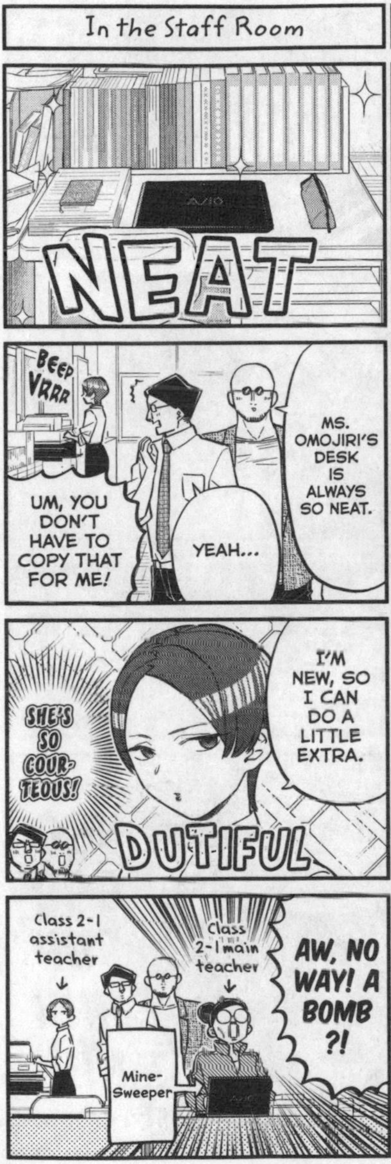
In the Staff Room
NEAT
MS. OMOJIRI'S DESK IS ALWAYS SO NEAT.
BEEP VRRR
YEAH...
UM, YOU DON'T HAVE TO COPY THAT FOR ME!
I'M NEW, SO I CAN DO A LITTLE EXTRA.
SHE'S SO COURTEOUS!
DUTIFUL
AW, NO WAY! A BOMB?!
Class 2-1 main teacher
Class 2-1 assistant teacher
Mine-Sweeper

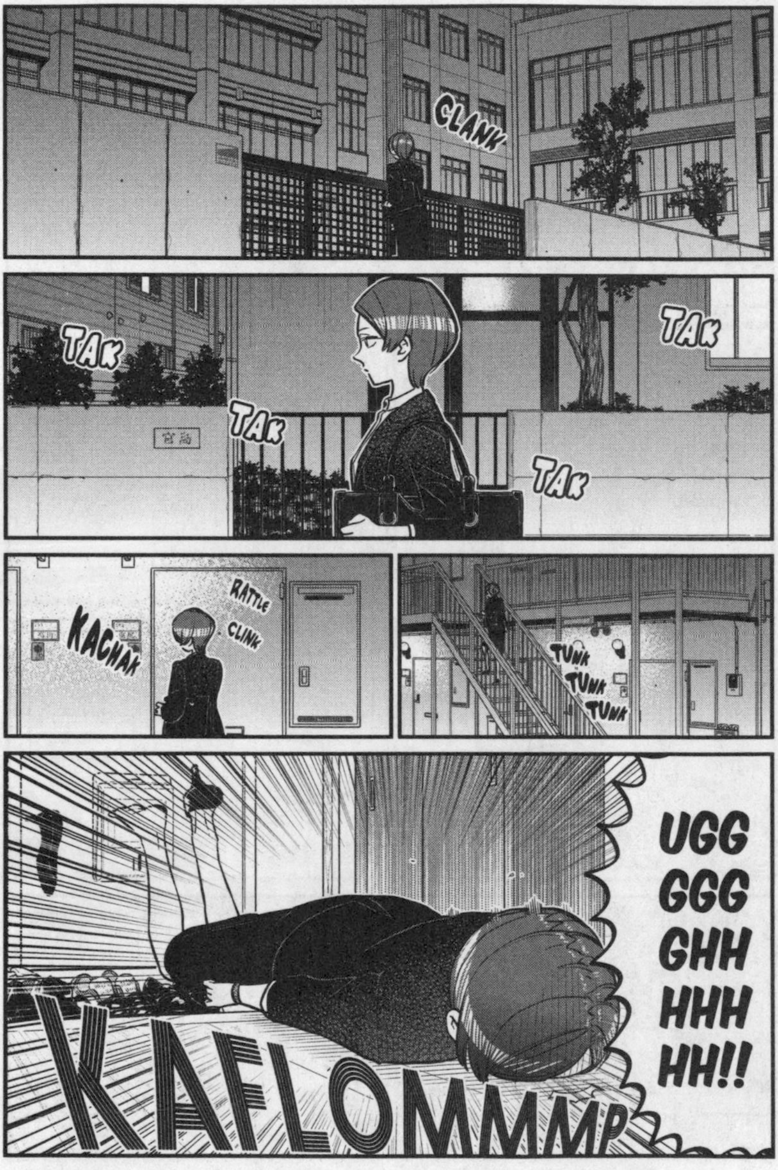

CLANK
TAK
TAK
TAK
TAK
TUNK
TUNK
TUNK
RATTLE
CLINK
KACHAK
UGGGGGGHHHHHHHH!!
KAFLOMMMP

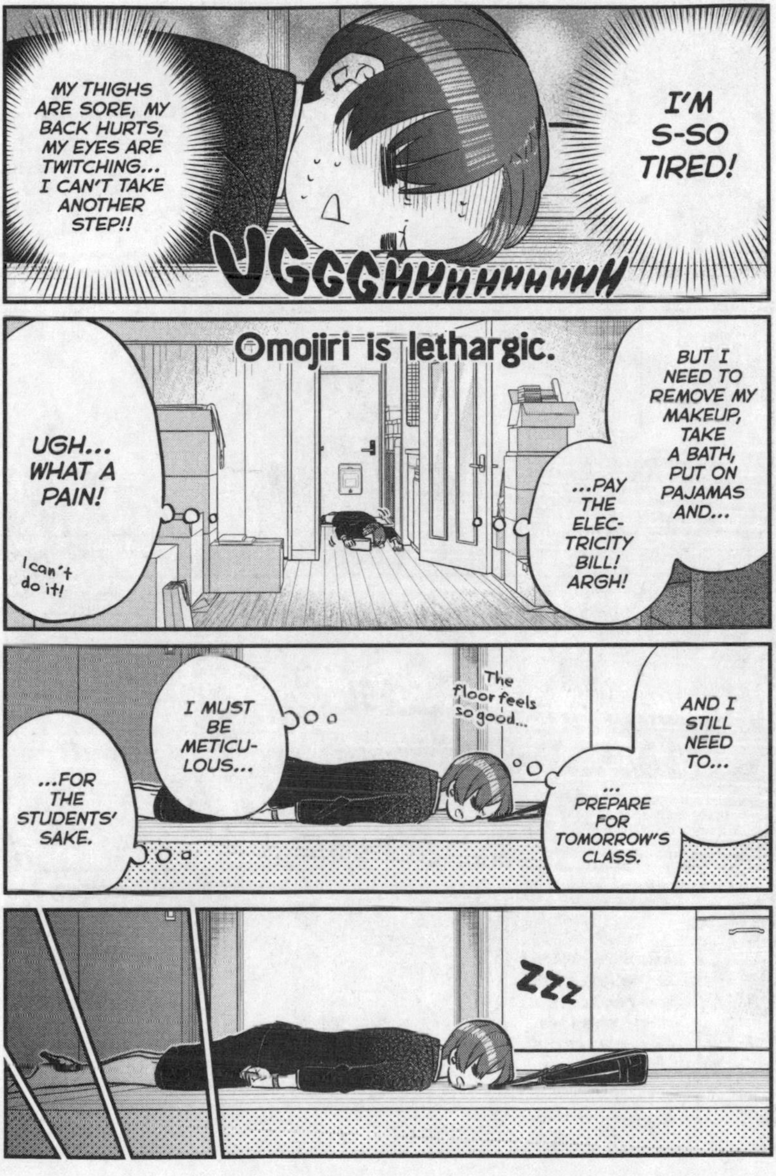
I'M S-SO TIRED!
MY THIGHS ARE SORE, MY BACK HURTS, MY EYES ARE TWITCHING... I CAN'T TAKE ANOTHER STEP!!
UGGGHHHHHHHHH
Omojiri is lethargic.
BUT I NEED TO REMOVE MY MAKEUP, TAKE A BATH, PUT ON PAJAMAS AND...
...PAY THE ELEC-TRICITY BILL! ARGH!
UGH... WHAT A PAIN!
I can't do it!
AND I STILL NEED TO...
... PREPARE FOR TOMORROW'S CLASS.
The floor feels so good...
I MUST BE METICU-LOUS...
...FOR THE STUDENTS' SAKE.
ZZZ

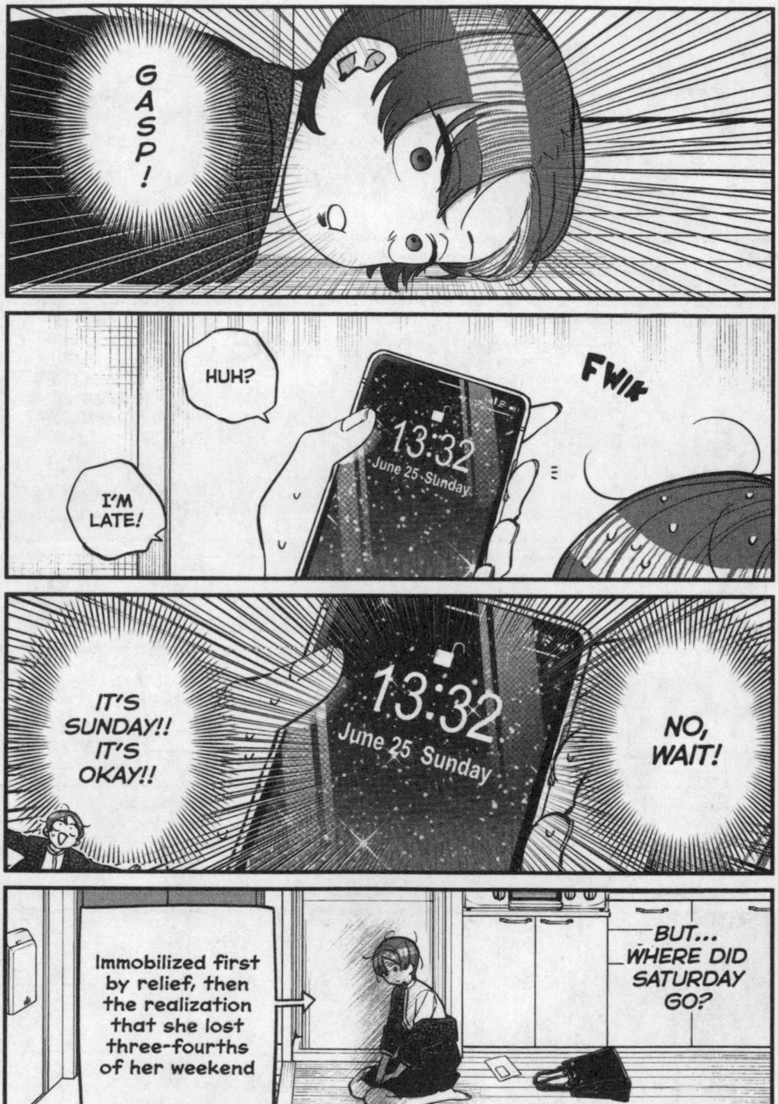
GASP!
FWIP
HUH?
13:32
June 25 Sunday
I'M LATE!
NO, WAIT!
13:32
June 25 Sunday
IT'S SUNDAY!! IT'S OKAY!!
BUT... WHERE DID SATURDAY GO?
Immobilized first by relief, then the realization that she lost three-fourths of her weekend

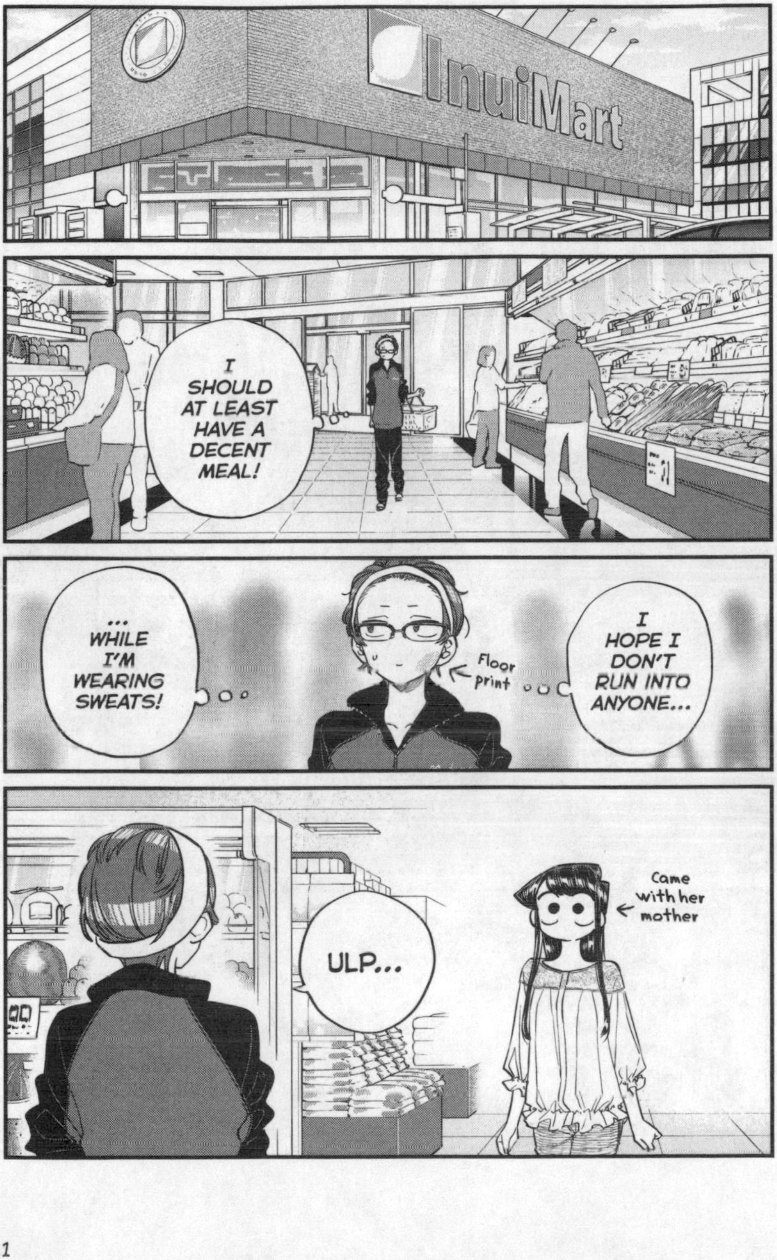
InuiMart
I SHOULD AT LEAST HAVE A DECENT MEAL!
I HOPE I DON'T RUN INTO ANYONE...
Floor print
...WHILE I'M WEARING SWEATS!
Came with her mother
ULP...

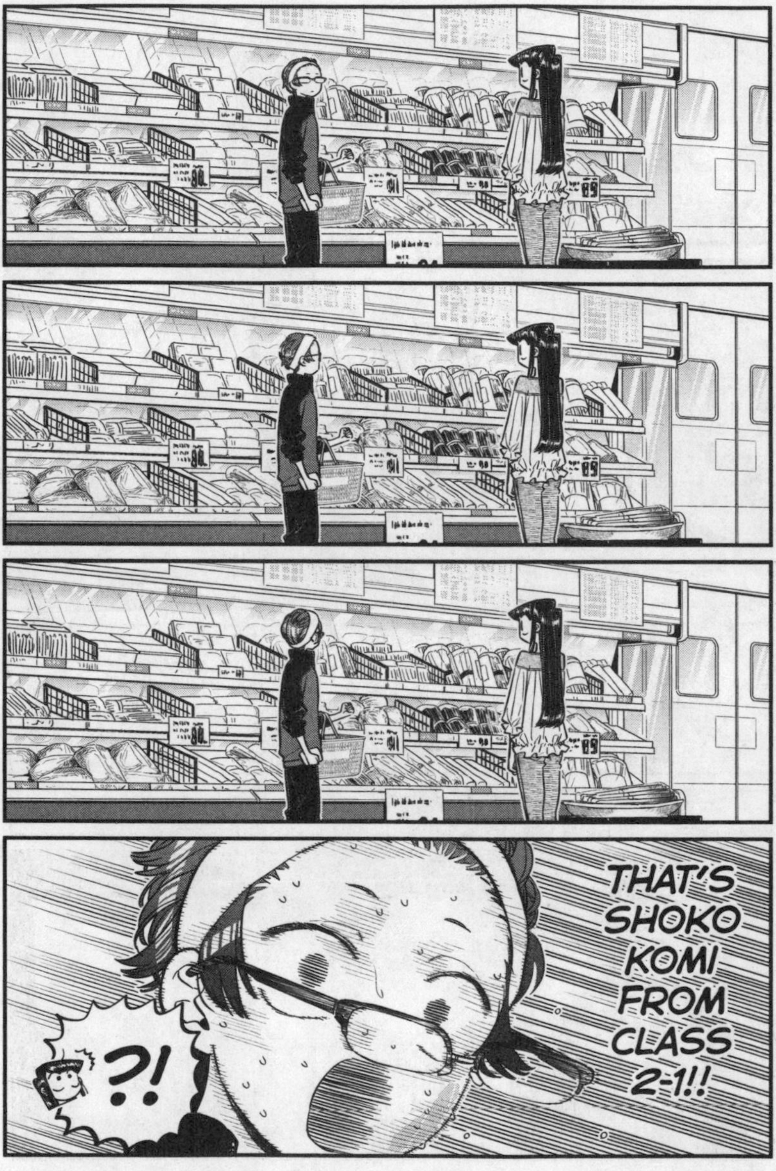
THAT'S SHOKO KOMI FROM CLASS 2-1!!
?!

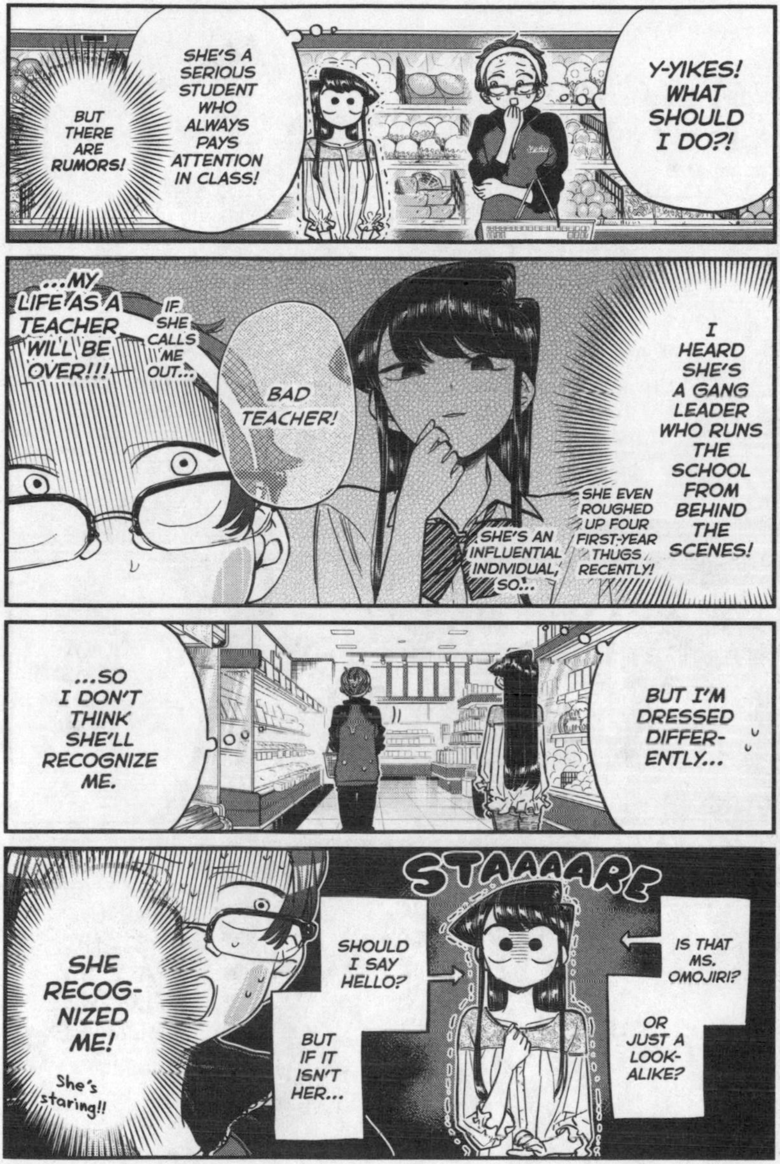
Y-YIKES! WHAT SHOULD I DO?!
SHE'S A SERIOUS STUDENT WHO ALWAYS PAYS ATTENTION IN CLASS!
BUT THERE ARE RUMORS!
I HEARD SHE'S A GANG LEADER WHO RUNS THE SCHOOL FROM BEHIND THE SCENES!
SHE EVEN ROUGHED UP FOUR FIRST-YEAR THUGS RECENTLY!
SHE'S AN INFLUENTIAL INDIVIDUAL, SO...
BAD TEACHER!
IF SHE CALLS ME OUT...
...MY LIFE AS A TEACHER WILL BE OVER!!!
BUT I'M DRESSED DIFFER-ENTLY...
...SO I DON'T THINK SHE'LL RECOGNIZE ME.
STAAAARE
IS THAT MS. OMOJIRI?
OR JUST A LOOK-ALIKE?
SHOULD I SAY HELLO?
BUT IF IT ISN'T HER...
SHE RECOG-NIZED ME!
She's staring!!

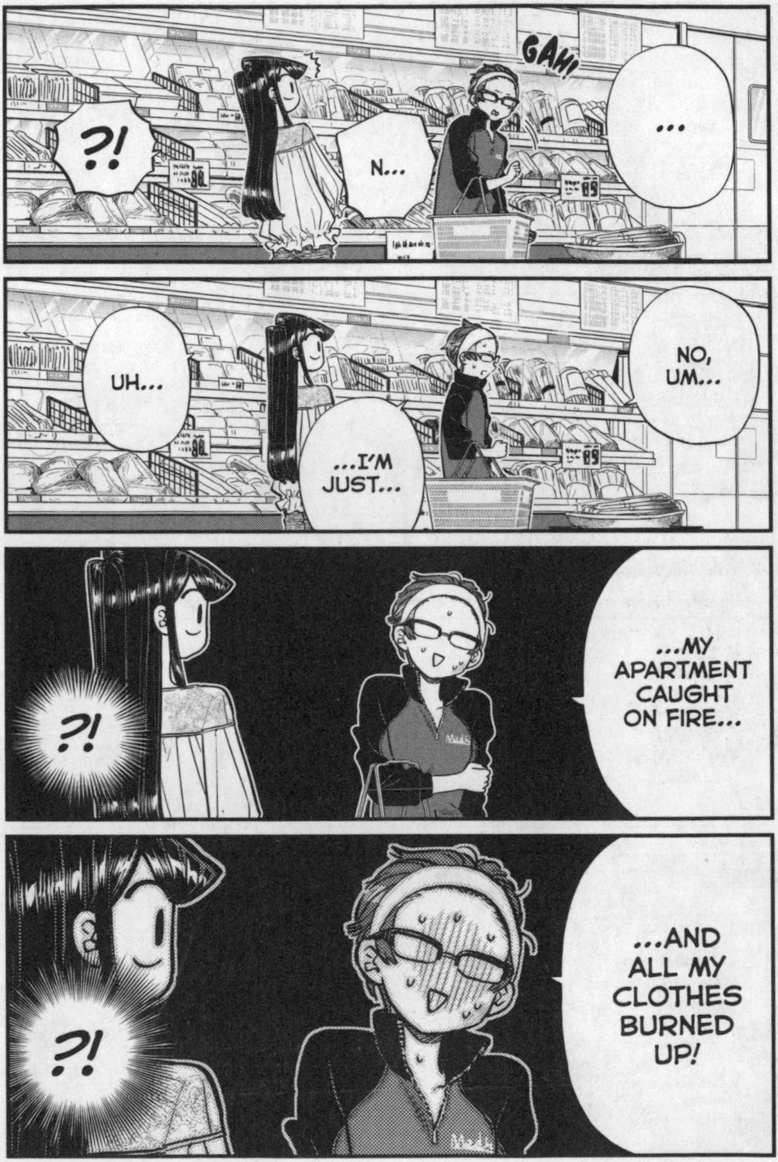
...
GAH!
N...
?!
NO, UM...
...I'M JUST...
UH...
...MY APARTMENT CAUGHT ON FIRE...
?!
...AND ALL MY CLOTHES BURNED UP!
?!

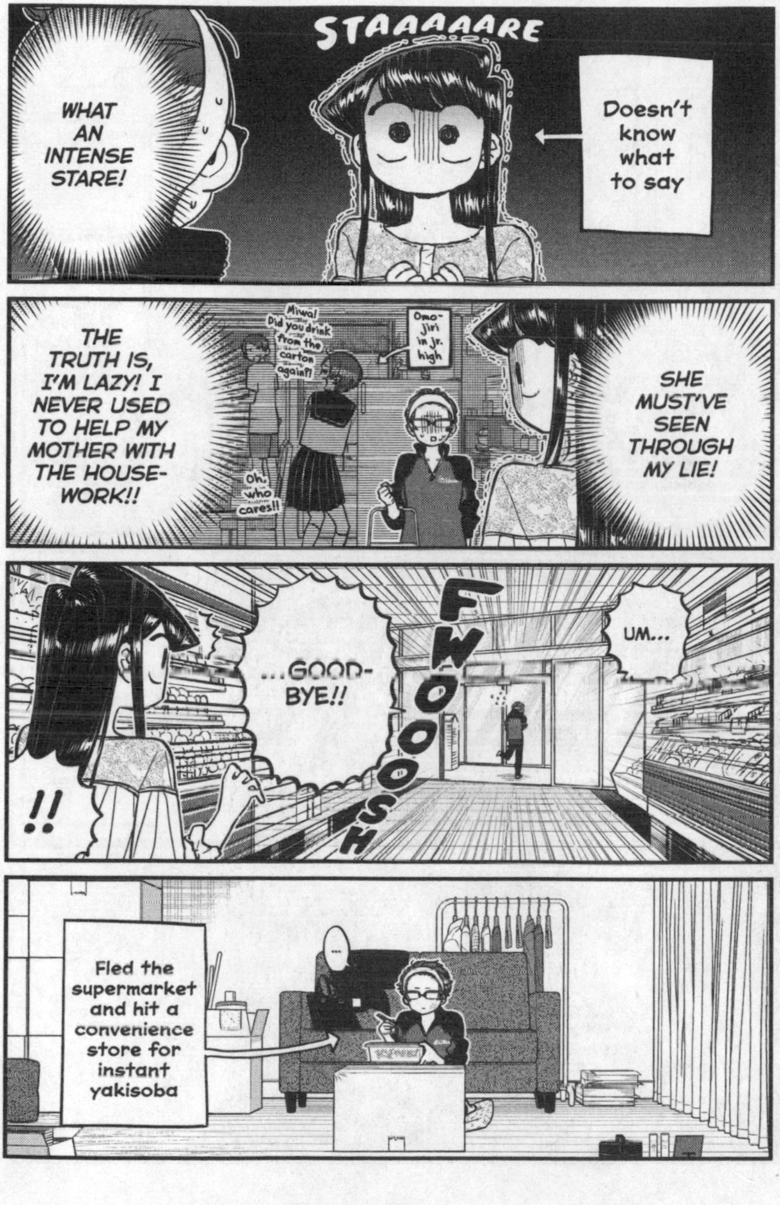
STAAAAARE
Doesn't know what to say
WHAT AN INTENSE STARE!
SHE MUST'VE SEEN THROUGH MY LIE!
Omo-jiri in jr. high
Miwa! Did you drink from the carton again?!
THE TRUTH IS, I'M LAZY! I NEVER USED TO HELP MY MOTHER WITH THE HOUSE-WORK!!
Oh, who cares!!
UM...
FWOOOOSH
...GOOD-BYE!!
!!
...
Fled the supermarket and hit a convenience store for instant yakisoba

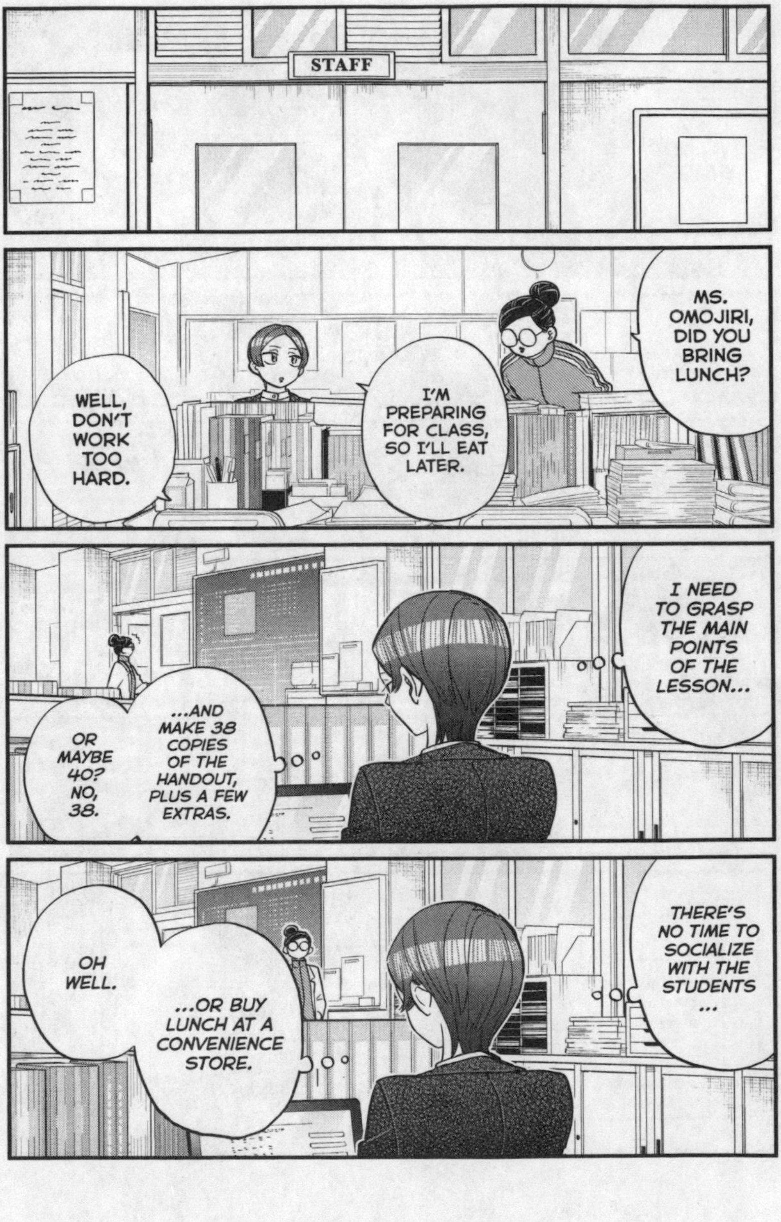
STAFF
MS. OMOJIRI, DID YOU BRING LUNCH?
I'M PREPARING FOR CLASS, SO I'LL EAT LATER.
WELL, DON'T WORK TOO HARD.
I NEED TO GRASP THE MAIN POINTS OF THE LESSON...
...AND MAKE 38 COPIES OF THE HANDOUT, PLUS A FEW EXTRAS.
OR MAYBE 40? NO, 38.
THERE'S NO TIME TO SOCIALIZE WITH THE STUDENTS ...
...OR BUY LUNCH AT A CONVENIENCE STORE.
OH WELL.

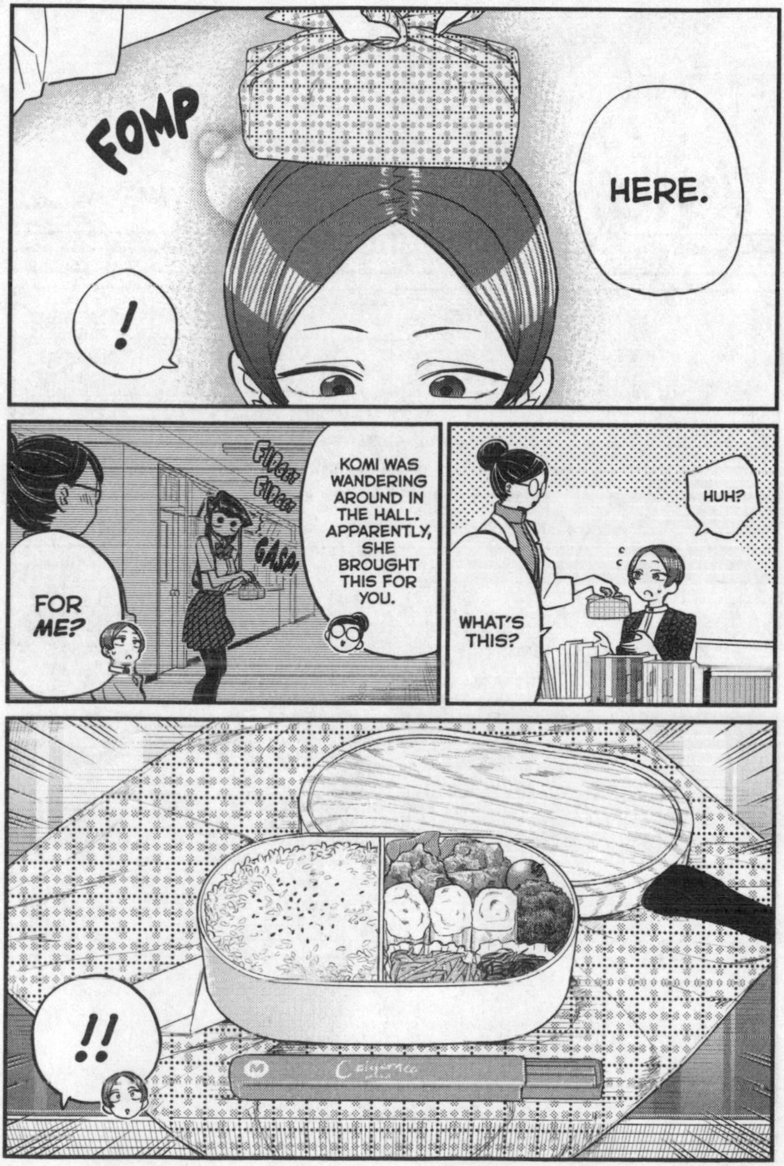
HERE.
FOMP
!
HUH?
WHAT'S THIS?
KOMI WAS WANDERING AROUND IN THE HALL. APPARENTLY, SHE BROUGHT THIS FOR YOU.
FIDGET FIDGET
GASP!
FOR *ME*?
!!

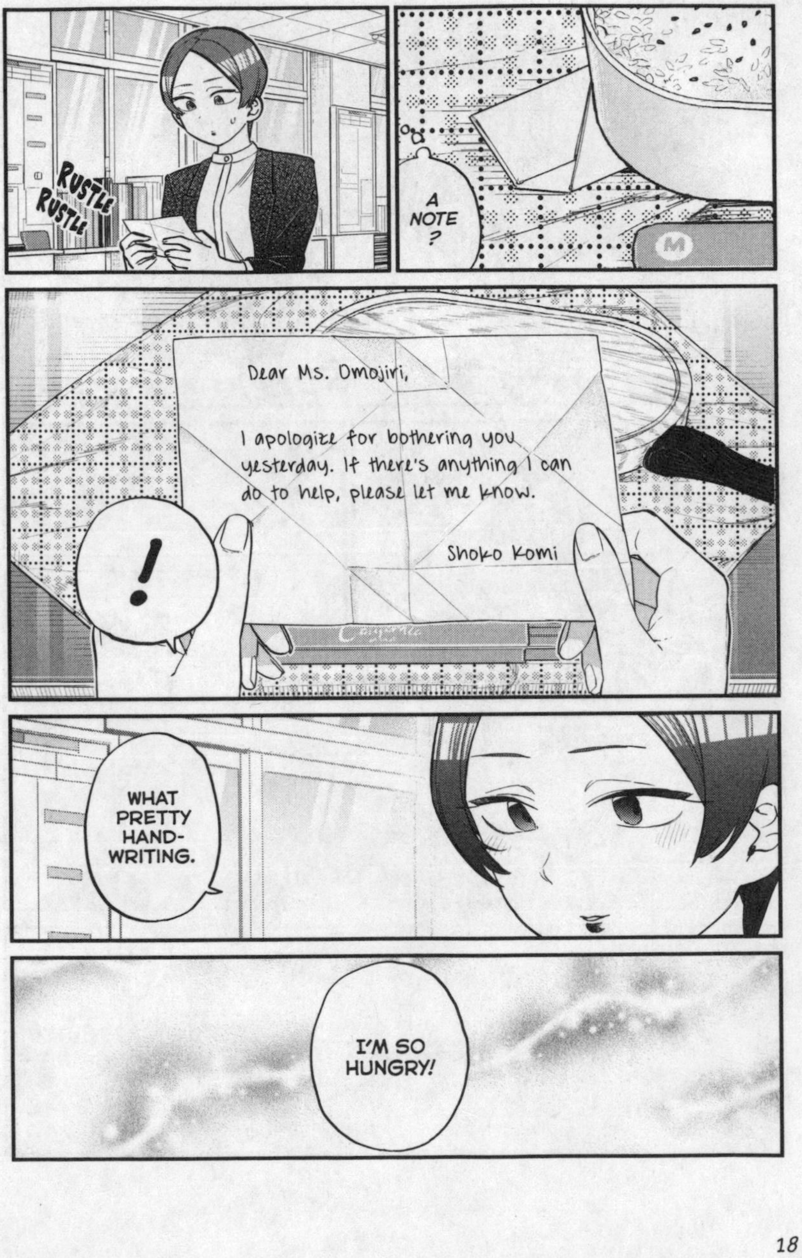
A NOTE ?
RUSTLE RUSTLE
Dear Ms. Omojiri,
I apologize for bothering you yesterday. If there's anything I can do to help, please let me know.
Shoko Komi
!
WHAT PRETTY HAND-WRITING.
I'M SO HUNGRY!

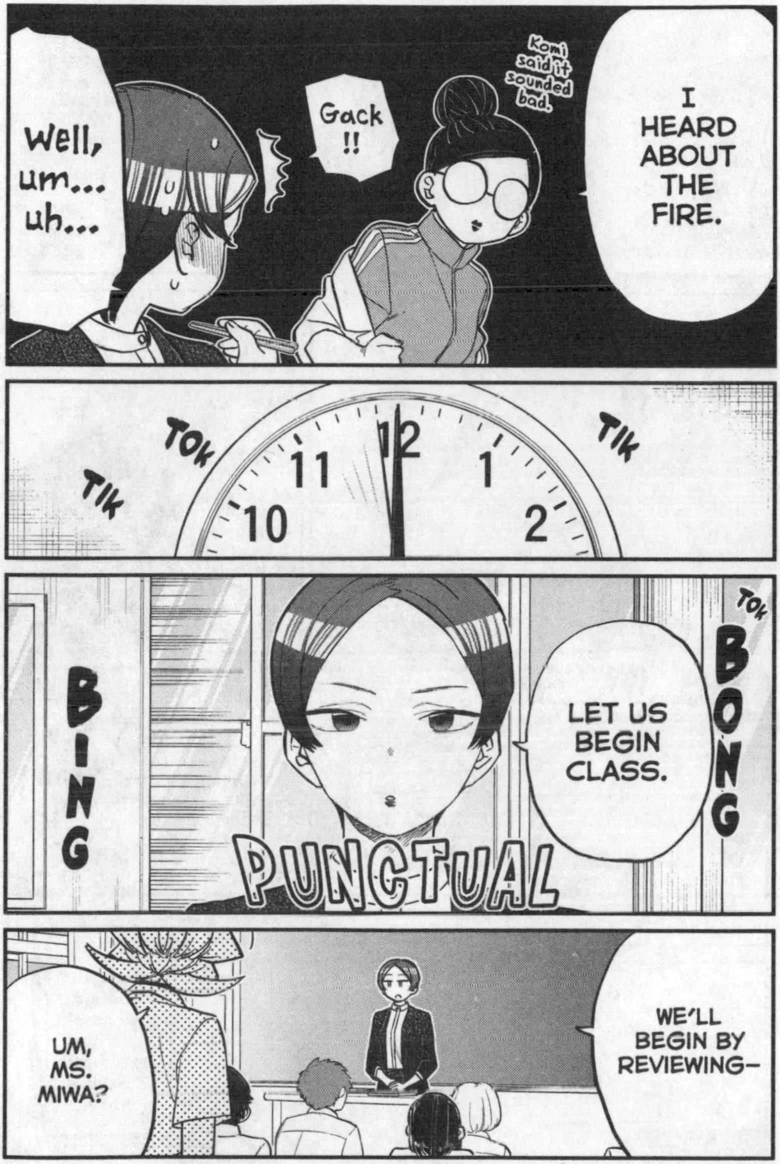
I HEARD ABOUT THE FIRE.
Komi said it sounded bad.
Gack!!
Well, um... uh...
TIK
TOK
TIK
TOK
BONG
LET US BEGIN CLASS.
PUNCTUAL
BING
WE'LL BEGIN BY REVIEWING—
UM, MS. MIWA?

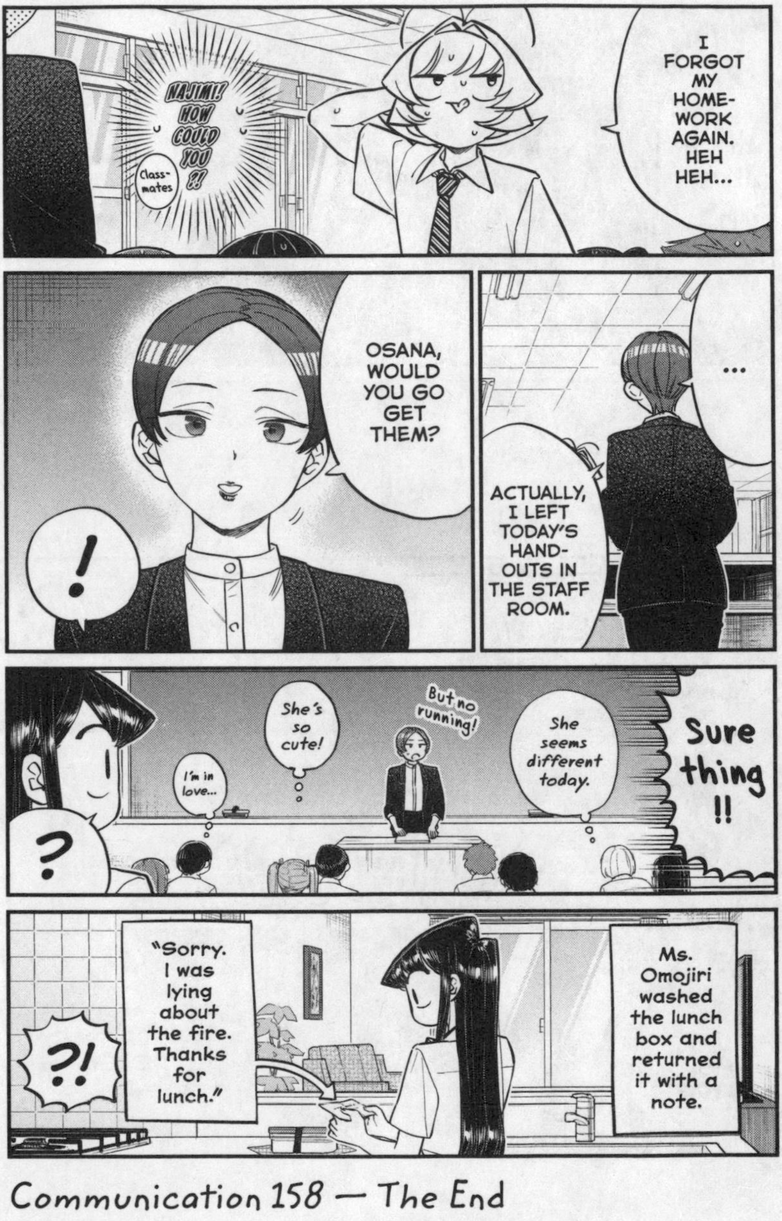
I FORGOT MY HOMEWORK AGAIN. HEH HEH...
NAJIMI! HOW COULD YOU?!
Class-mates
...
ACTUALLY, I LEFT TODAY'S HAND-OUTS IN THE STAFF ROOM.
OSANA, WOULD YOU GO GET THEM?
!
Sure thing!!
She seems different today.
But no running!
She's so cute!
I'm in love...
?
Ms. Omojiri washed the lunch box and returned it with a note.
"Sorry. I was lying about the fire. Thanks for lunch."
?!

Communication 158 — The End

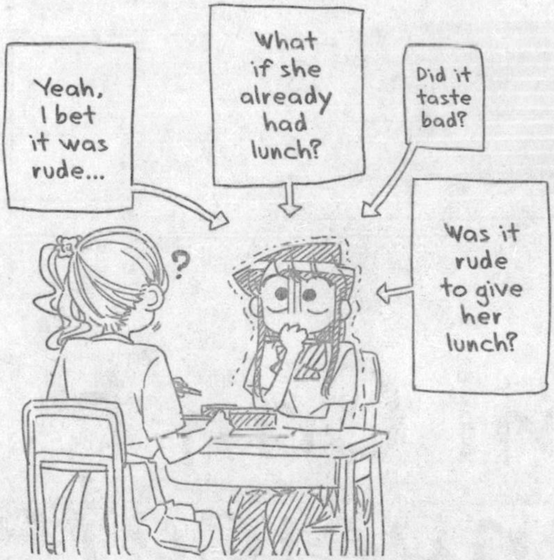
Did it taste bad?
What if she already had lunch?
Was it rude to give her lunch?
Yeah, I bet it was rude...
?

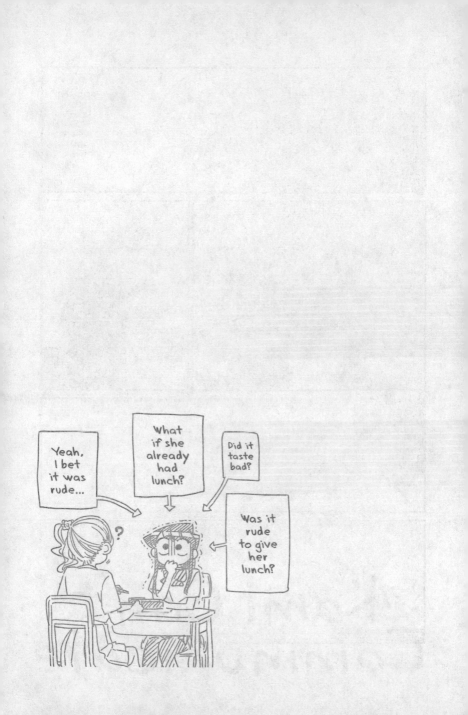

Komi Can't
Communicate

Komi Can't Communicate

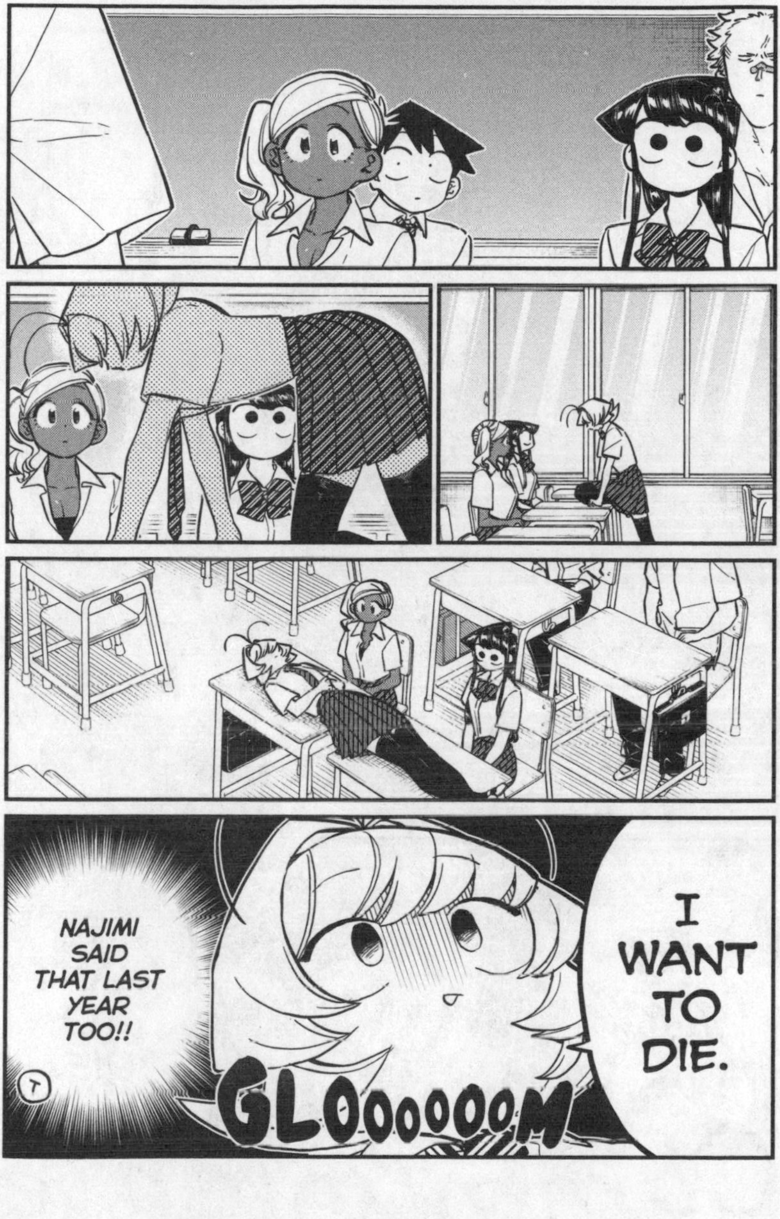
I WANT TO DIE.
NAJIMI SAID THAT LAST YEAR TOO!!
GLOOOOOOM

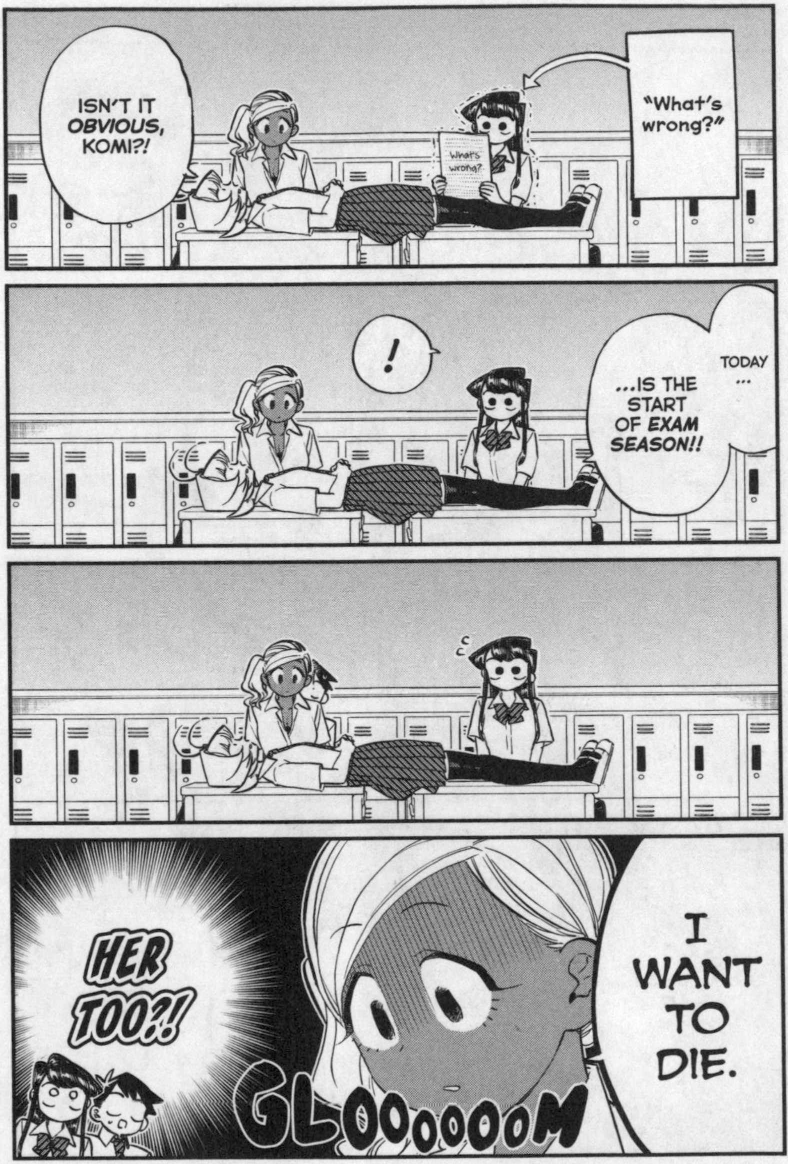
"What's wrong?"
What's wrong?
ISN'T IT OBVIOUS, KOMI?!
TODAY ...
...IS THE START OF EXAM SEASON!!
!
I WANT TO DIE.
GLOOOOOOM
HER TOO?!

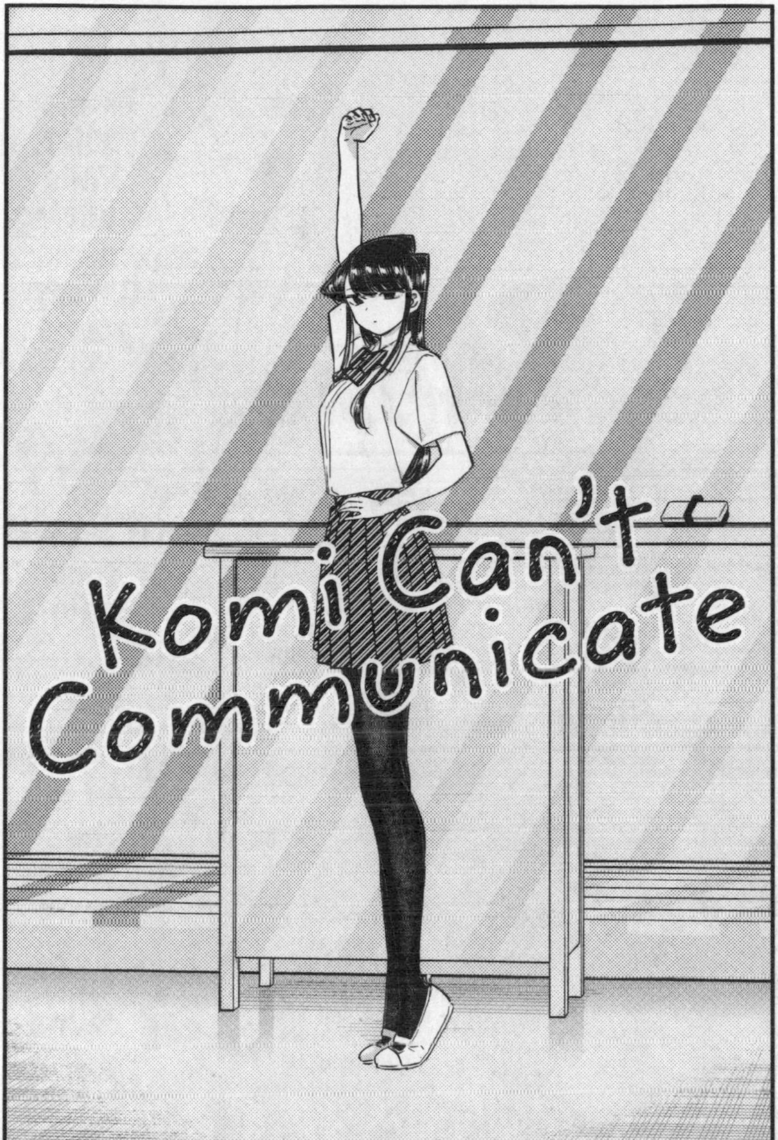
Komi Can't Communicate

Communication 159: Quiet While Studying in the Library, Round 4

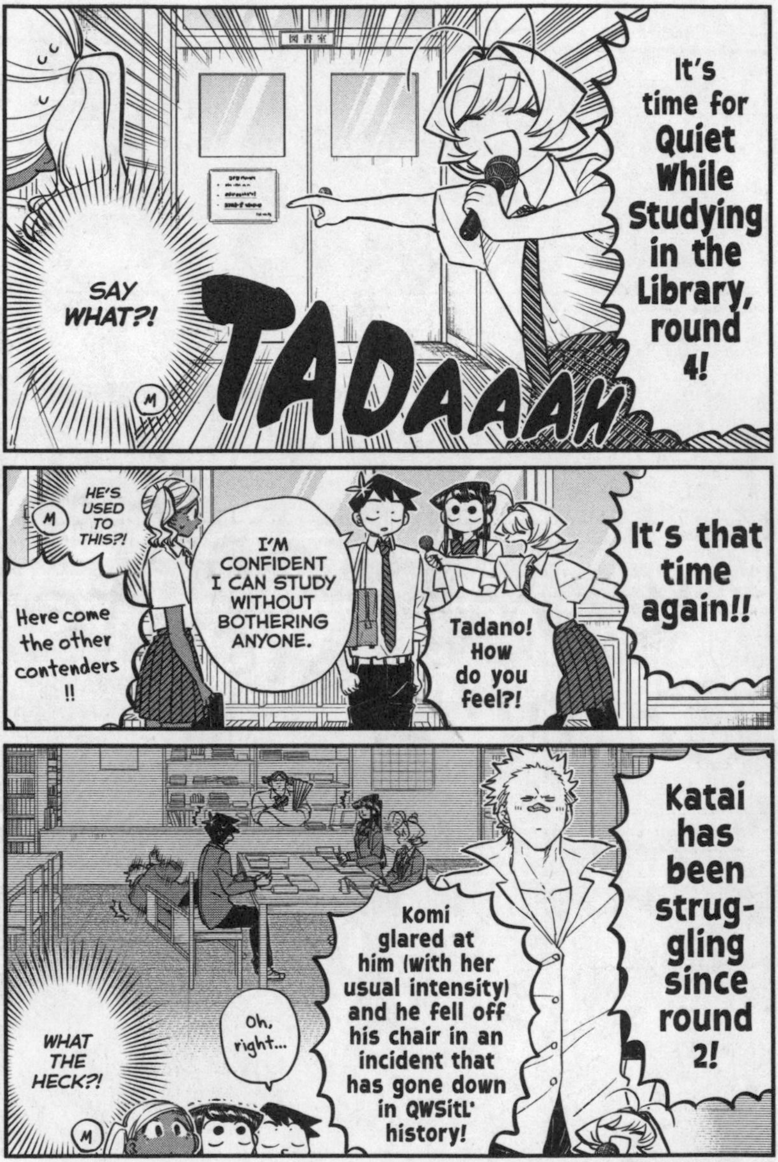
It's time for Quiet While Studying in the Library, round 4!
TADAAAH
SAY WHAT?!
M
It's that time again!!
Tadano! How do you feel?!
I'M CONFIDENT I CAN STUDY WITHOUT BOTHERING ANYONE.
HE'S USED TO THIS?!
M
Here come the other contenders!!
Katai has been strug-gling since round 2!
Komi glared at him (with her usual intensity) and he fell off his chair in an incident that has gone down in QWSitL* history!
Oh, right...
WHAT THE HECK?!
M

* QWSITL = QUIET WHILE STUDYING IN THE LIBRARY

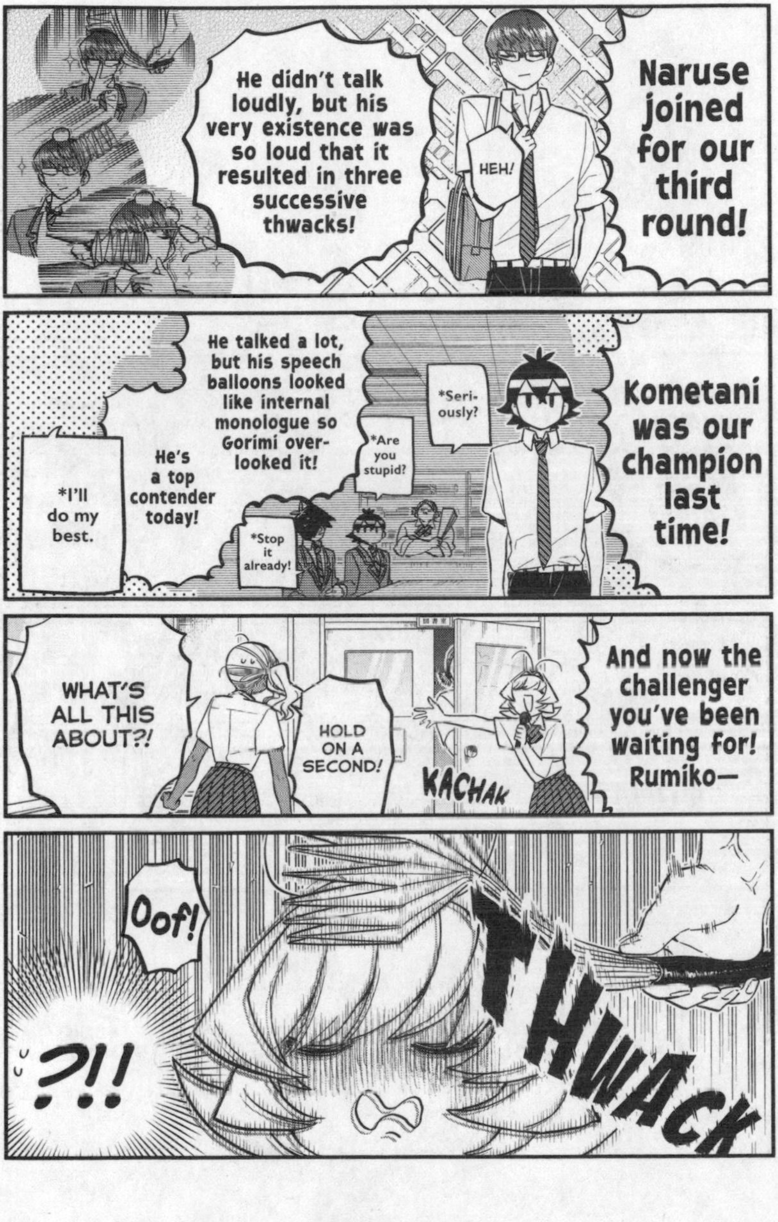
Naruse joined for our third round!
HEH!
He didn't talk loudly, but his very existence was so loud that it resulted in three successive thwacks!
Kometani was our champion last time!
*Seriously?
He talked a lot, but his speech balloons looked like internal monologue so Gorimi over-looked it!
*Are you stupid?
*Stop it already!
He's a top contender today!
*I'll do my best.
And now the challenger you've been waiting for! Rumiko—
KACHAK
HOLD ON A SECOND!
WHAT'S ALL THIS ABOUT?!
THWACK
Oof!
?!!

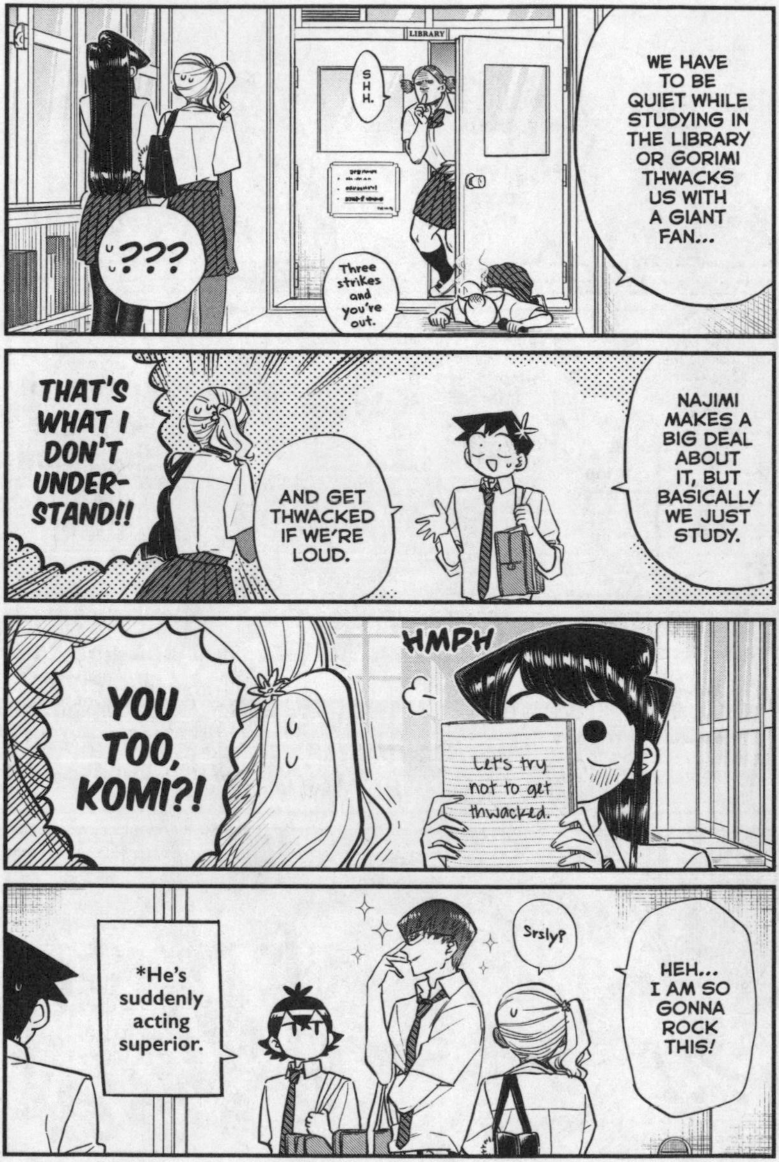
WE HAVE TO BE QUIET WHILE STUDYING IN THE LIBRARY OR GORIMI THWACKS US WITH A GIANT FAN...
LIBRARY
SHH.
Three strikes and you're out.
???
NAJIMI MAKES A BIG DEAL ABOUT IT, BUT BASICALLY WE JUST STUDY.
AND GET THWACKED IF WE'RE LOUD.
THAT'S WHAT I DON'T UNDER-STAND!!
HMPH
Let's try not to get thwacked.
YOU TOO, KOMI?!
HEH... I AM SO GONNA ROCK THIS!
Srsly?
*He's suddenly acting superior.

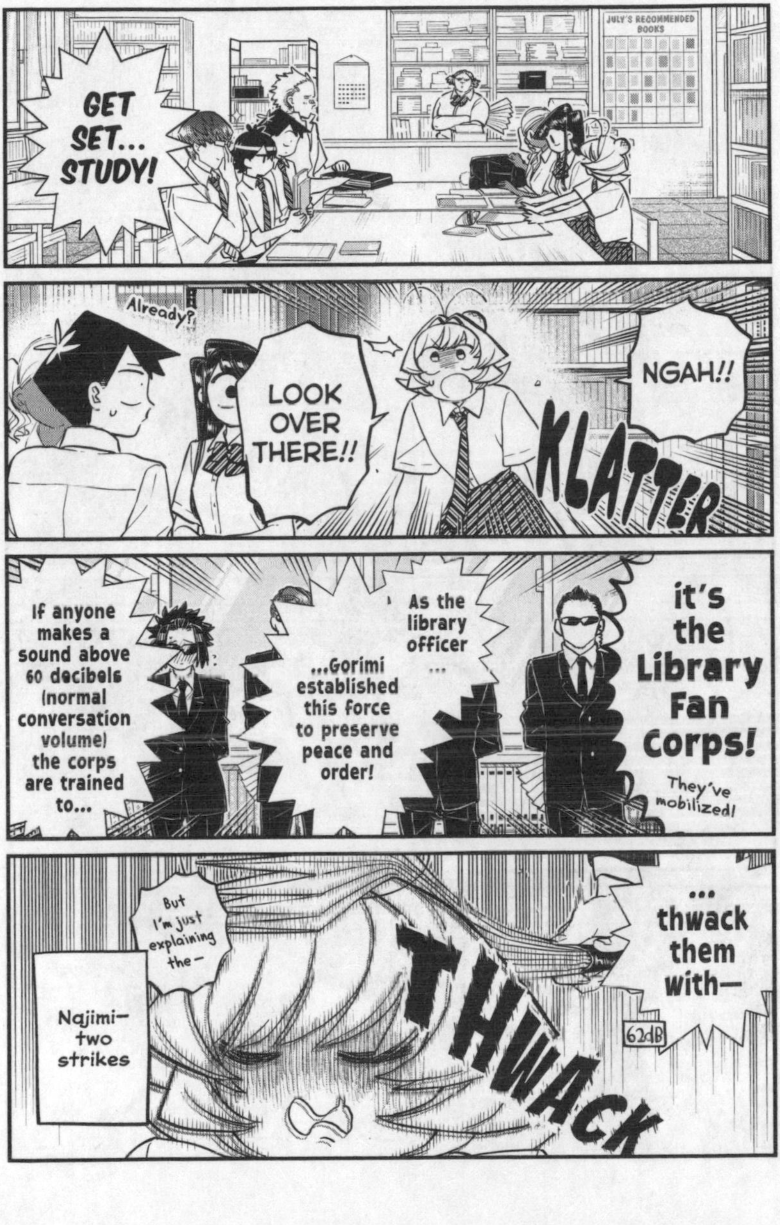
JULY'S RECOMMENDED BOOKS
GET SET... STUDY!
NGAH!!
KLATTER
LOOK OVER THERE!!
Already?
it's the Library Fan Corps!
They've mobilized!
As the library officer...
...Gorimi established this force to preserve peace and order!
If anyone makes a sound above 60 decibels (normal conversation volume) the corps are trained to...
...thwack them with—
THWACK
62dB
But I'm just explaining the—
Najimi—two strikes

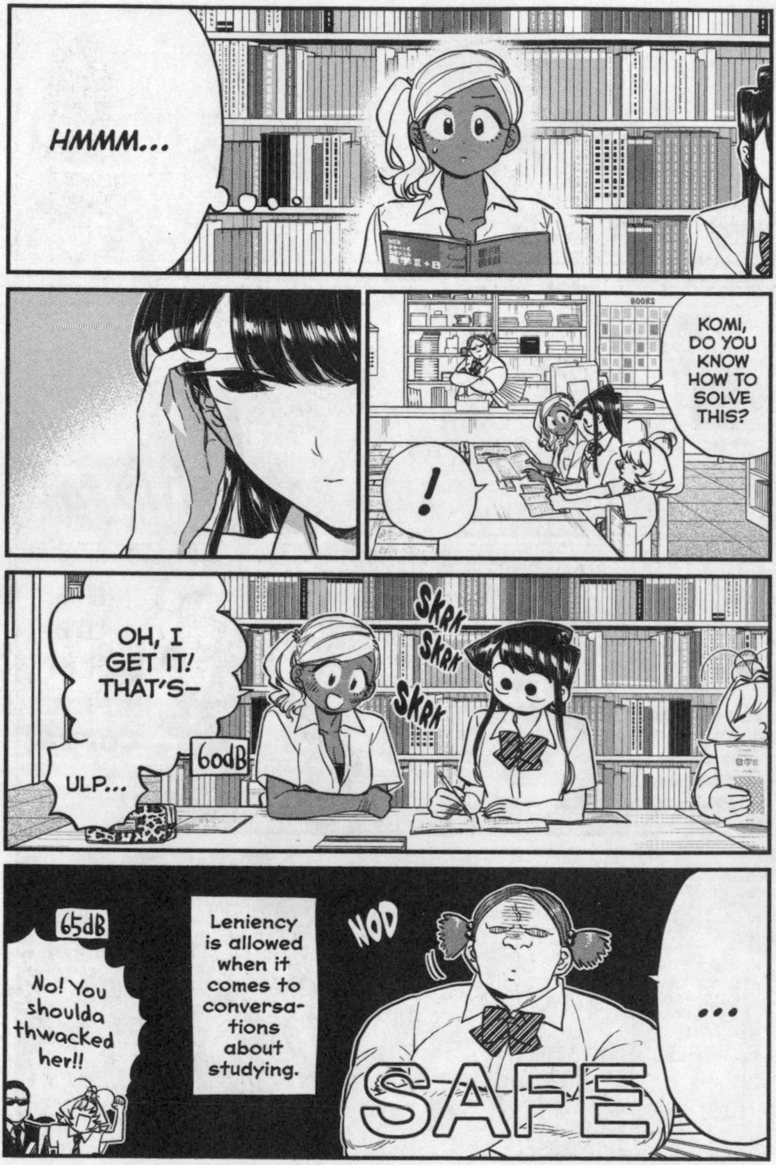
HMMM...
KOMI, DO YOU KNOW HOW TO SOLVE THIS?
!
SKRK SKRK SKRK
OH, I GET IT! THAT'S—
60dB
ULP...
...
SAFE
NOD
Leniency is allowed when it comes to conversations about studying.
65dB
No! You shoulda thwacked her!!

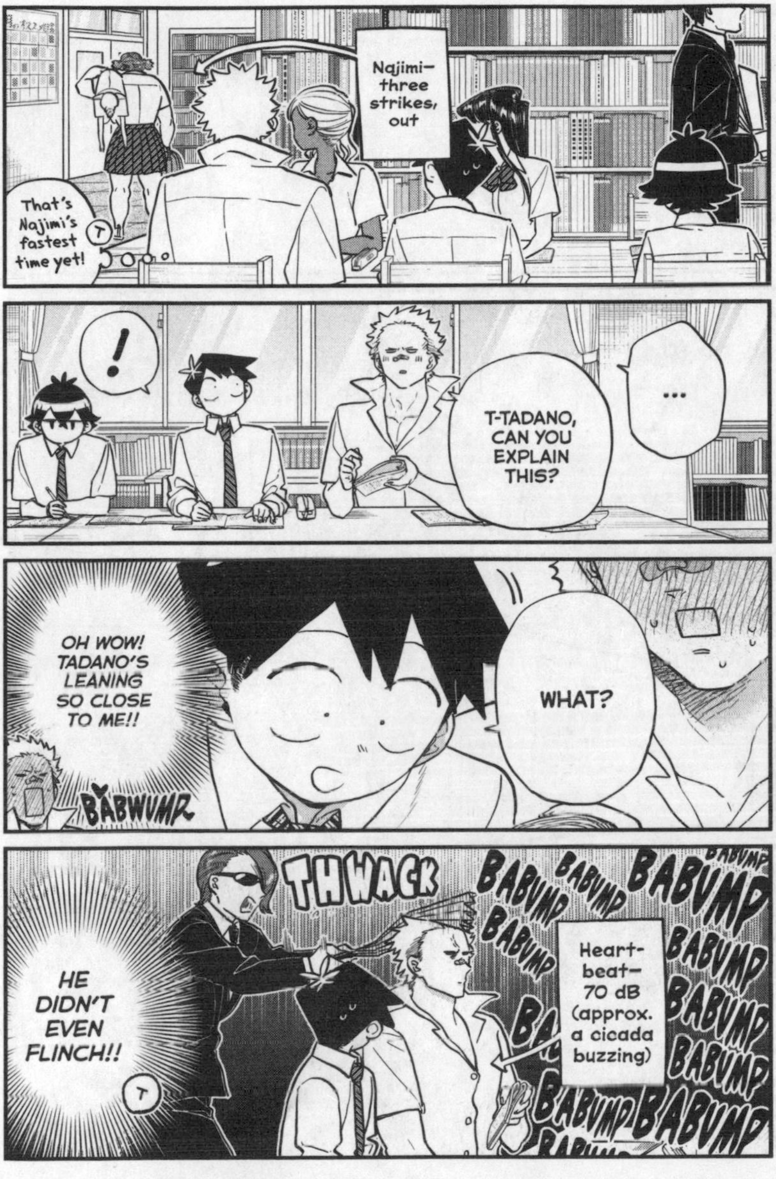
Najimi—three strikes, out
That's Najimi's fastest time yet!
...
T-TADANO, CAN YOU EXPLAIN THIS?
!
WHAT?
OH WOW! TADANO'S LEANING SO CLOSE TO ME!!
BABWUMP
BABUMP
Heart-beat—70 dB (approx. a cicada buzzing)
THWACK
HE DIDN'T EVEN FLINCH!!

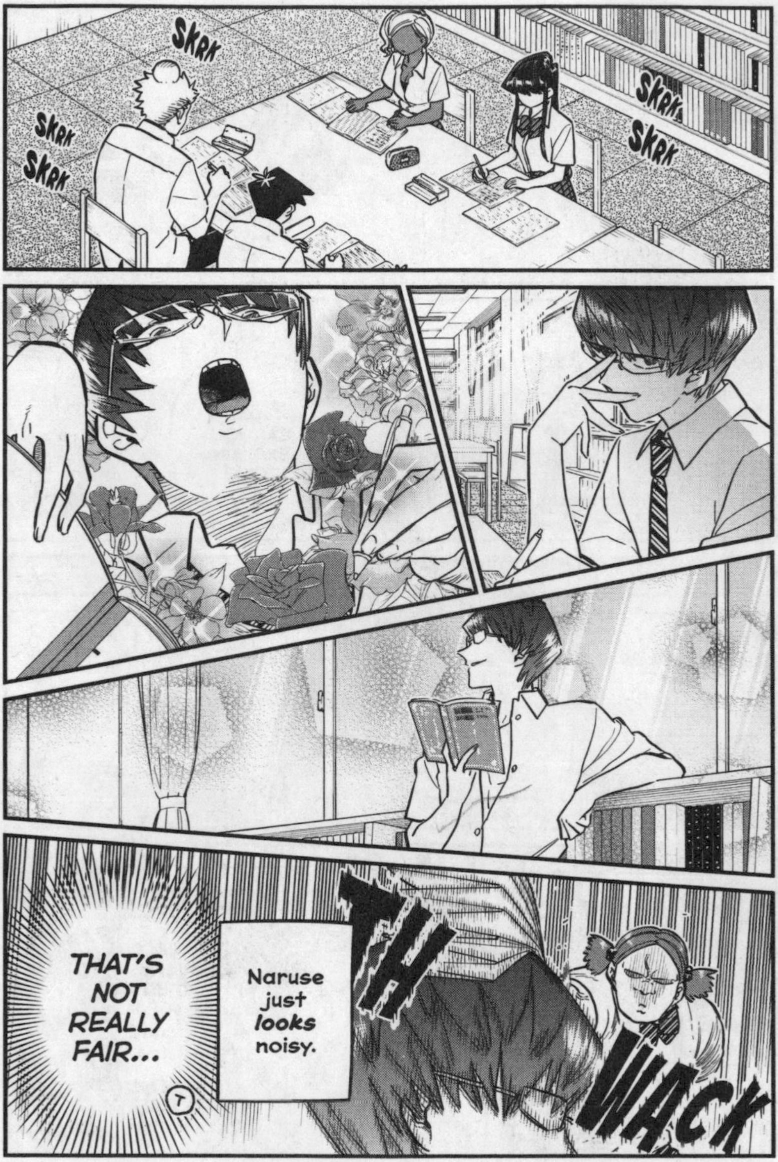
SKRK
SKRK
SKRK
SKRK
SKRK
THWACK
Naruse just looks noisy.
THAT'S NOT REALLY FAIR...

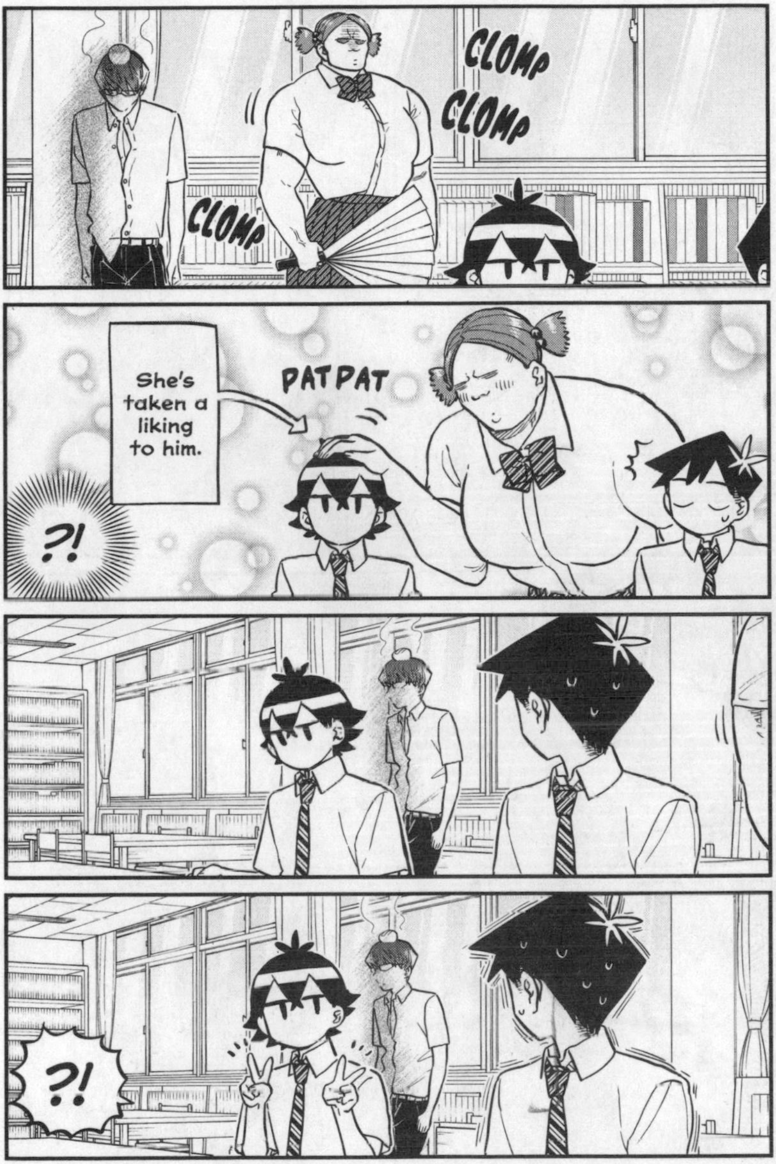
CLOMP
CLOMP
CLOMP
PATPAT
She's taken a liking to him.
?!
?!

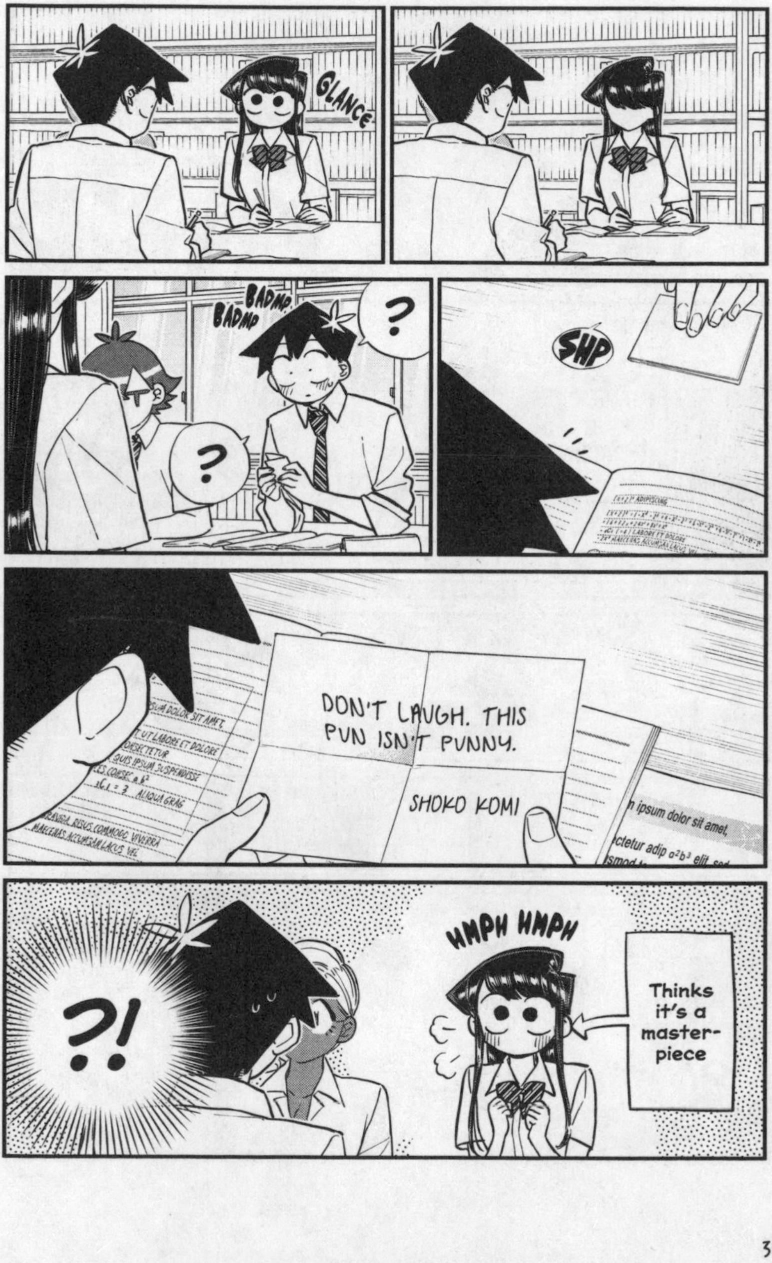
GLANCE
SHP
BADMP BADMP
?
?
DON'T LAUGH. THIS PUN ISN'T PUNNY.
SHOKO KOMI
Thinks it's a masterpiece
HMPH HMPH
?!

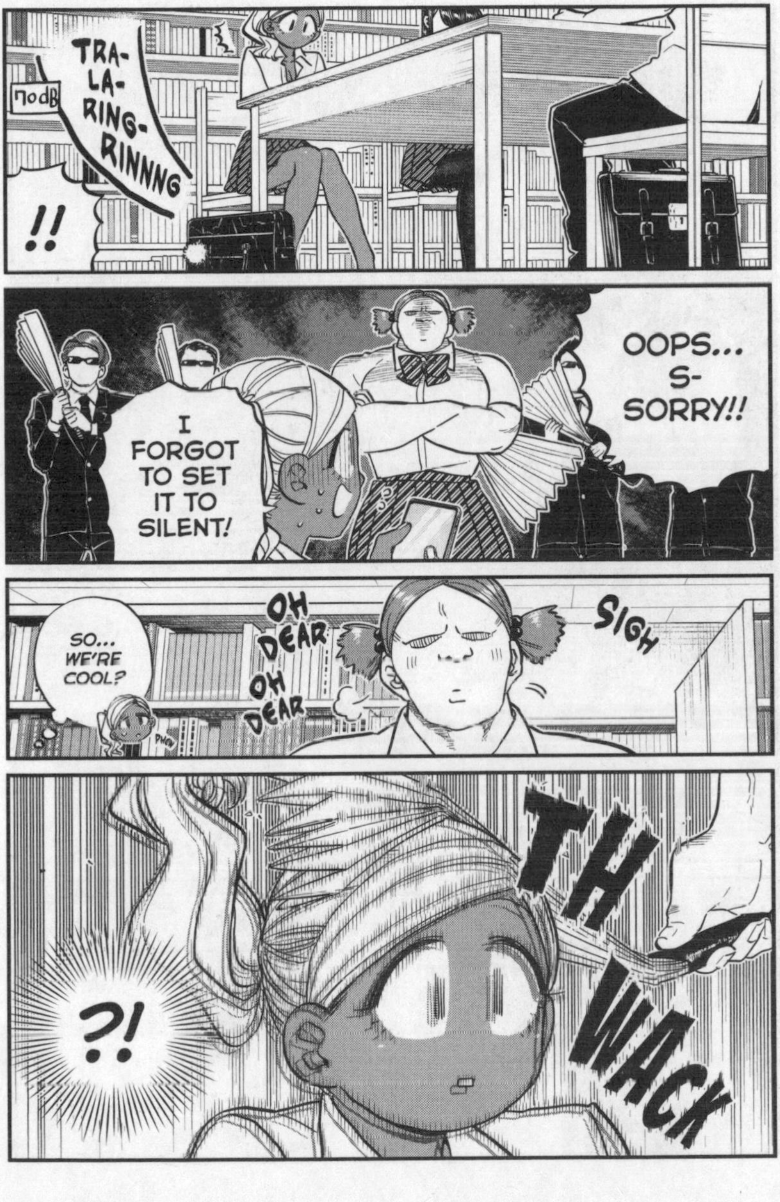

TRA-LA-RING-RINNNG
70dB
!!
OOPS... S-SORRY!!
I FORGOT TO SET IT TO SILENT!
SIGH
OH DEAR OH DEAR
SO... WE'RE COOL?
THWACK
?!

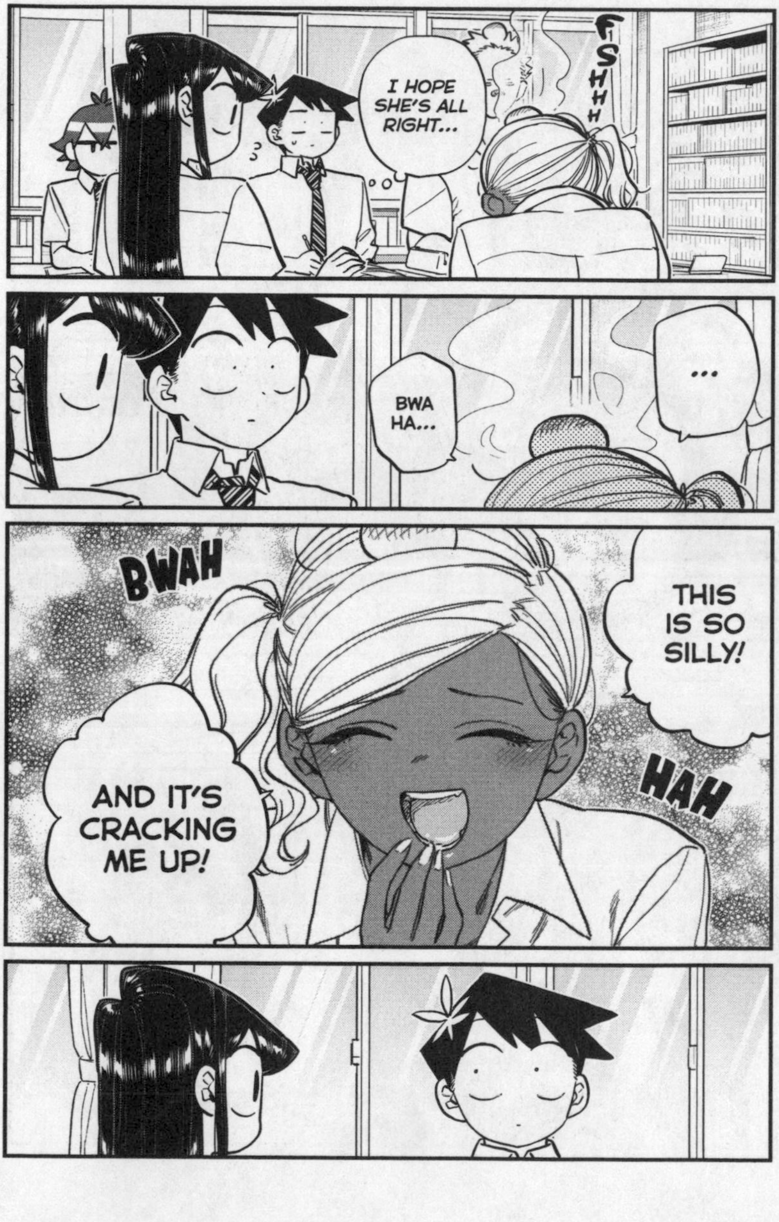
FSHHH
I HOPE SHE'S ALL RIGHT...
...
BWA HA...
THIS IS SO SILLY!
HAH
BWAH
AND IT'S CRACKING ME UP!

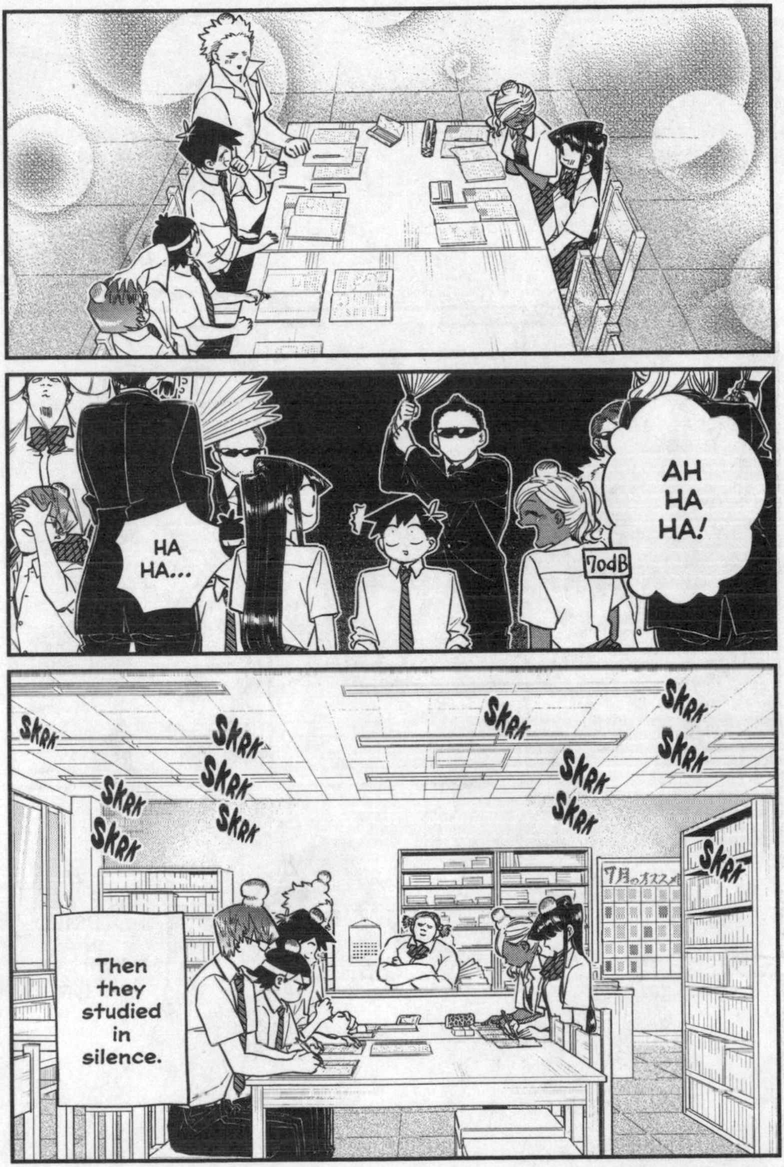
AH HA HA!
70dB
HA HA...
SKRK
SKRK
SKRK
SKRK
SKRK
SKRK
SKRK
SKRK
SKRK
SKRK
SKRK
SKRK
Then they studied in silence.

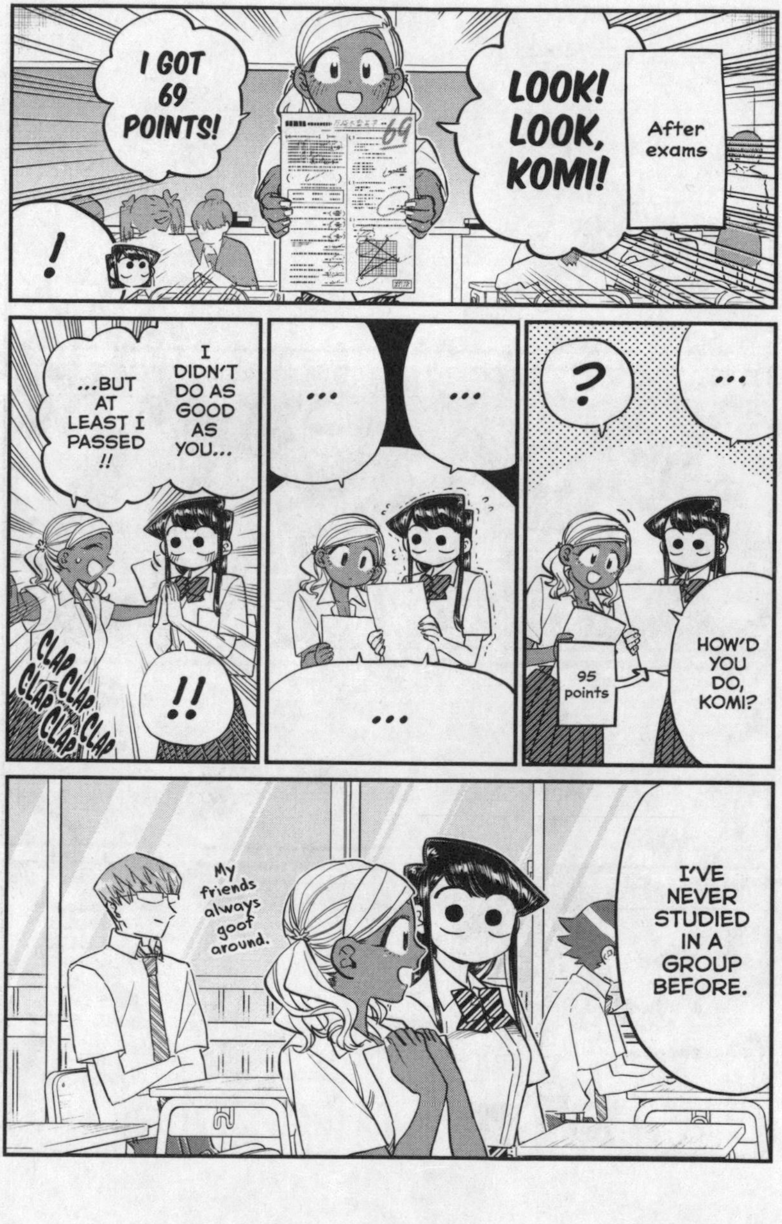
After exams
LOOK! LOOK, KOMI!
I GOT 69 POINTS!
!
...
?
HOW'D YOU DO, KOMI?
95 points
...
...
...
I DIDN'T DO AS GOOD AS YOU...
...BUT AT LEAST I PASSED!!
!!
CLAP CLAP CLAP CLAP CLAP
I'VE NEVER STUDIED IN A GROUP BEFORE.
My friends always goof around.

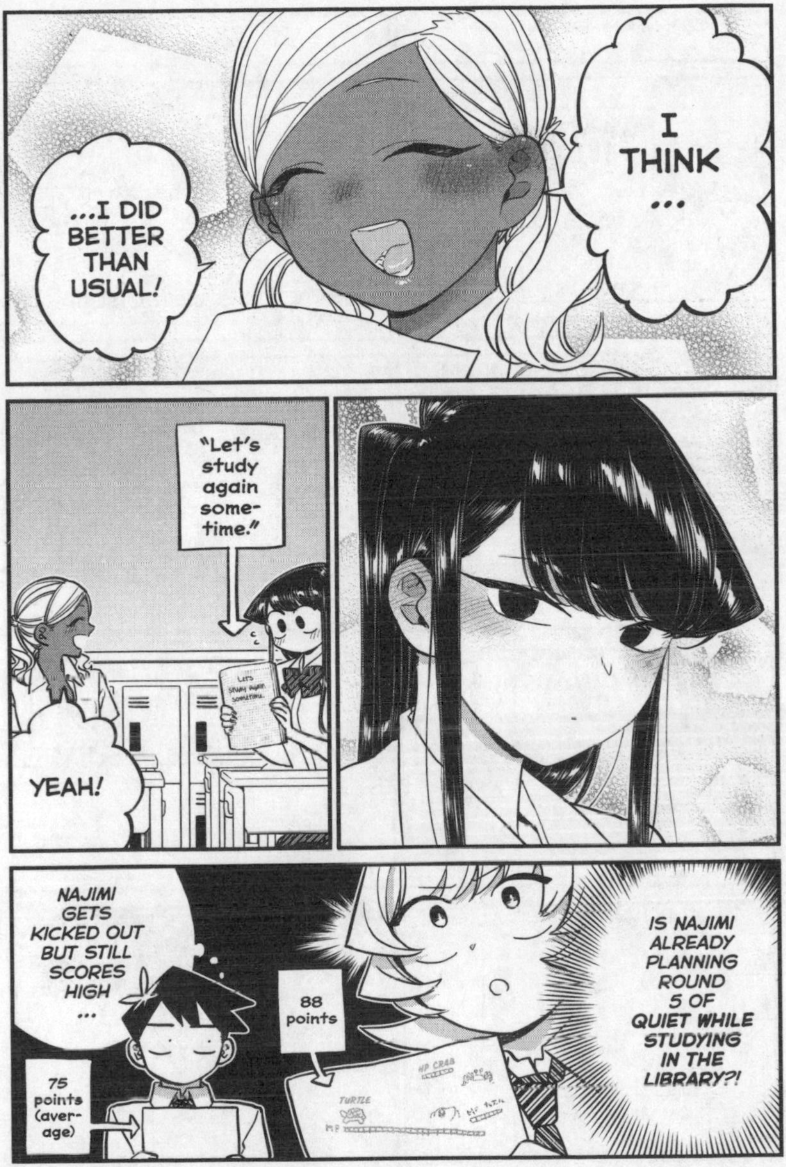
I THINK...
...I DID BETTER THAN USUAL!
"Let's study again sometime."
YEAH!
IS NAJIMI ALREADY PLANNING ROUND 5 OF QUIET WHILE STUDYING IN THE LIBRARY?!
88 points
HP CRAB
TURTLE
NAJIMI GETS KICKED OUT BUT STILL SCORES HIGH...
75 points (average)

Communication 159 — The End

Surprising

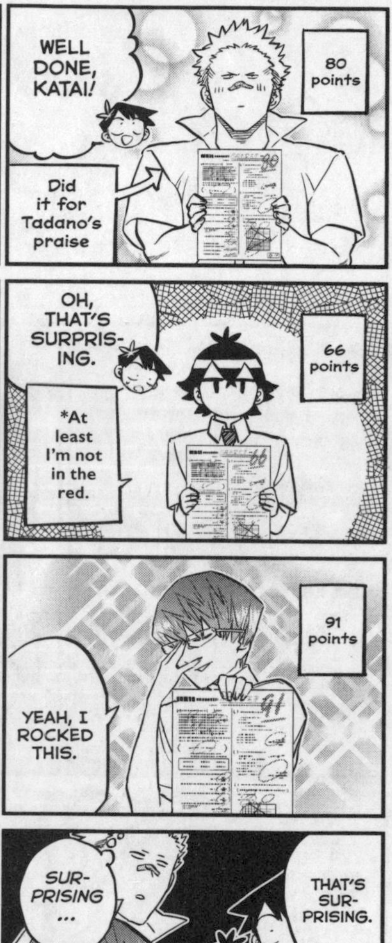
80 points
WELL DONE, KATAI!
Did it for Tadano's praise
66 points
OH, THAT'S SURPRIS-ING.
*At least I'm not in the red.
91 points
YEAH, I ROCKED THIS.
THAT'S SUR-PRISING.
SUR-PRISING ...
*Yes, sur-prising.
WHY ?!

Previous Rounds of Quiet While Studying in the Library

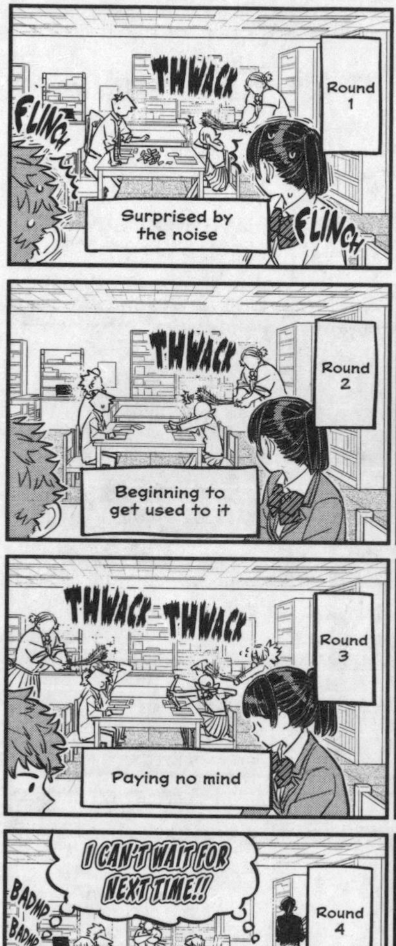
Round 1
THWACK
FLINCH
FLINCH
Surprised by the noise
Round 2
THWACK
Beginning to get used to it
Round 3
THWACK THWACK
Paying no mind
Round 4
I CAN'T WAIT FOR NEXT TIME!!
BADMP BADMP
YAY YAY
Looking forward to it

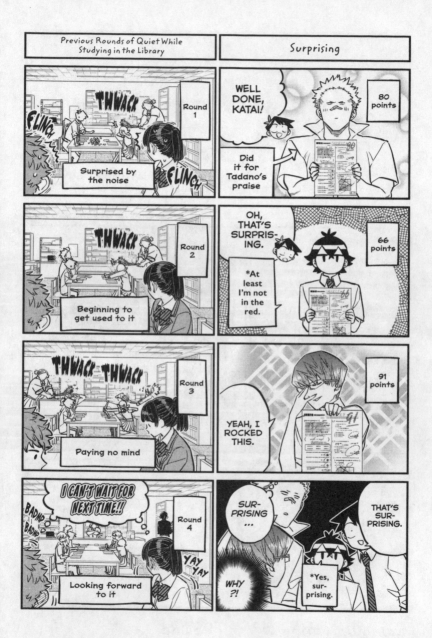

24TH TERM EXAM RESULTS!!

KOMI, SHOKO #3

SHIROKI, YUKA (YUKAPOYO) #4

AGARI, HIMIKO #7

MAEDA, HOSHIO JUKUJOSKY #9

FUWA, MASUKO #11

NARUSE, SHISUTO #13

KATO, MIKUNI #16

BODO, KANAME #22

SEIKIMATSU, TOSHIO #23

YAMAI, REN #36

NAKANAKA, OMOHARU #36

FUKUSUKI, NATSU #40

OSANA, NAJIMI #46

SHINOBINO, MONO #54

SONODA, TAISEI #61

ASE, SHIBUKI #68

SATO AMAMI #70

USHIRODA, EIKO #71

TADANO, HITOHITO #75

ODOKA, SHIZUKA #76

ONIGASHIMA, AKAKO #78

KUROITA, MUTSUMI (MUTAN) #82

ONEMINE, NENE #87

SAMURAI, SAM # 88

FUSHIMA, SAKU #89

MANBAGI, RUMIKO #98

INAKA, NOKOKO #102

YADANO, MAKERU #108

KOMETANI, CHUSHAKU #111

OTAKU, YUJI #114

CHIARAI, SHIGEO #123

KISHI, HIMEKO #125

OTORI, KAEDE #126 (TEST INCOMPLETE)

ISU, SHIORI (GONZALES) #134

OHAI, SHUKI #139

SASAKI, AYAMI #143

TOTOI, SON #144

SUKIDA, LILY #150

Komi Can't Communicate

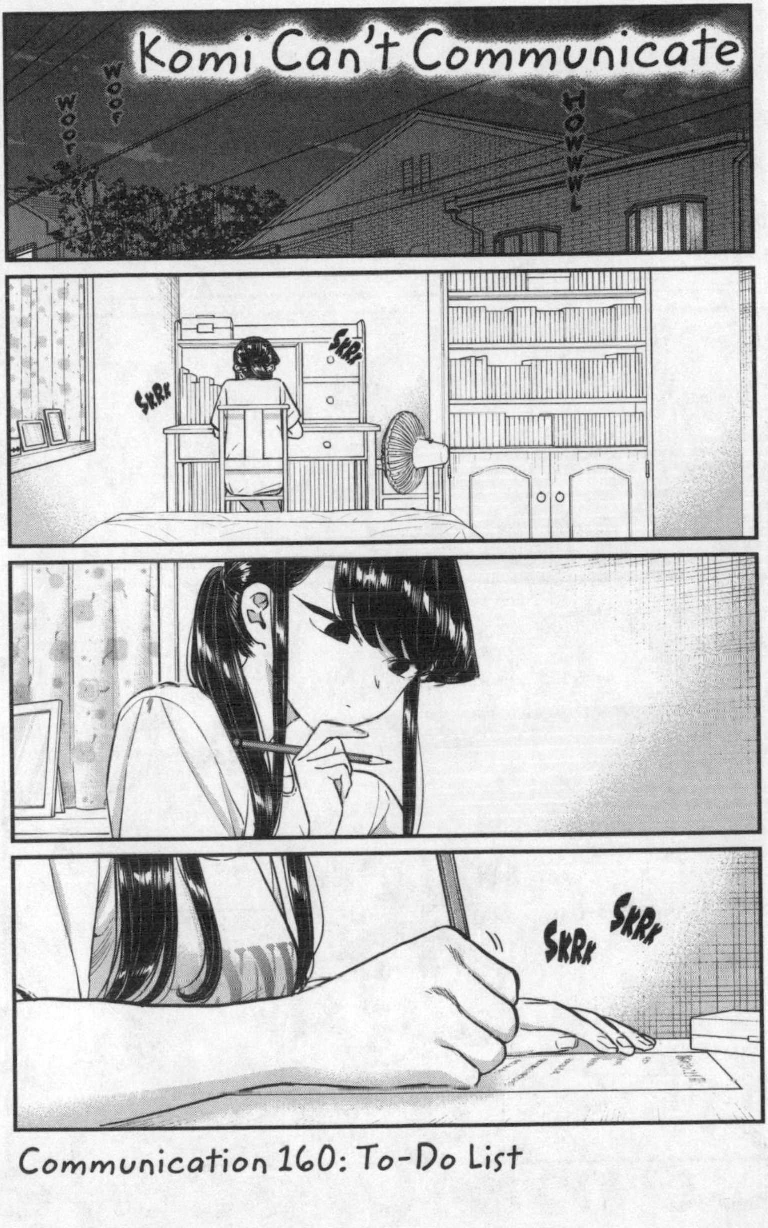
Komi Can't Communicate
HOWWWL
WOOF
WOOF
SKRK
SKRK
SKRK
SKRK

Communication 160: To-Do List

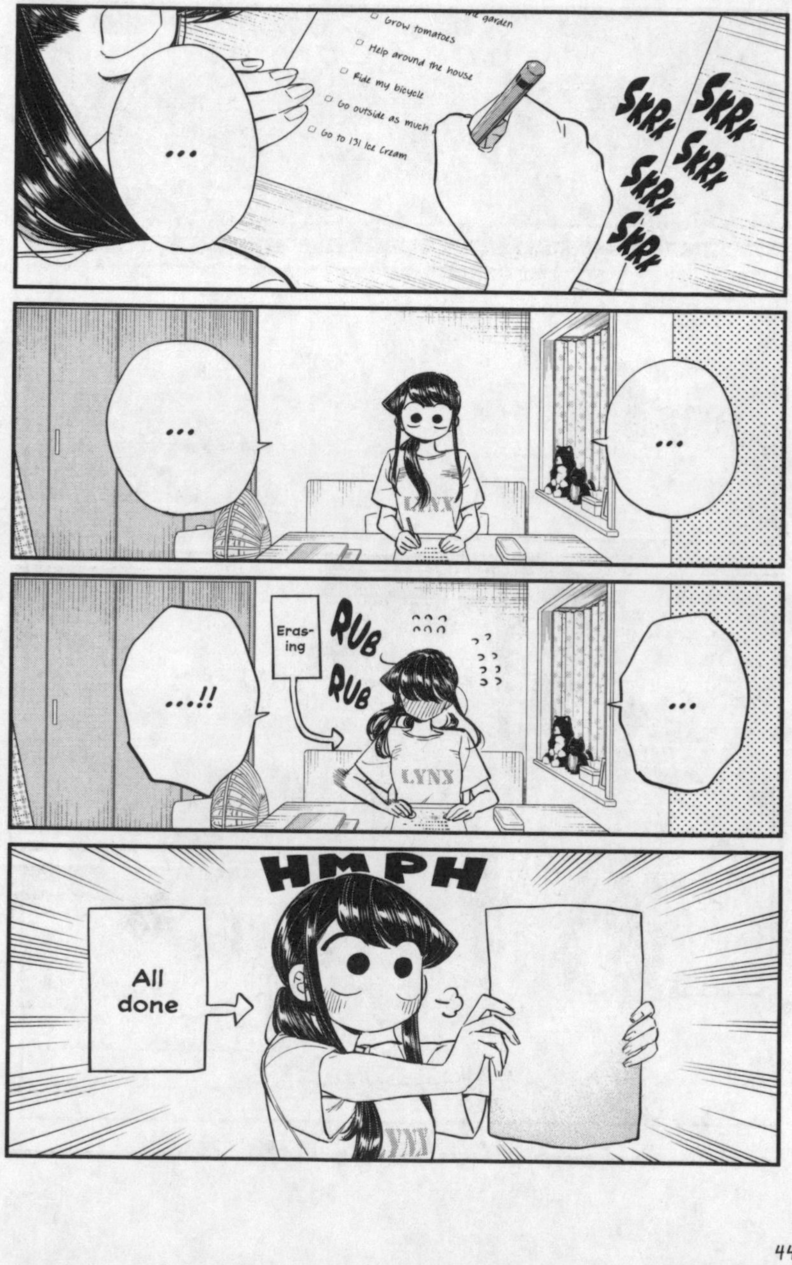

SKRK SKRK
SKRK SKRK
SKRK
Grow tomatoes
Help around the house
Ride my bicycle
Go outside as much
Go to 131 Ice Cream
...
...
...
...
RUB RUB
Erasing
...!!
HMPH
All done

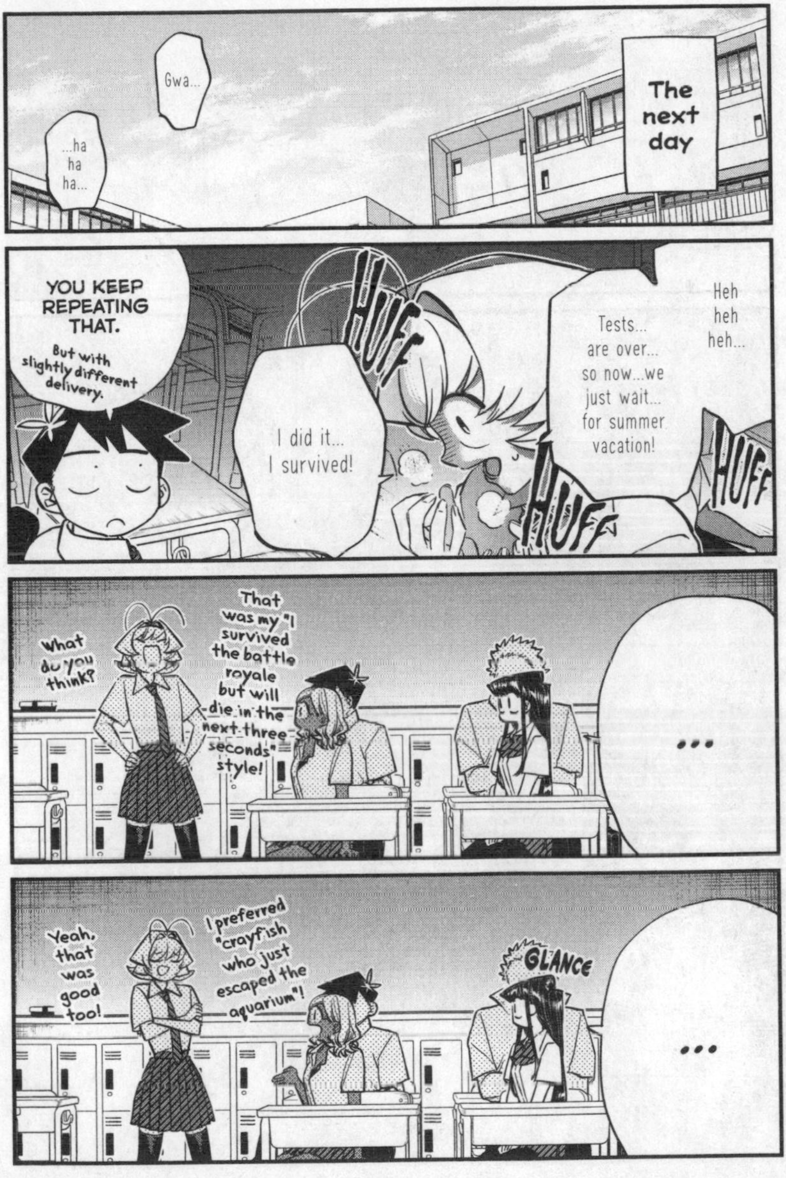
The next day
Gwa...
...ha ha ha...
Heh heh heh...
Tests... are over... so now...we just wait... for summer vacation!
HUFF
HUFF
HUFF
I did it... I survived!
YOU KEEP REPEATING THAT.
But with slightly different delivery.
...
That was my "I survived the battle royale but will die in the next three seconds" style!
What do you think?
...
GLANCE
I preferred "crayfish who just escaped the aquarium"!
Yeah, that was good too!

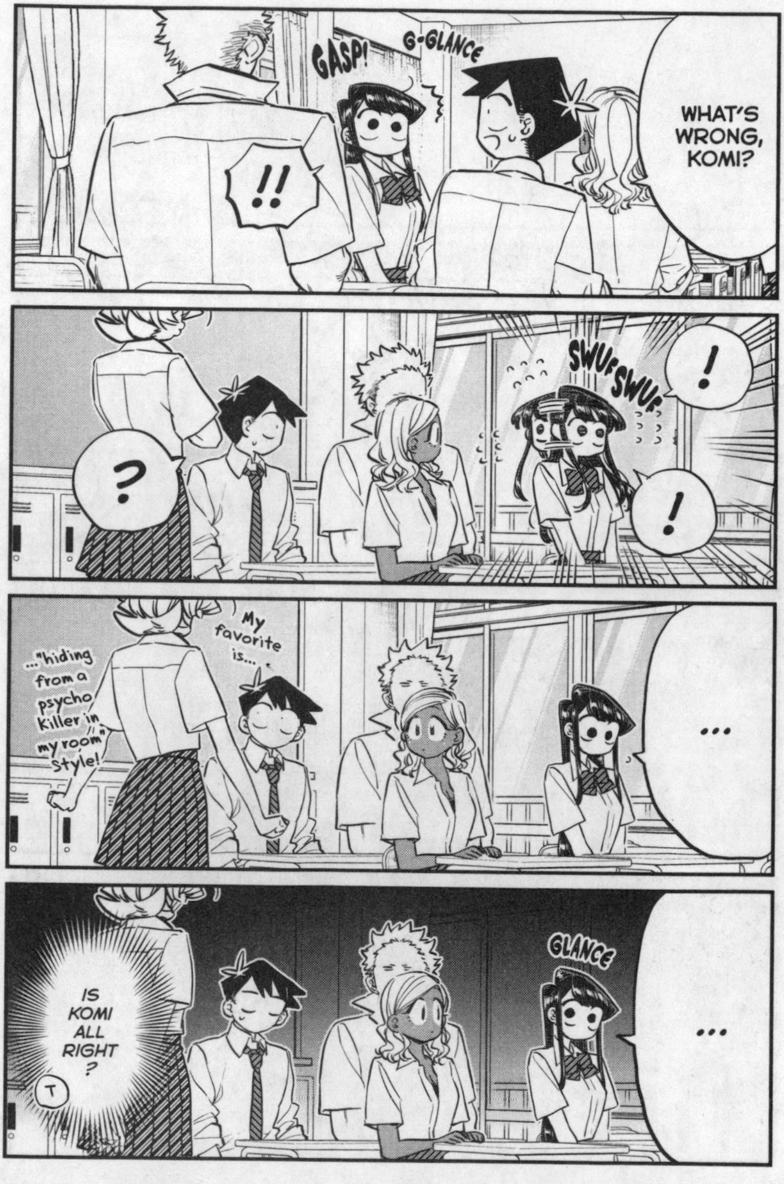
WHAT'S WRONG, KOMI?
G-GLANCE
GASP!
!!
!
SWUF SWUF
!
?
...
My favorite is...
..."hiding from a psycho killer in my room" style!
...
GLANCE
IS KOMI ALL RIGHT?
T

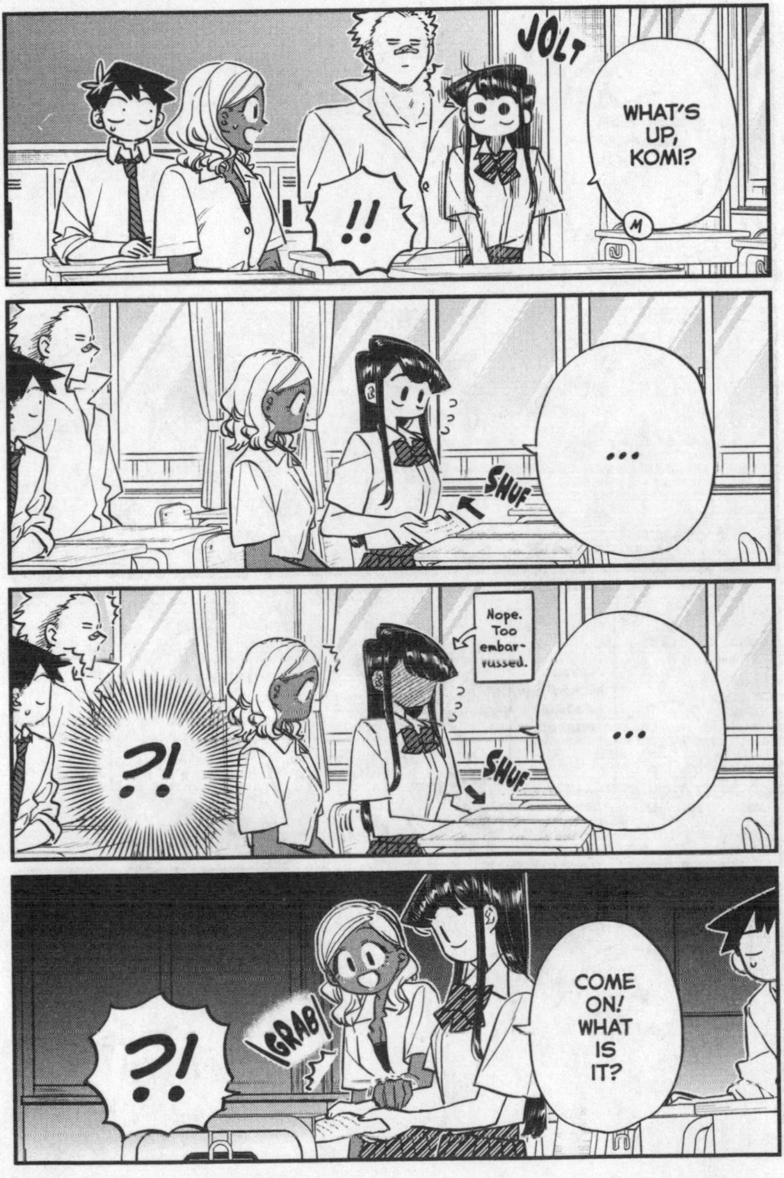
WHAT'S UP, KOMI?
JOLT
!!
...
SHUF
...
Nope. Too embar-rassed.
SHUF
?!
COME ON! WHAT IS IT?
GRAB
?!

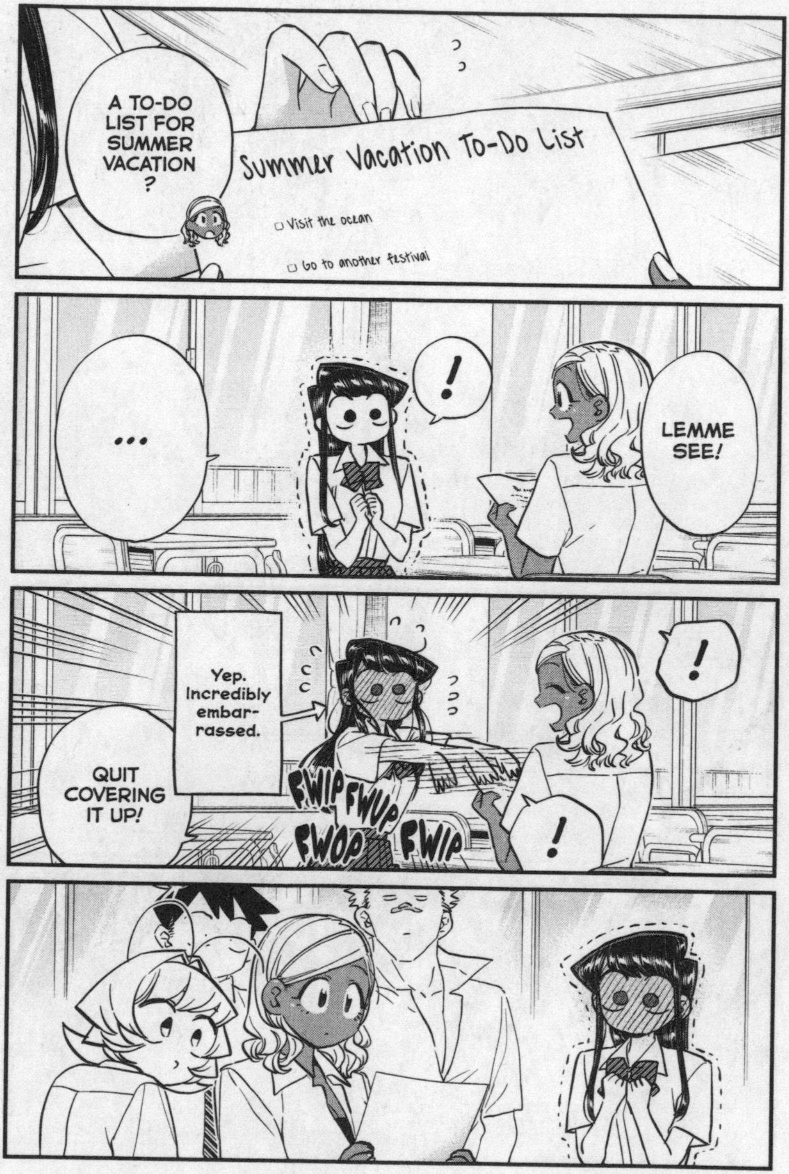
Summer Vacation To-Do List
Visit the ocean
Go to another festival
A TO-DO LIST FOR SUMMER VACATION?
LEMME SEE!
!
...
!
!
FWIP FWUP
FWOP FWIP
Yep. Incredibly embar-rassed.
QUIT COVERING IT UP!

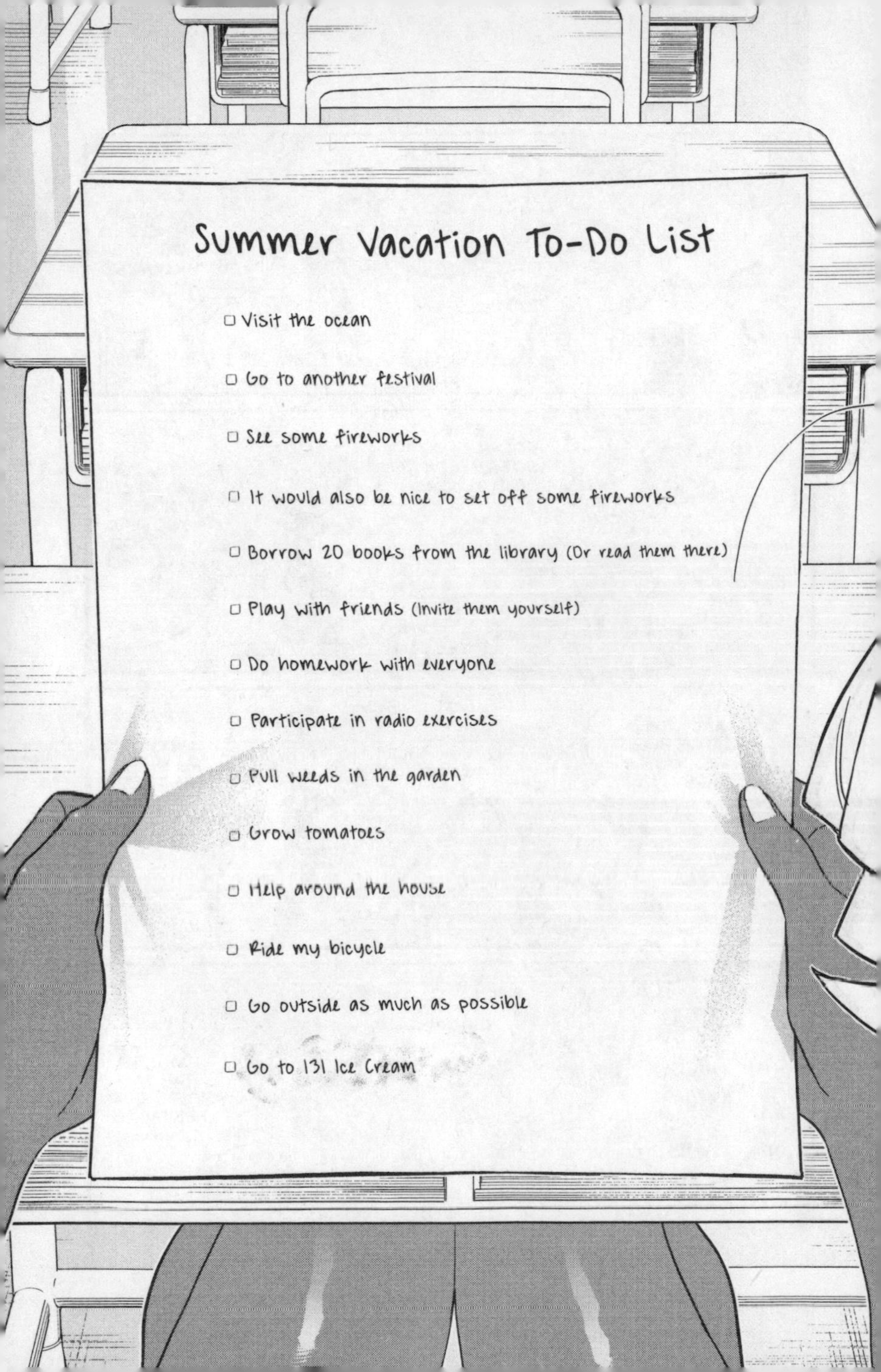
Summer Vacation To-Do List
☐ Visit the ocean
☐ Go to another festival
☐ See some fireworks
☐ It would also be nice to set off some fireworks
☐ Borrow 20 books from the library (Or read them there)
☐ Play with friends (Invite them yourself)
☐ Do homework with everyone
☐ Participate in radio exercises
☐ Pull weeds in the garden
☐ Grow tomatoes
☐ Help around the house
☐ Ride my bicycle
☐ Go outside as much as possible
☐ Go to 131 Ice Cream

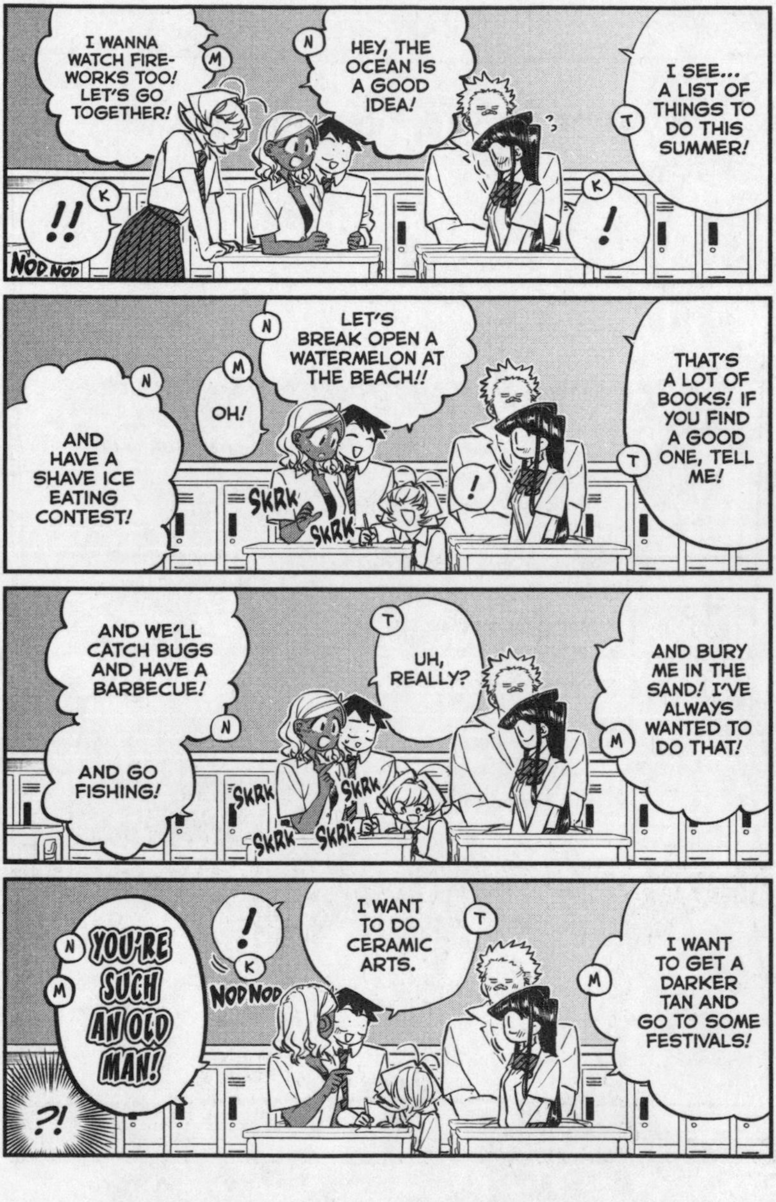
I SEE... A LIST OF THINGS TO DO THIS SUMMER!
!
HEY, THE OCEAN IS A GOOD IDEA!
I WANNA WATCH FIRE-WORKS TOO! LET'S GO TOGETHER!
!!
NOD NOD
THAT'S A LOT OF BOOKS! IF YOU FIND A GOOD ONE, TELL ME!
!
LET'S BREAK OPEN A WATERMELON AT THE BEACH!!
OH!
AND HAVE A SHAVE ICE EATING CONTEST!
SKRK
SKRK
AND BURY ME IN THE SAND! I'VE ALWAYS WANTED TO DO THAT!
UH, REALLY?
AND WE'LL CATCH BUGS AND HAVE A BARBECUE!
AND GO FISHING!
SKRK
SKRK
SKRK
SKRK
I WANT TO GET A DARKER TAN AND GO TO SOME FESTIVALS!
I WANT TO DO CERAMIC ARTS.
!
NOD NOD
YOU'RE SUCH AN OLD MAN!
?!

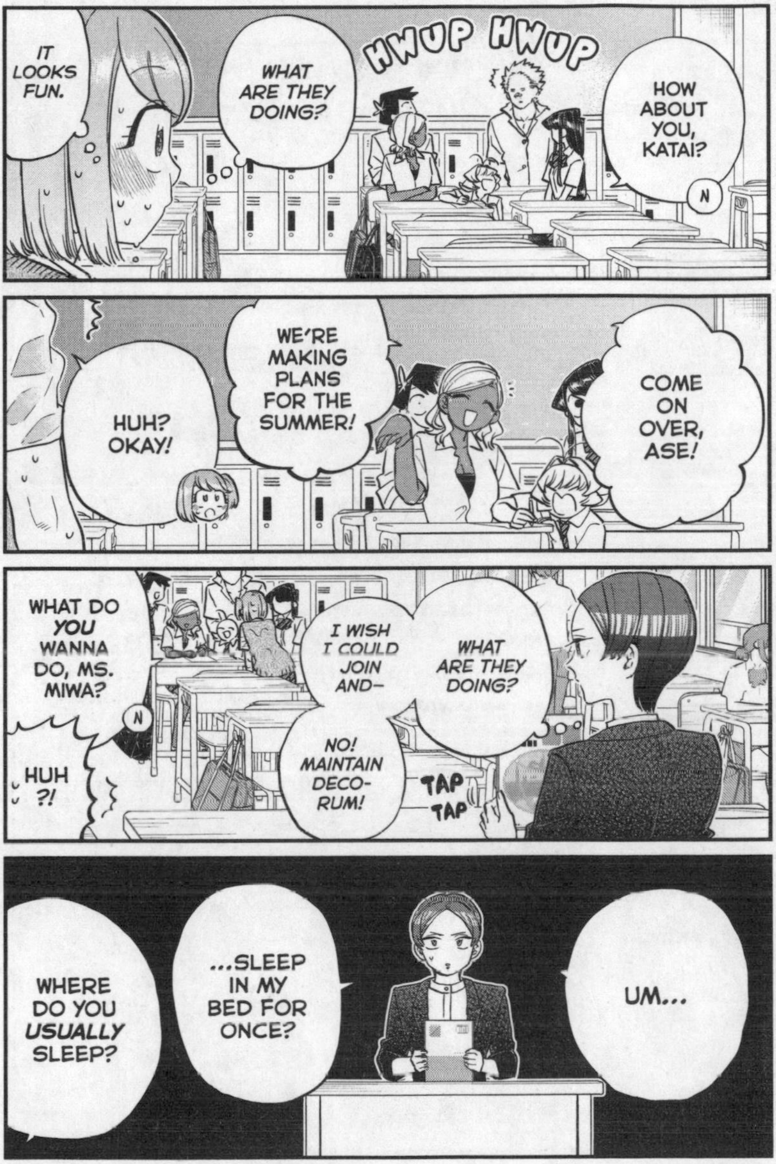
HOW ABOUT YOU, KATAI?
N
HWUP HWUP
WHAT ARE THEY DOING?
IT LOOKS FUN.
COME ON OVER, ASE!
WE'RE MAKING PLANS FOR THE SUMMER!
HUH? OKAY!
WHAT ARE THEY DOING?
I WISH I COULD JOIN AND—
NO! MAINTAIN DECO-RUM!
TAP TAP
WHAT DO YOU WANNA DO, MS. MIWA?
N
HUH ?!
UM...
...SLEEP IN MY BED FOR ONCE?
WHERE DO YOU USUALLY SLEEP?

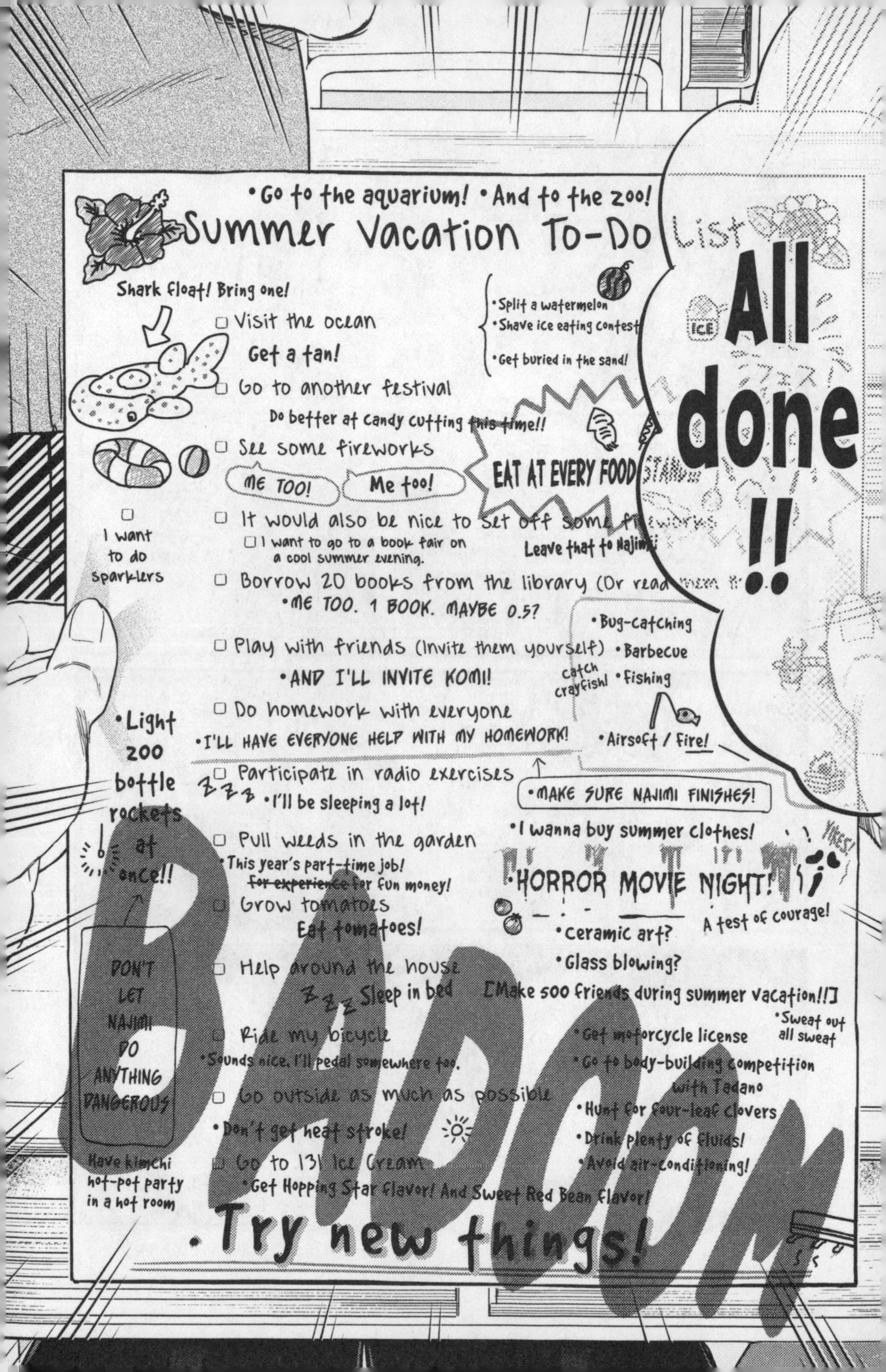

• Go to the aquarium! • And to the zoo!
Summer Vacation To-Do List
All done!!
Shark float! Bring one!
☐ Visit the ocean
Get a tan!
• Split a watermelon
• Shave ice eating contest
• Get buried in the sand!
☐ Go to another festival
Do better at candy cutting this time!!
☐ See some fireworks
ME TOO!
Me too!
EAT AT EVERY FOOD
☐ It would also be nice to set off some
☐ I want to do sparklers
☐ I want to go to a book fair on a cool summer evening.
Leave that to Najimi
☐ Borrow 20 books from the library (Or read
• ME TOO. 1 BOOK. MAYBE 0.5?
• Bug-catching
☐ Play with friends (Invite them yourself)
• Barbecue
• AND I'LL INVITE KOMI!
catch crayfish!
• Fishing
☐ Do homework with everyone
• I'LL HAVE EVERYONE HELP WITH MY HOMEWORK!
• Airsoft / Fire!
• Light 200 bottle rockets at once!!
☐ Participate in radio exercises
Z Z Z • I'll be sleeping a lot!
• MAKE SURE NAJIMI FINISHES!
☐ Pull weeds in the garden
• I wanna buy summer clothes!
• This year's part-time job! For experience For fun money!
• HORROR MOVIE NIGHT!
YIKES!
☐ Grow tomatoes
Eat tomatoes!
A test of courage!
• Ceramic art?
• Glass blowing?
DON'T LET NAJIMI DO ANYTHING DANGEROUS
☐ Help around the house
Z Z Z Sleep in bed
[Make 500 friends during summer vacation!!]
☐ Ride my bicycle
• Sounds nice. I'll pedal somewhere too.
• Get motorcycle license
• Sweat out all sweat
• Go to body-building competition with Tadano
☐ Go outside as much as possible
• Hunt for four-leaf clovers
• Don't get heat stroke!
• Drink plenty of fluids!
• Avoid air-conditioning!
☐ Go to 131 Ice Cream
Have kimchi hot-pot party in a hot room
• Get Hopping Star flavor! And Sweet Red Bean flavor!
• Try new things!
BADOOM

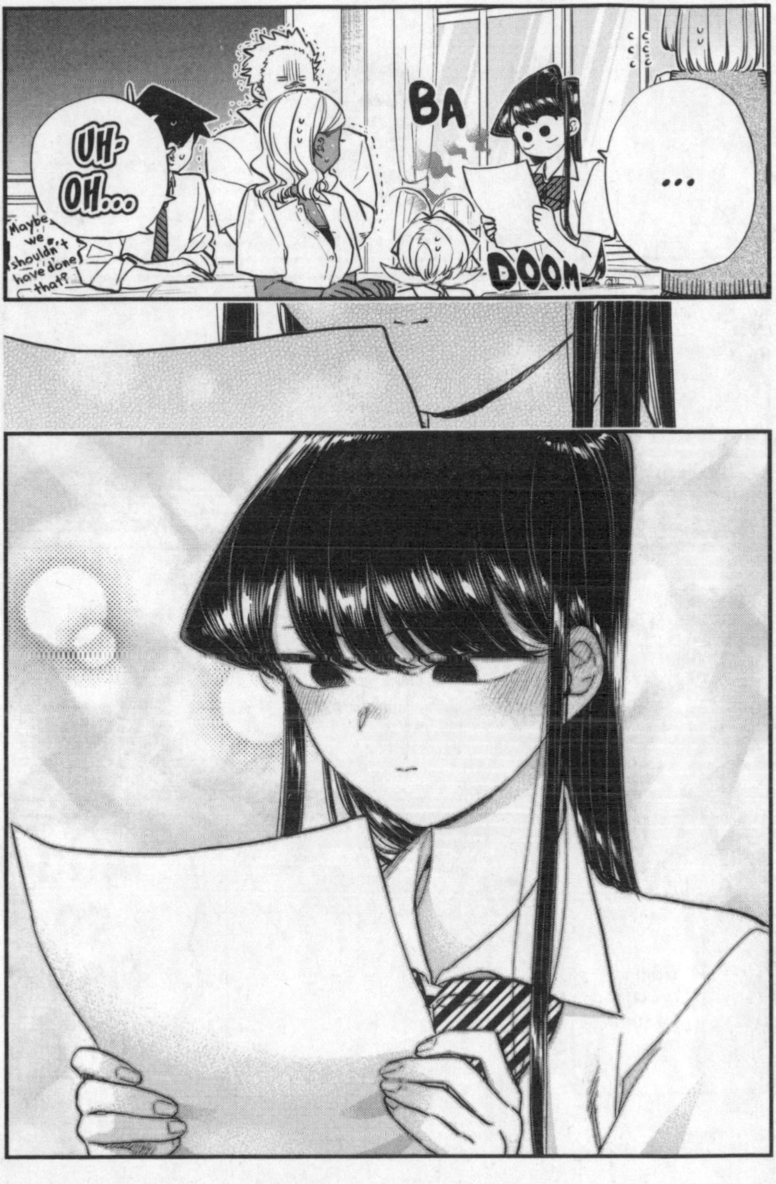
...
BA
DOOM
UH-OH...
Maybe we shouldn't have done that?

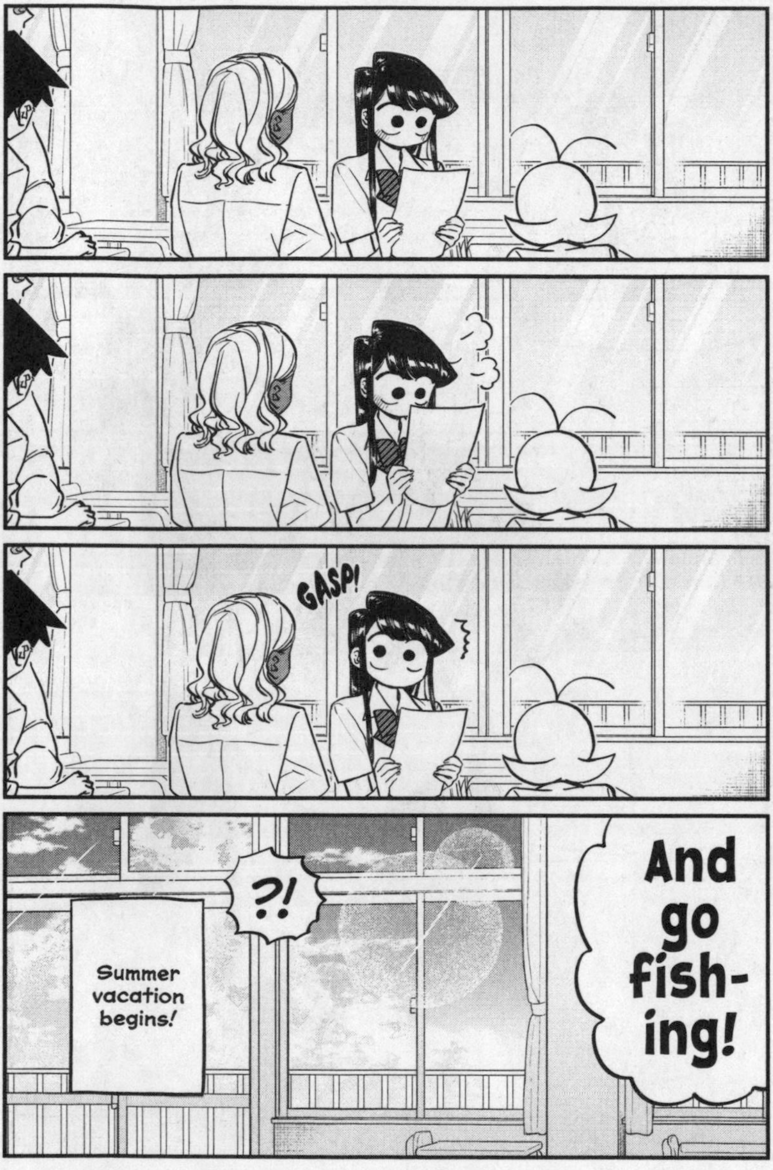
GASP!
And go fish-ing!
?!
Summer vacation begins!

Communication 160 — The End

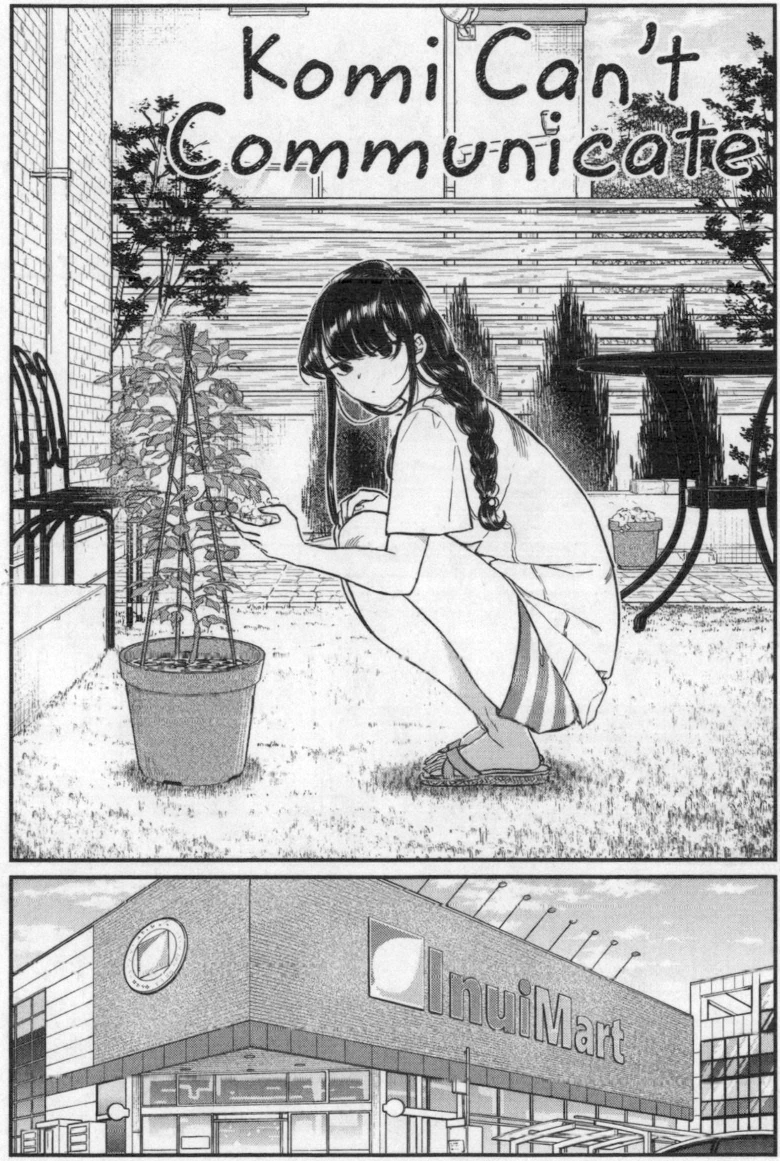
Komi Can't Communicate
InuiMart

Communication 161: Cherry Tomatoes

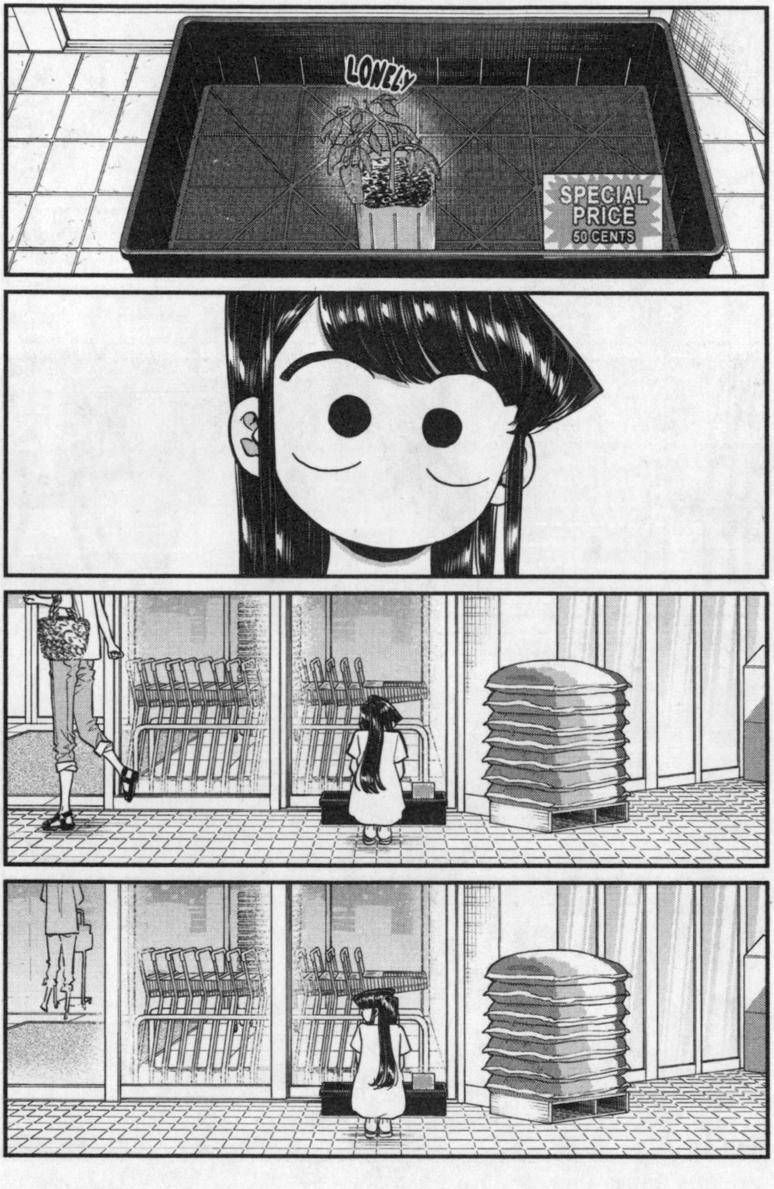
LONELY
SPECIAL PRICE 50 CENTS

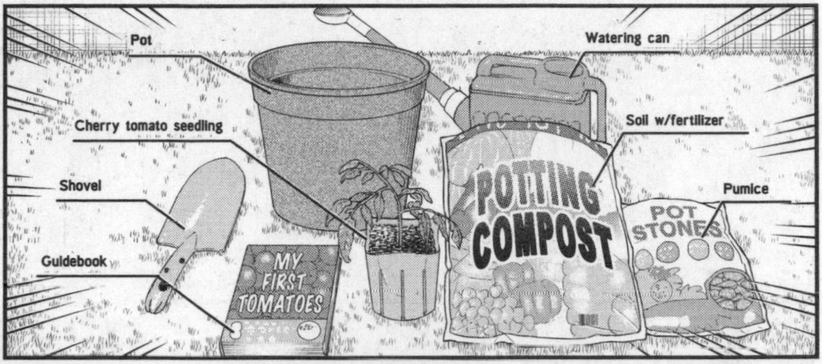
Watering can
Soil w/fertilizer
Pumice
Pot
Cherry tomato seedling
Shovel
Guidebook
POTTING COMPOST
POT STONES
MY FIRST TOMATOES

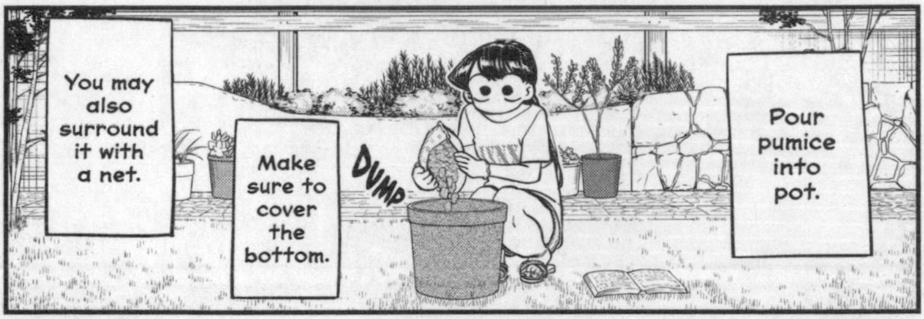
Pour pumice into pot.
DUMP
Make sure to cover the bottom.
You may also surround it with a net.

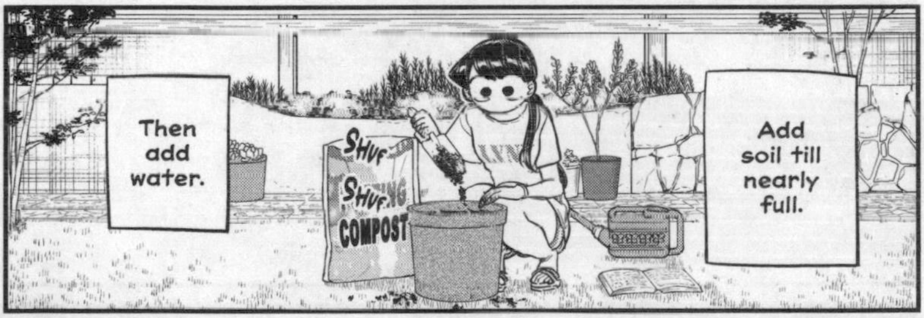
Add soil till nearly full.
SHUF
SHUF
COMPOST
Then add water.

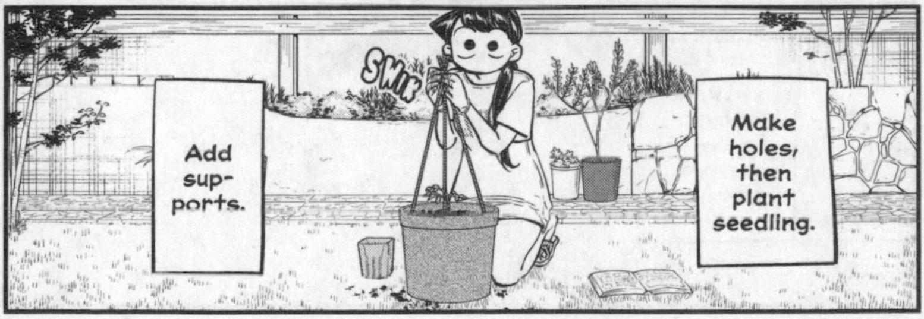
Make holes, then plant seedling.
SWIK
Add sup-ports.

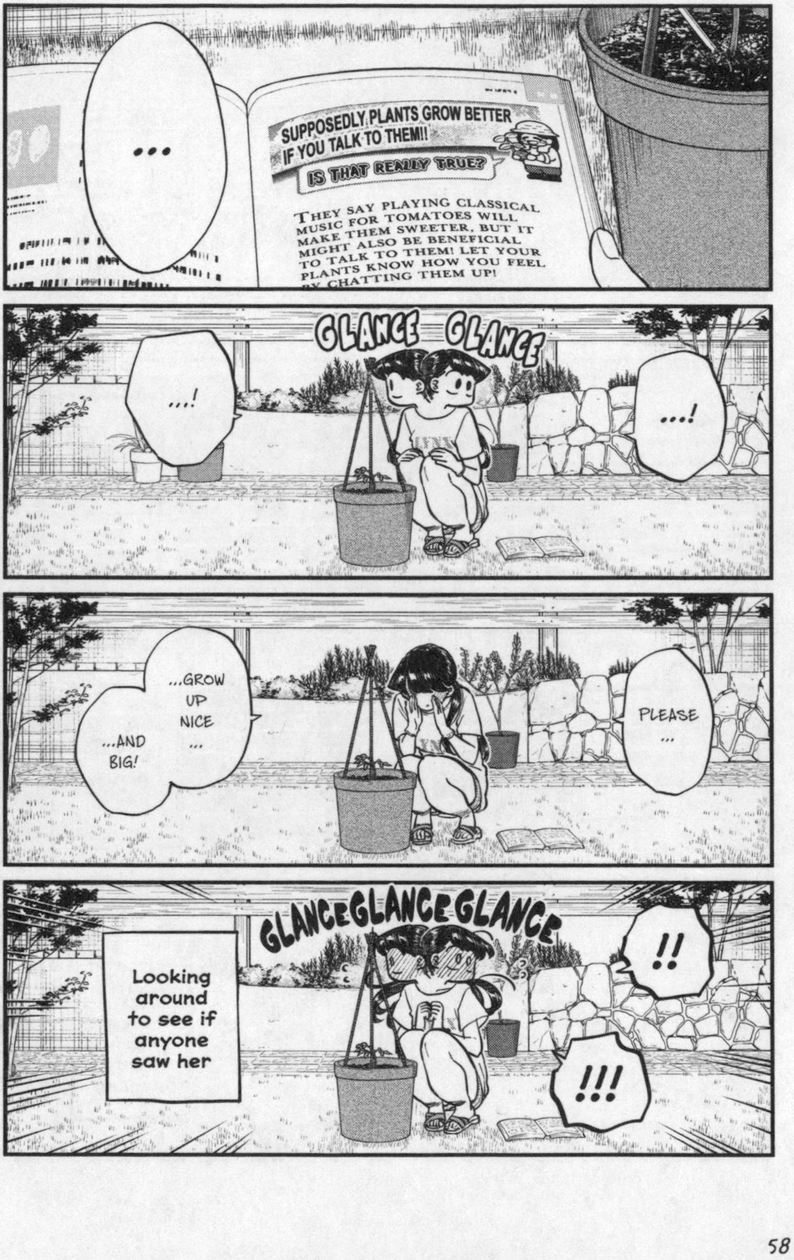
SUPPOSEDLY PLANTS GROW BETTER IF YOU TALK TO THEM!!
IS THAT REALLY TRUE?
THEY SAY PLAYING CLASSICAL MUSIC FOR TOMATOES WILL MAKE THEM SWEETER, BUT IT MIGHT ALSO BE BENEFICIAL TO TALK TO THEM! LET YOUR PLANTS KNOW HOW YOU FEEL BY CHATTING THEM UP!
...
GLANCE GLANCE
...!
...!
PLEASE ...
...GROW UP NICE ... ...AND BIG!
GLANCEGLANCEGLANCE
!!
!!!
Looking around to see if anyone saw her

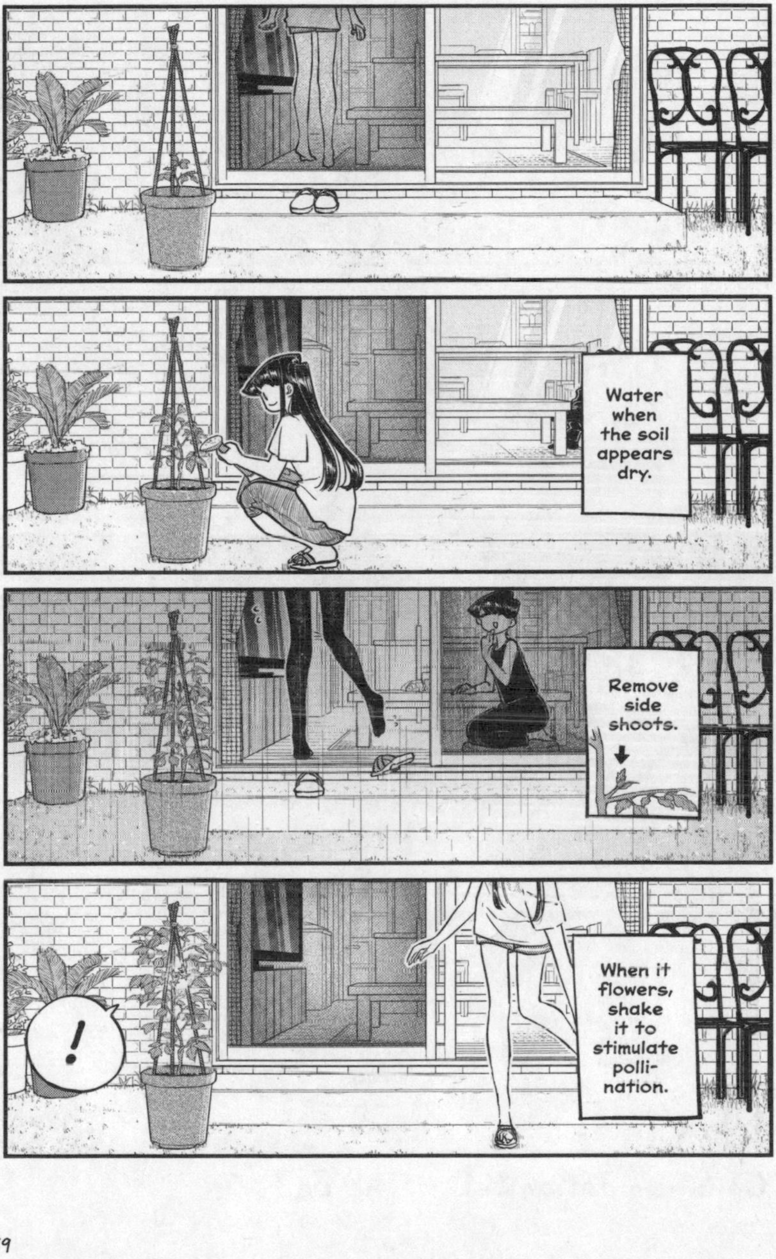
Water when the soil appears dry.
Remove side shoots.
When it flowers, shake it to stimulate polli-nation.
!

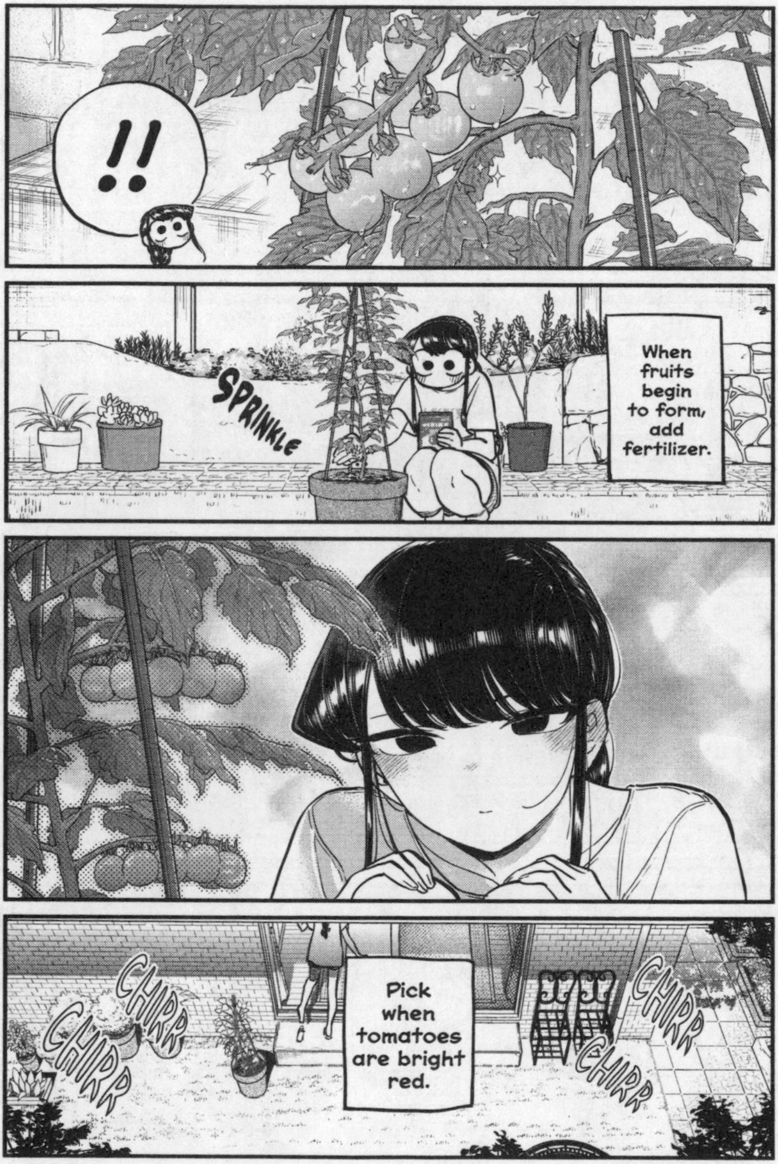
!!
When fruits begin to form, add fertilizer.
SPRINKLE
CHIRR
CHIRR
Pick when tomatoes are bright red.
CHIRR
CHIRR

Communication 161 — The End

Komi Can't Communicate

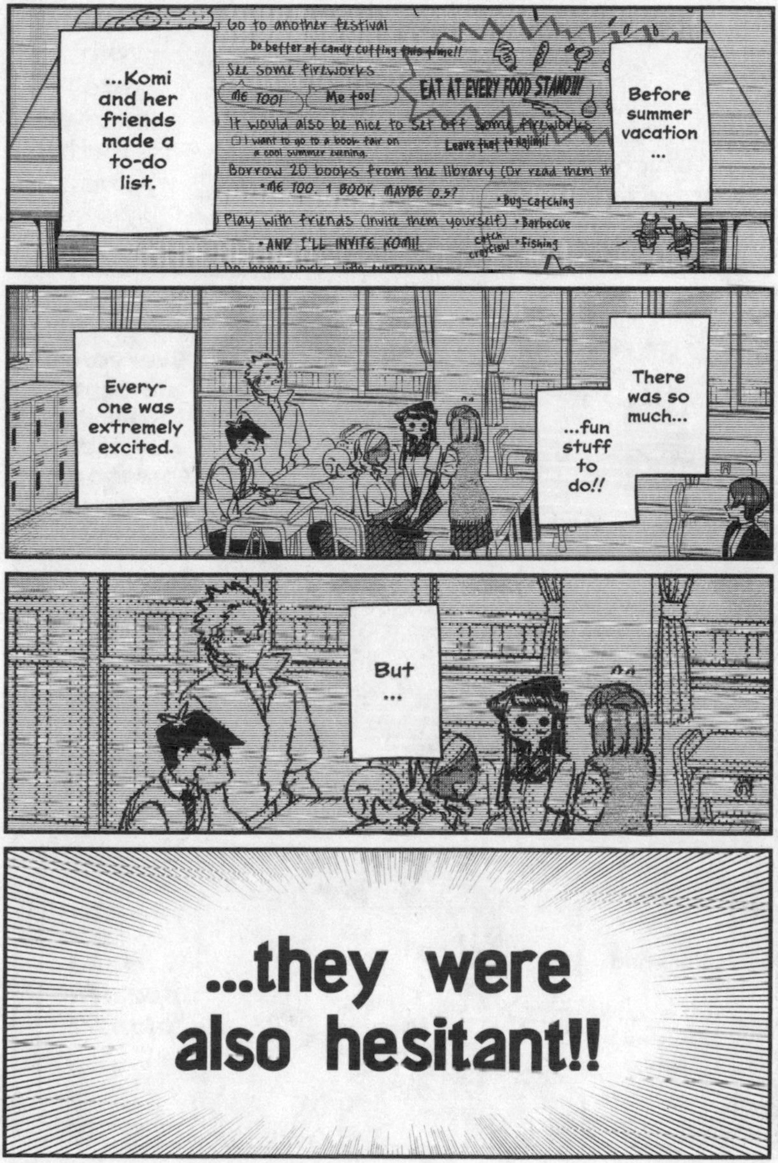
Before summer vacation ...
...Komi and her friends made a to-do list.
Go to another festival
Do better at candy cutting this time!!
See some fireworks
ME TOO!
Me too!
EAT AT EVERY FOOD STAND!!!
It would also be nice to set off some fireworks
I want to go to a book fair on a cool summer evening.
Leave that to Najimi!
Borrow 20 books from the library (Or read them th
•ME TOO. 1 BOOK. MAYBE 0.5?
•Bug-catching
Play with friends (invite them yourself)
•Barbecue
•AND I'LL INVITE KOMI!
catch crayfish!
•Fishing
There was so much...
...fun stuff to do!!
Every-one was extremely excited.
But ...
...they were also hesitant!!

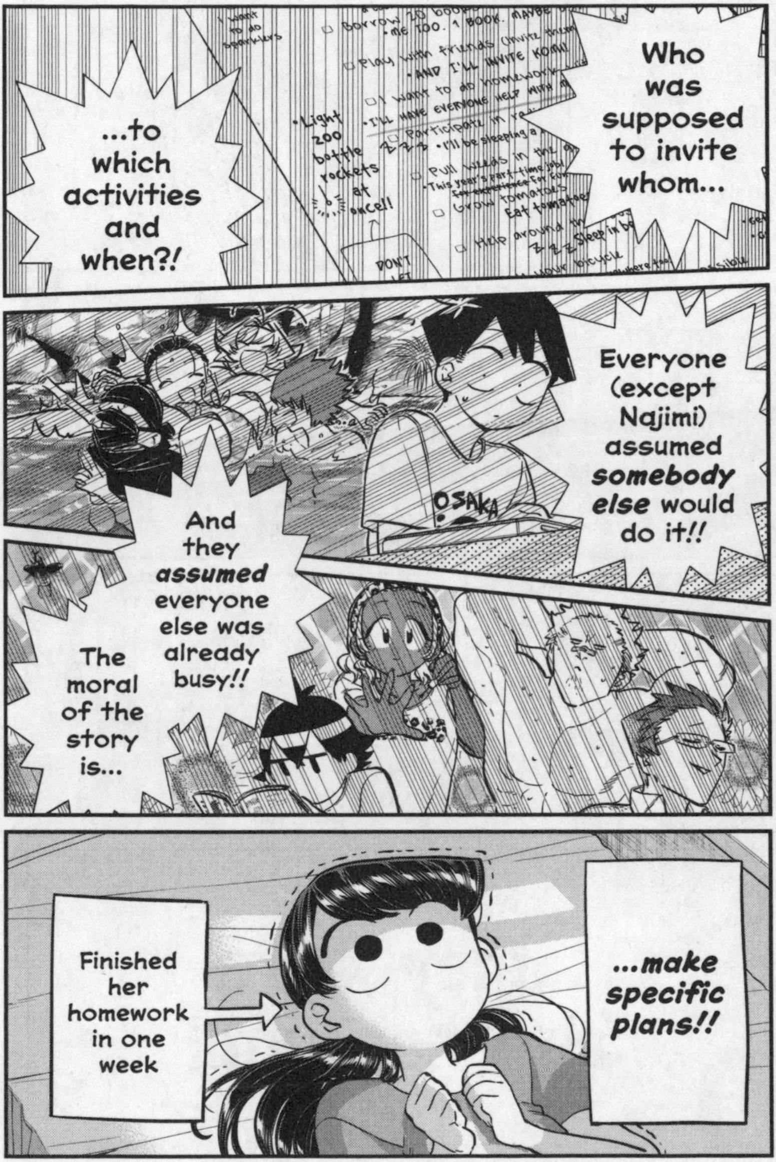
Who was supposed to invite whom...
...to which activities and when?!
Everyone (except Najimi) assumed *somebody else* would do it!!
OSAKA
And they *assumed* everyone else was already busy!!
The moral of the story is...
...make specific plans!!
Finished her homework in one week

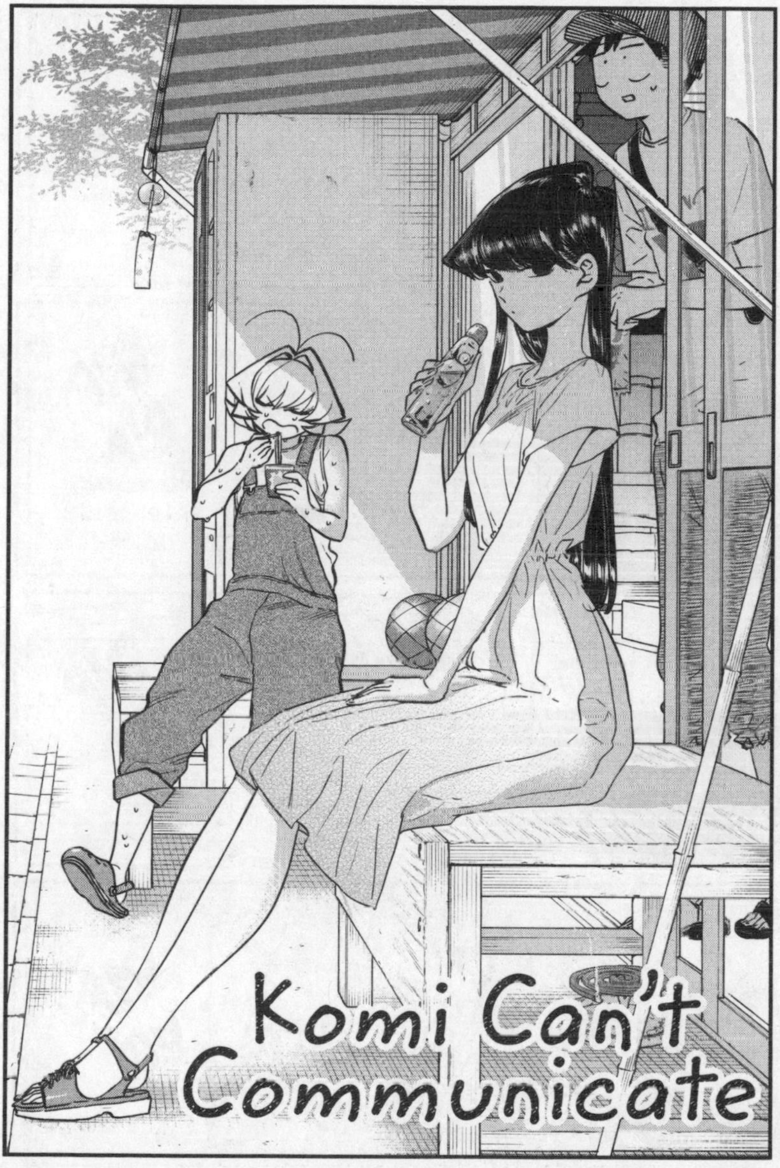
Komi Can't Communicate

Communication 162: The Invitation

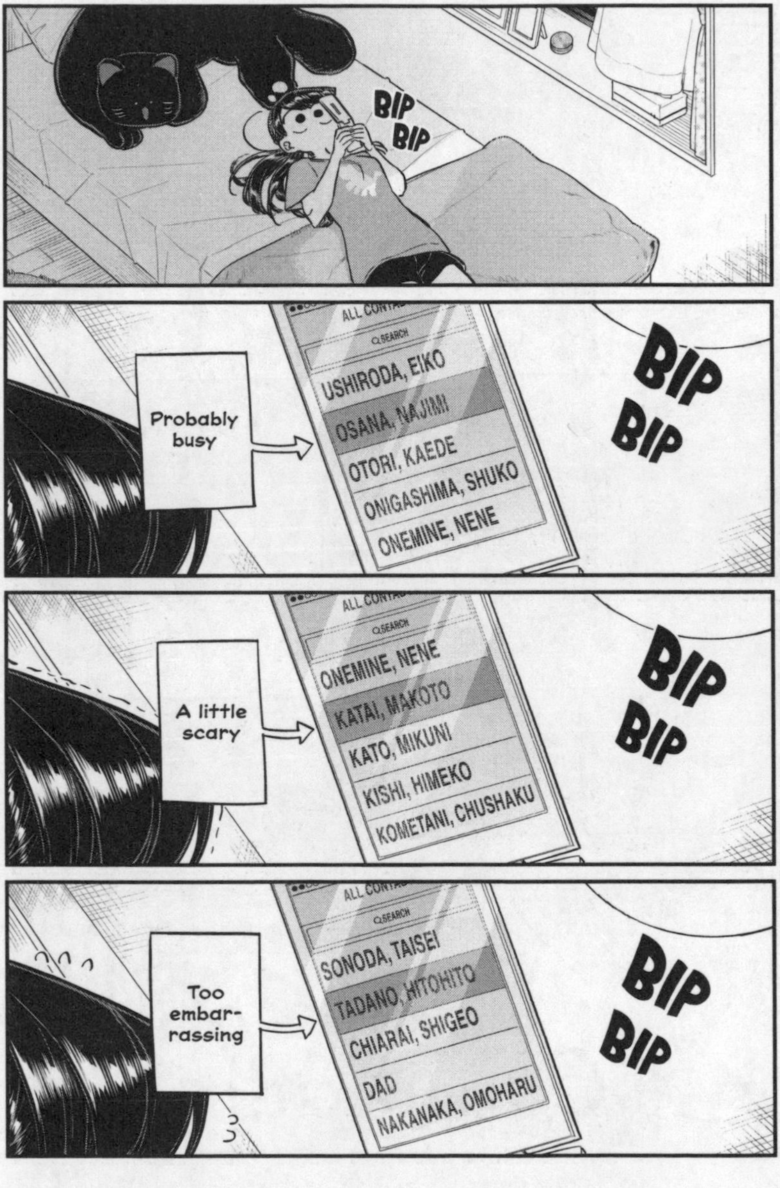
BIP
BIP
BIP
BIP
SEARCH
USHIRODA, EIKO
OSANA, NAJIMI
OTORI, KAEDE
ONIGASHIMA, SHUKO
ONEMINE, NENE
Probably busy
BIP
BIP
SEARCH
ONEMINE, NENE
KATAI, MAKOTO
KATO, MIKUNI
KISHI, HIMEKO
KOMETANI, CHUSHAKU
A little scary
BIP
BIP
SEARCH
SONODA, TAISEI
TADANO, HITOHITO
CHIARAI, SHIGEO
DAD
NAKANAKA, OMOHARU
Too embar-rassing

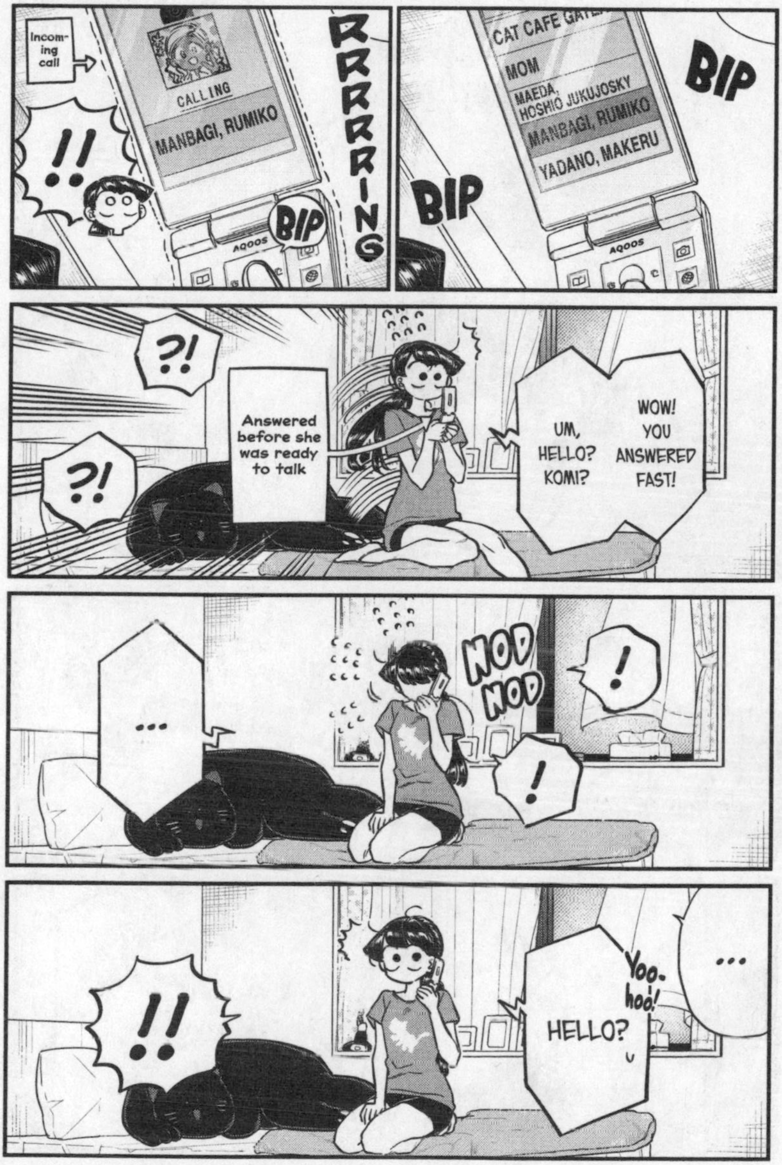
BIP
CAT CAFE
MOM
MAEDA, HOSHIO JUKUJOSKY
MANBAGI, RUMIKO
YADANO, MAKERU
BIP
AQOOS
RRRRRING
CALLING
MANBAGI, RUMIKO
Incom-ing call
!!
BIP
AQOOS
WOW! YOU ANSWERED FAST!
UM, HELLO? KOMI?
Answered before she was ready to talk
?!
?!
!
!
NOD NOD
...
...
Yoo-hoo!
HELLO?
!!

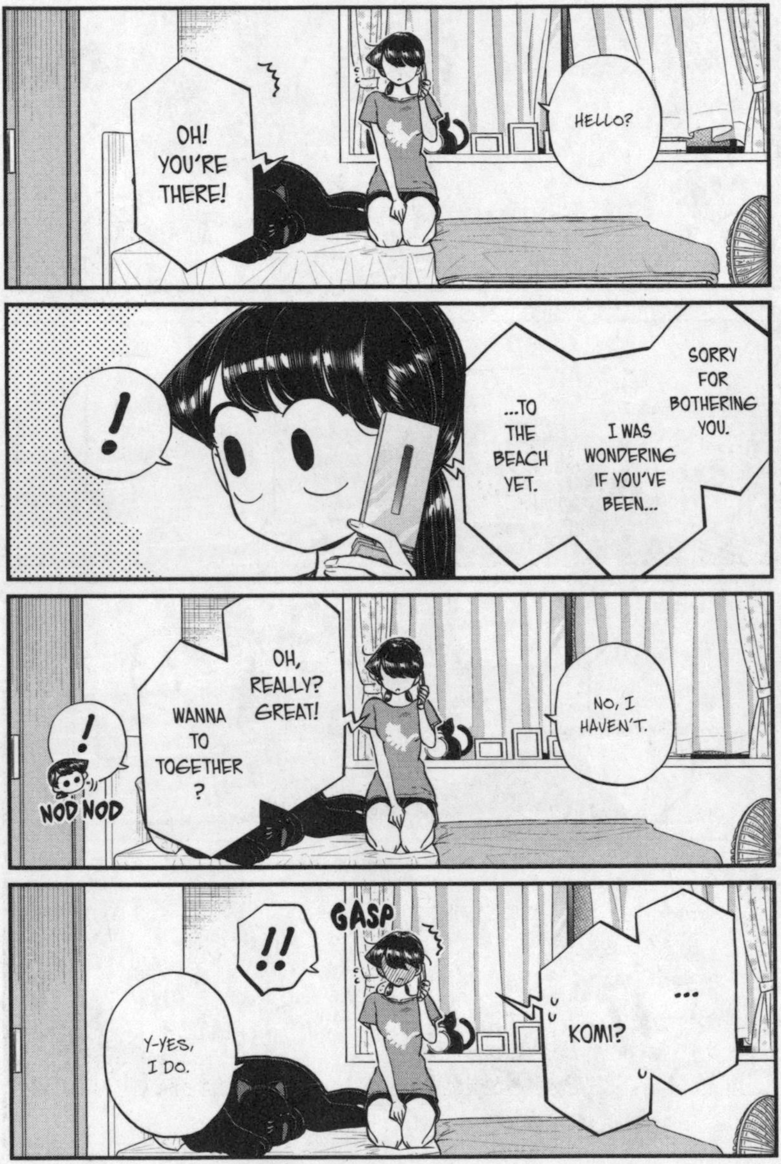
HELLO?
OH! YOU'RE THERE!
SORRY FOR BOTHERING YOU. I WAS WONDERING IF YOU'VE BEEN... ...TO THE BEACH YET.
!
NO, I HAVEN'T.
OH, REALLY? GREAT! WANNA TO TOGETHER ?
!
NOD NOD
... KOMI?
GASP
!!
Y-YES, I DO.

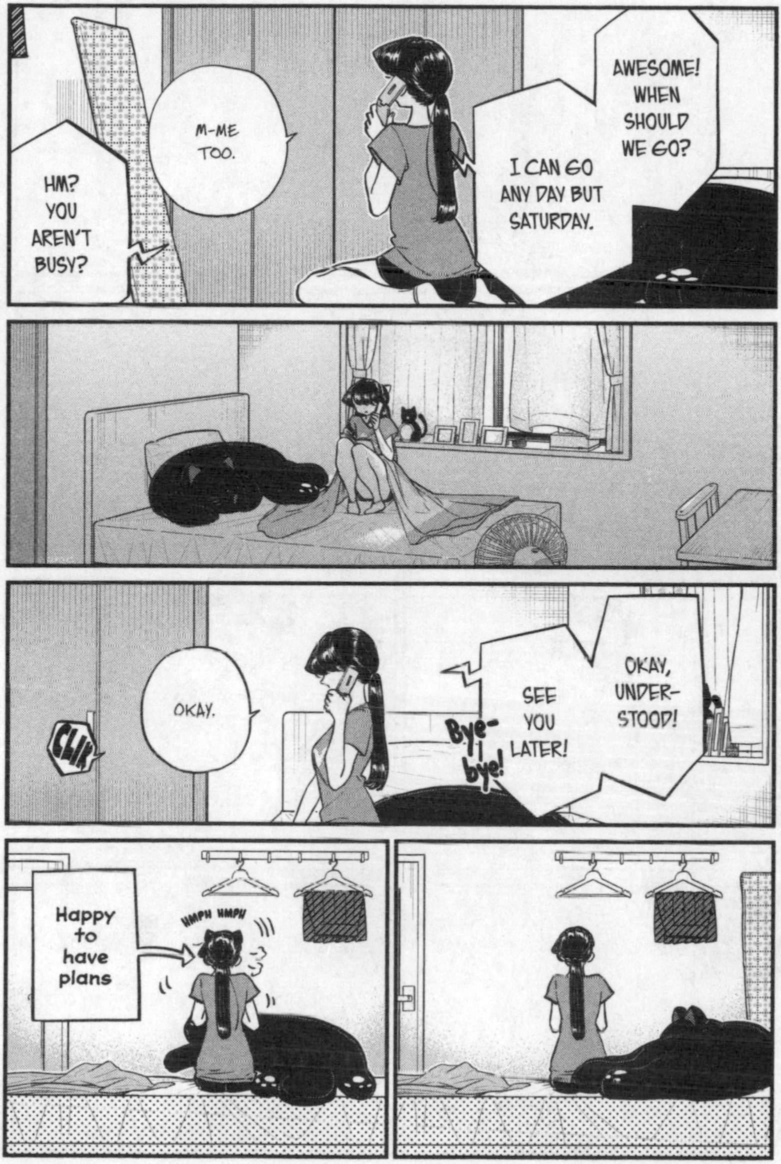
AWESOME! WHEN SHOULD WE GO?
I CAN GO ANY DAY BUT SATURDAY.
M-ME TOO.
HM? YOU AREN'T BUSY?
OKAY, UNDER-STOOD!
SEE YOU LATER!
Bye-bye!
OKAY.
CLIK
HMPH HMPH
Happy to have plans

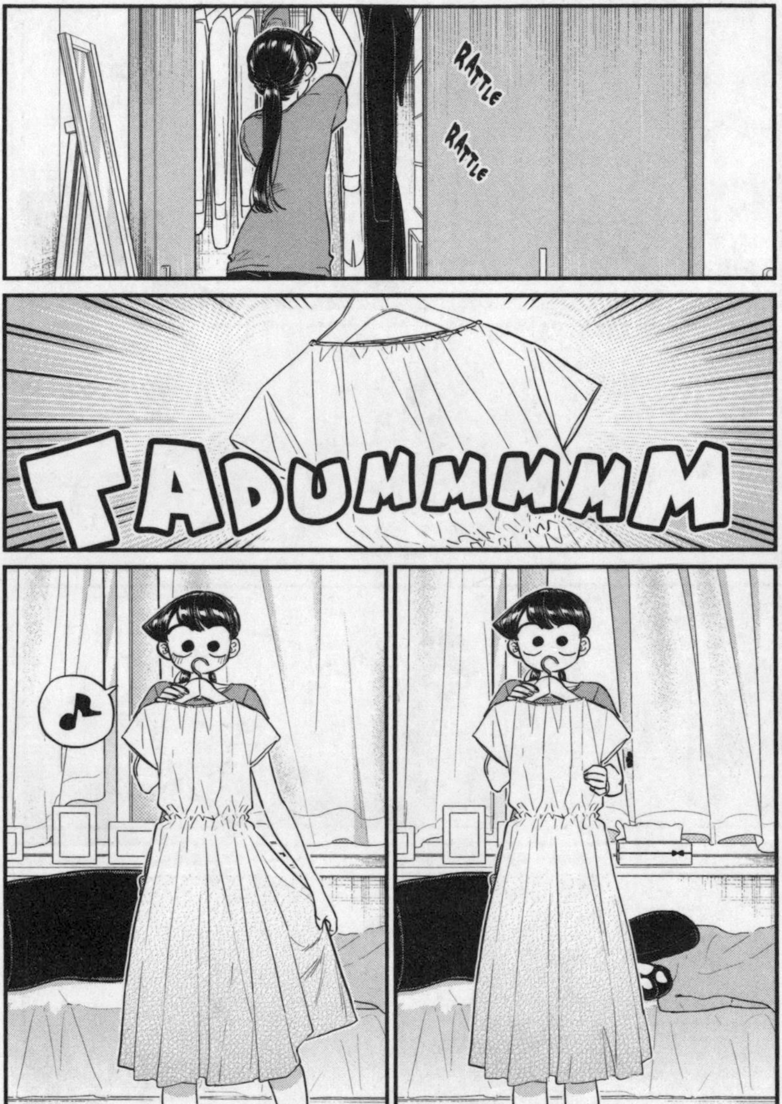
RATTLE
RATTLE
TADUMMMMMM

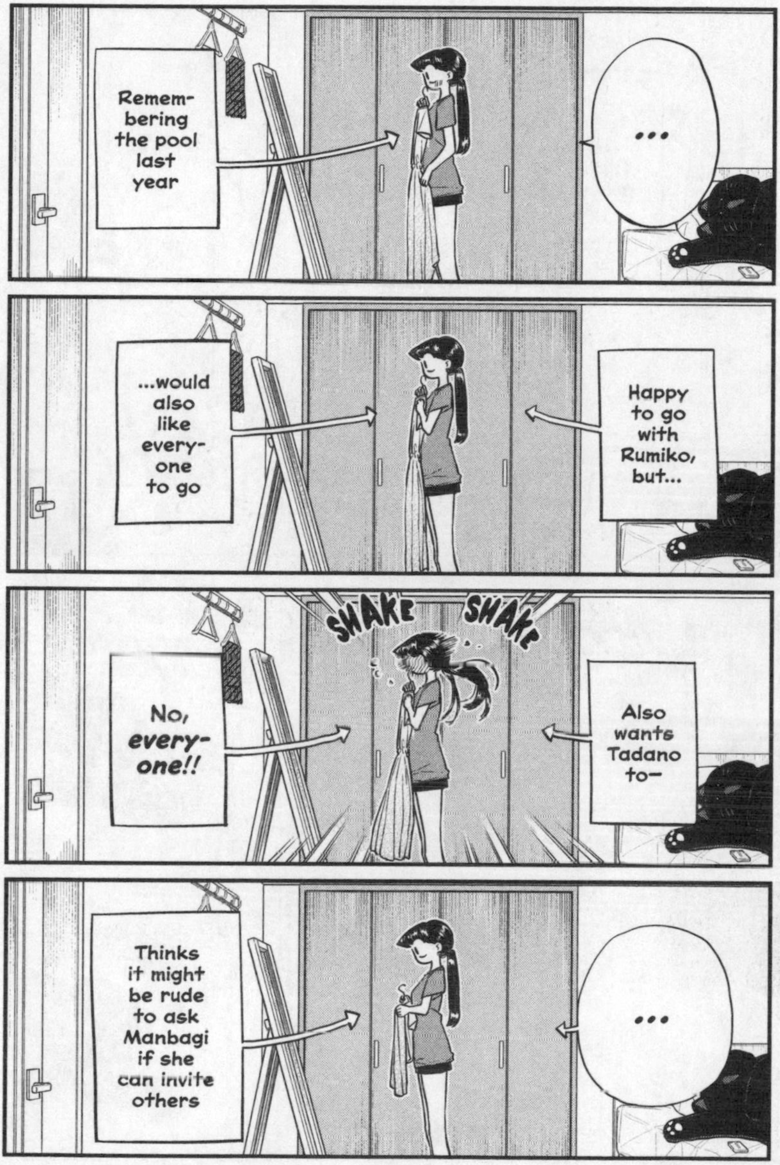
...
Remembering the pool last year
Happy to go with Rumiko, but...
...would also like everyone to go
SHAKE
SHAKE
Also wants Tadano to–
No, *everyone!!*
...
Thinks it might be rude to ask Manbagi if she can invite others

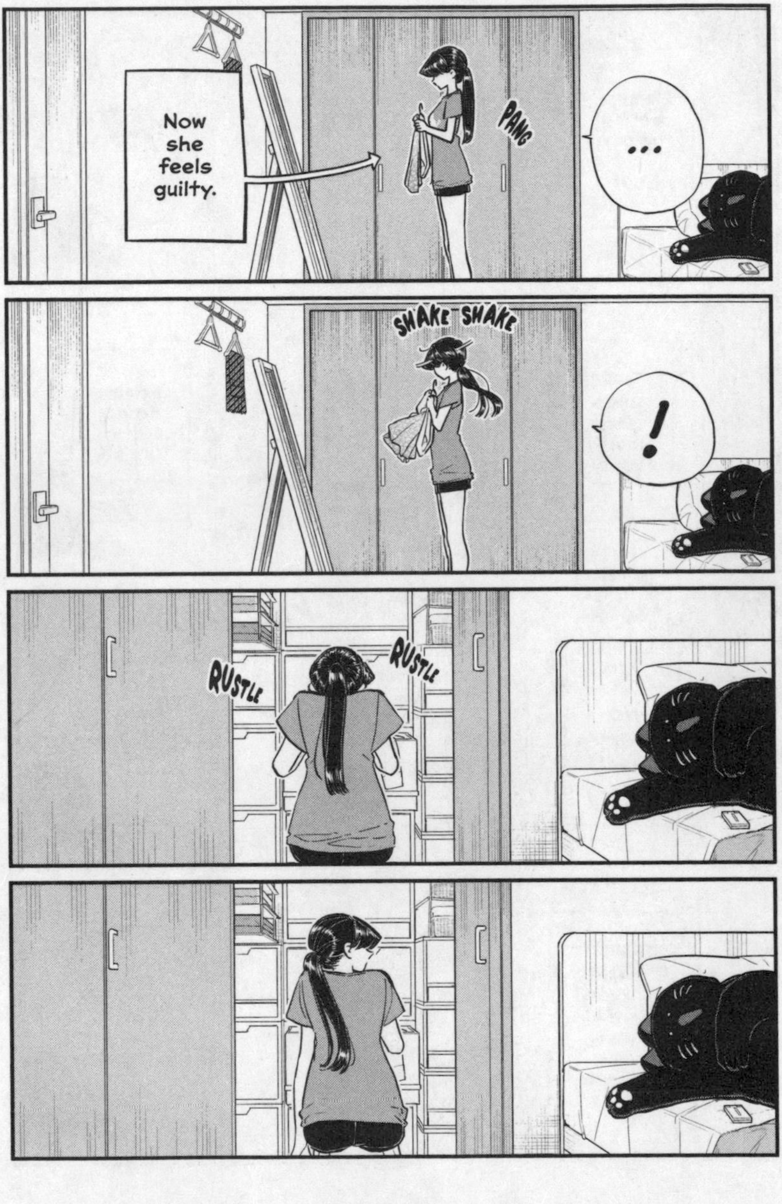
...
PANG
Now she feels guilty.
!
SHAKE SHAKE
RUSTLE
RUSTLE

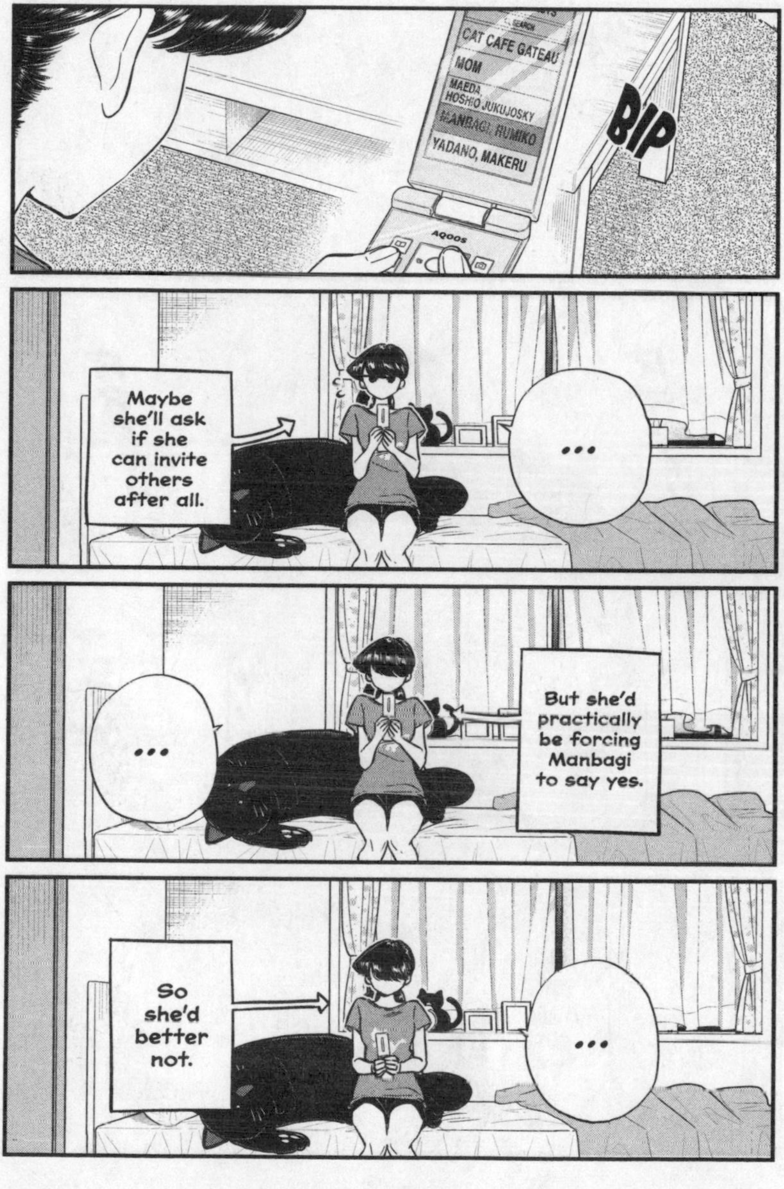
CAT CAFE GATEAU
MOM
MAEDA, HOSHIO JUKUJOSKY
MANBAGI, RUMIKO
YADANO, MAKERU
AQOOS
BIP
...
Maybe she'll ask if she can invite others after all.
But she'd practically be forcing Manbagi to say yes.
...
...
So she'd better not.

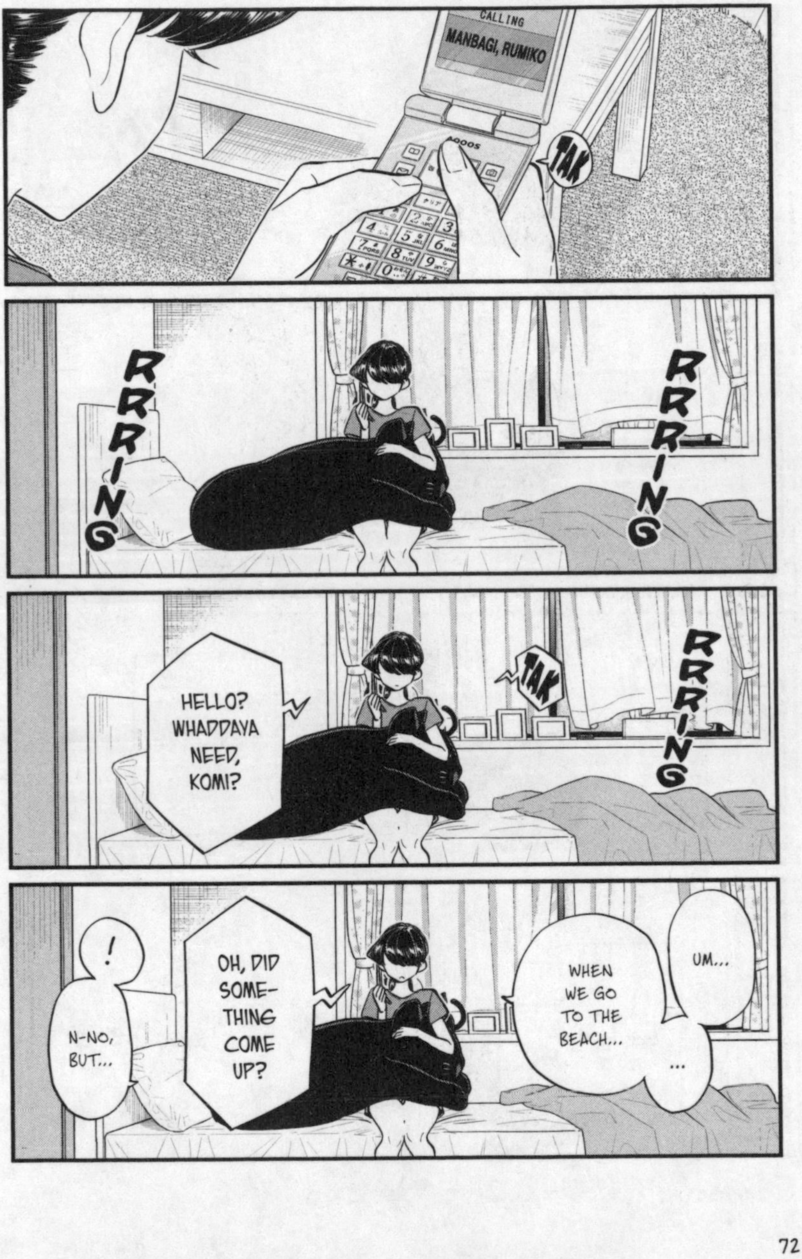

CALLING
MANBAGI, RUMIKO
TAK
RRRING
RRRING
RRRING
TAK
HELLO? WHADDAYA NEED, KOMI?
UM... ...
WHEN WE GO TO THE BEACH...
OH, DID SOME-THING COME UP?
!
N-NO, BUT...

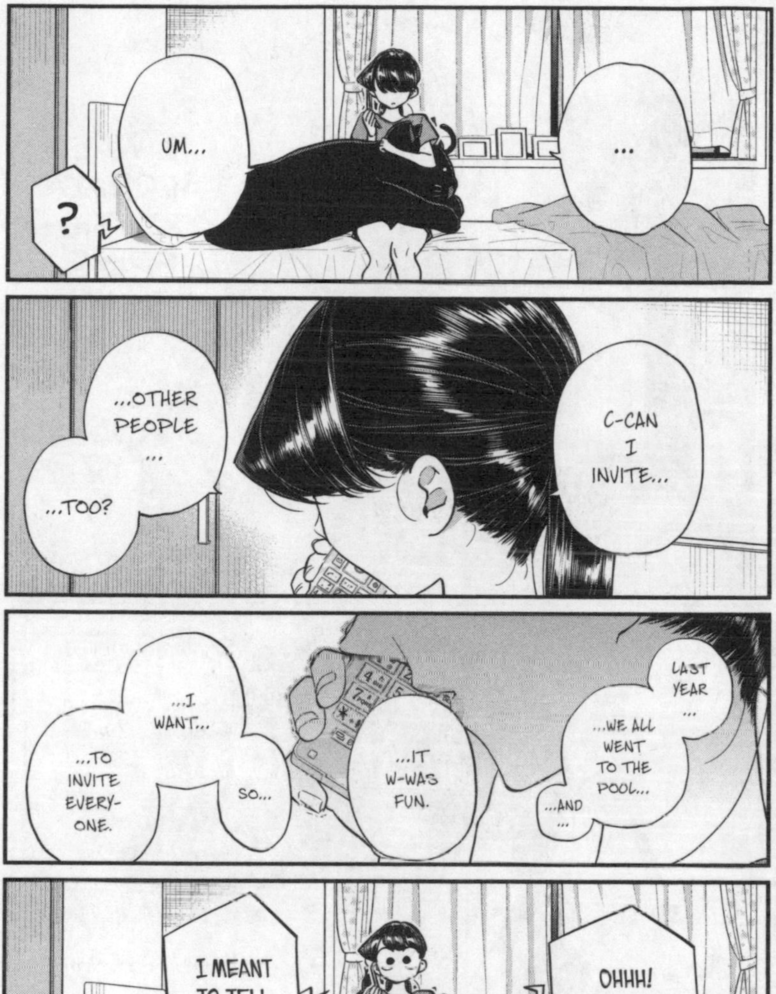
...
UM...
?
C-CAN I INVITE...
...OTHER PEOPLE ... ...TOO?
LAST YEAR ...
...WE ALL WENT TO THE POOL...
...AND ...
...IT W-WAS FUN.
...I WANT...
...TO INVITE EVERY-ONE.
SO...
OHHH! RIGHT! ABOUT THAT!
I MEANT TO TELL YOU EARLIER!
!

Communication 162 — The End

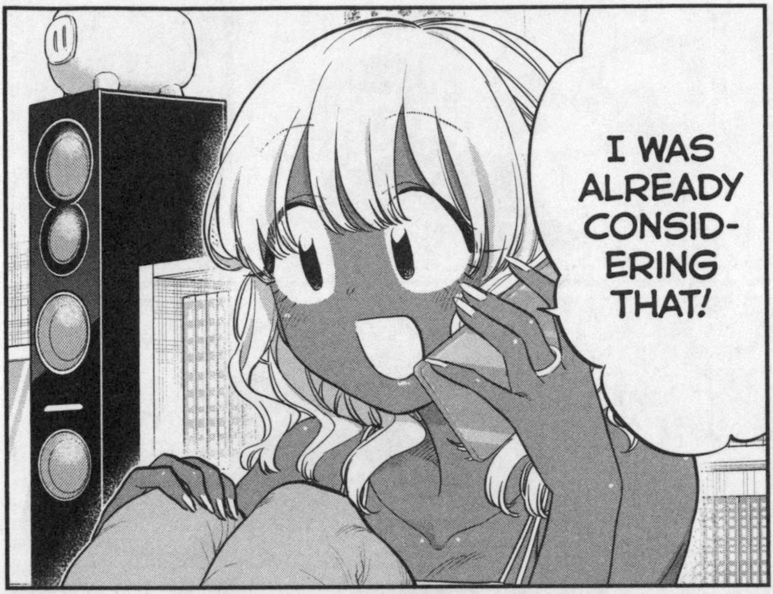
I WAS ALREADY CONSID- ERING THAT!
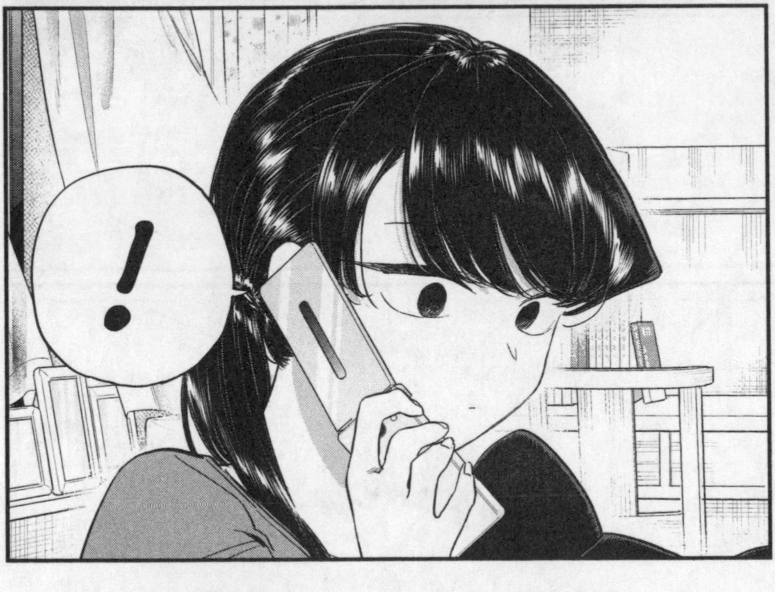
!

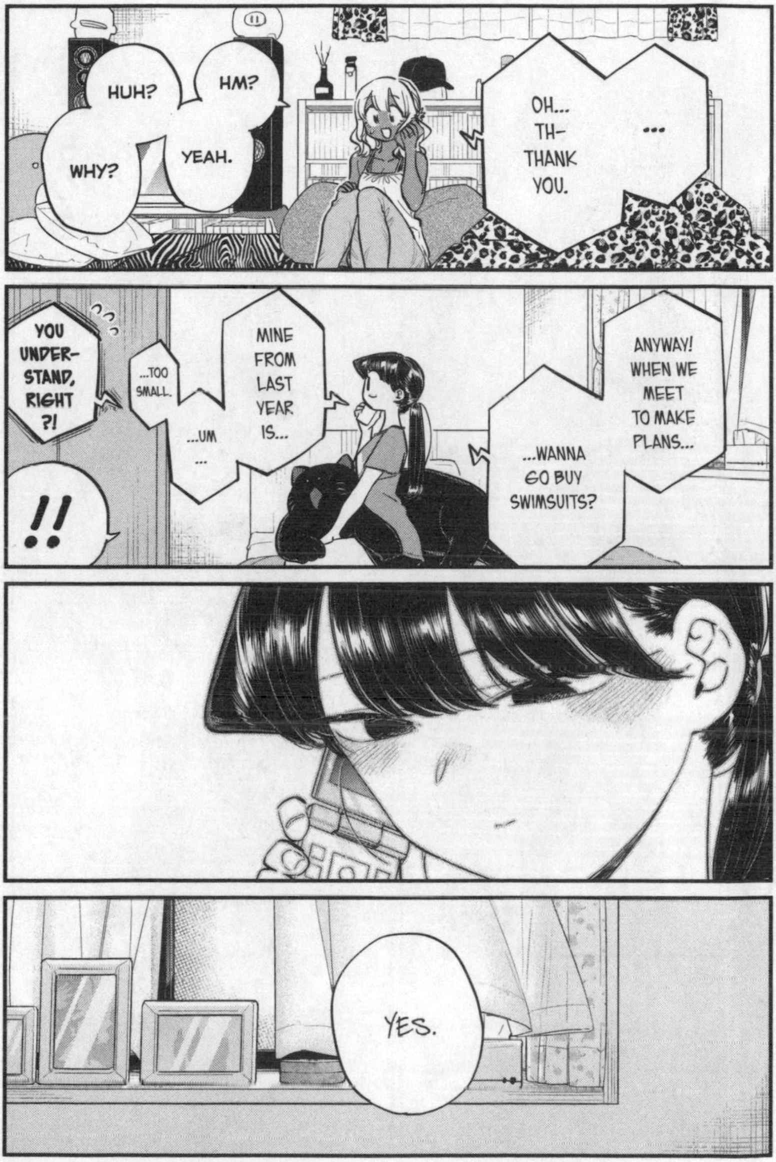
...
OH... TH- THANK YOU.
HM?
HUH?
YEAH.
WHY?
ANYWAY! WHEN WE MEET TO MAKE PLANS...
...WANNA GO BUY SWIMSUITS?
MINE FROM LAST YEAR IS...
...UM ...
...TOO SMALL.
YOU UNDER-STAND, RIGHT ?!
!!
YES.

Komi Can't Communicate

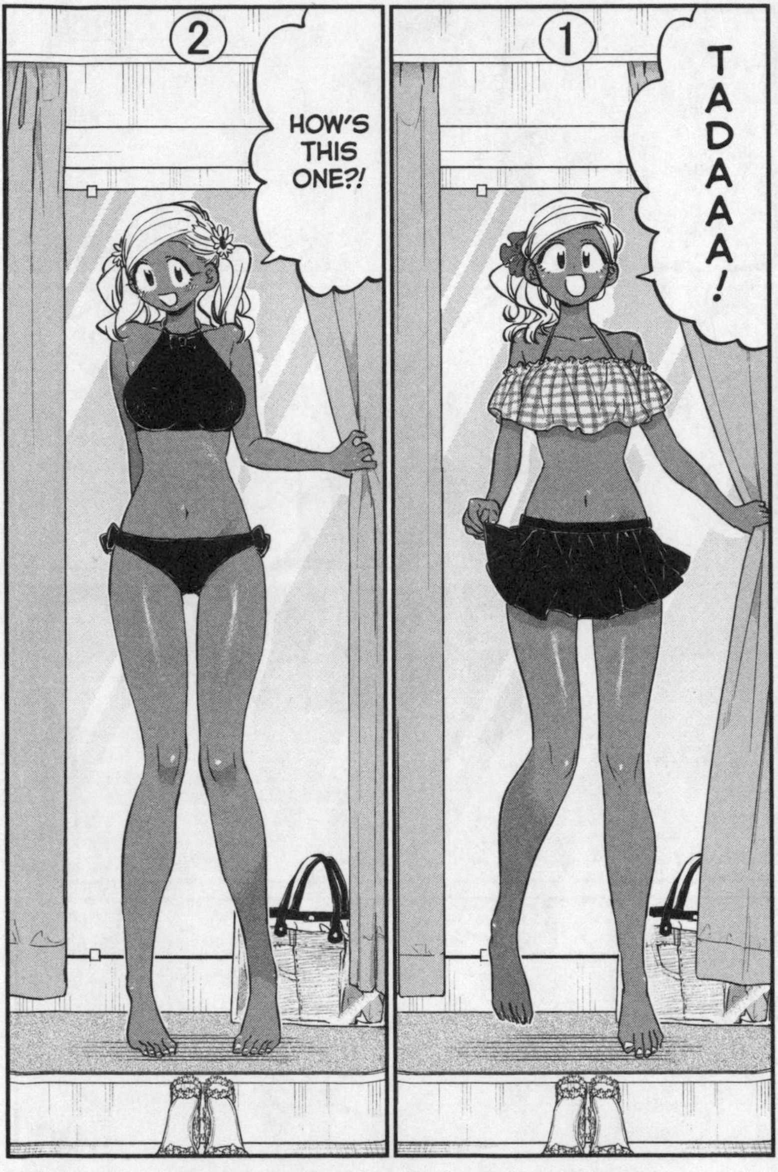
1
TADAAAA!
2
HOW'S THIS ONE?!

Communication 163: Swimsuit Shopping

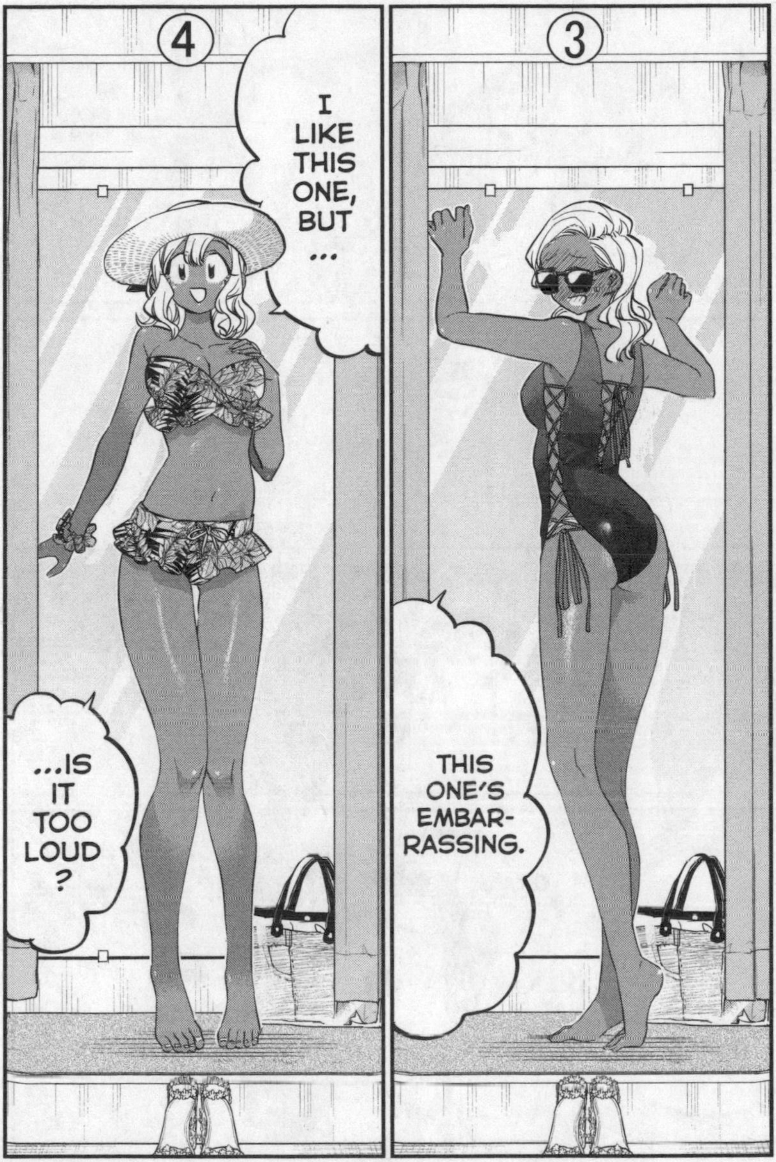
3
THIS ONE'S EMBARRASSING.
4
I LIKE THIS ONE, BUT...
...IS IT TOO LOUD?

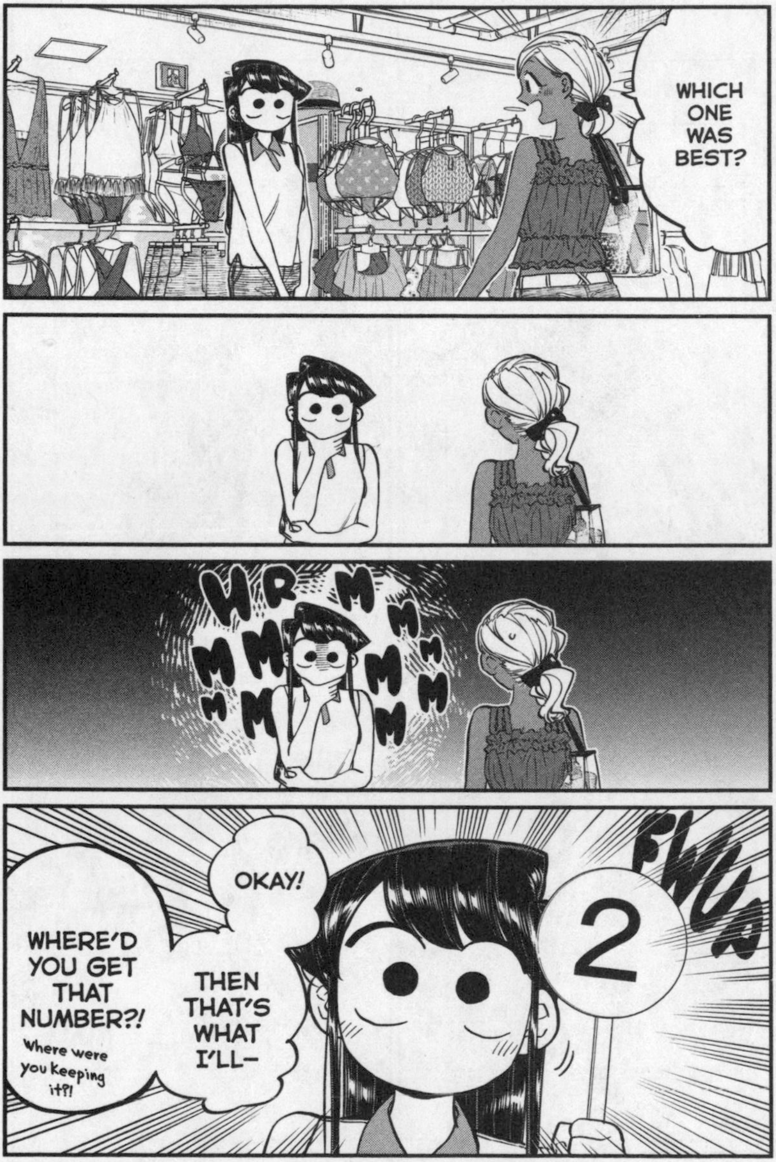
WHICH ONE WAS BEST?
HRMMMMMMMMMMMMMMMM
FWUP
2
OKAY!
THEN THAT'S WHAT I'LL—
WHERE'D YOU GET THAT NUMBER?!
Where were you keeping it?!

Communication 163 — The End

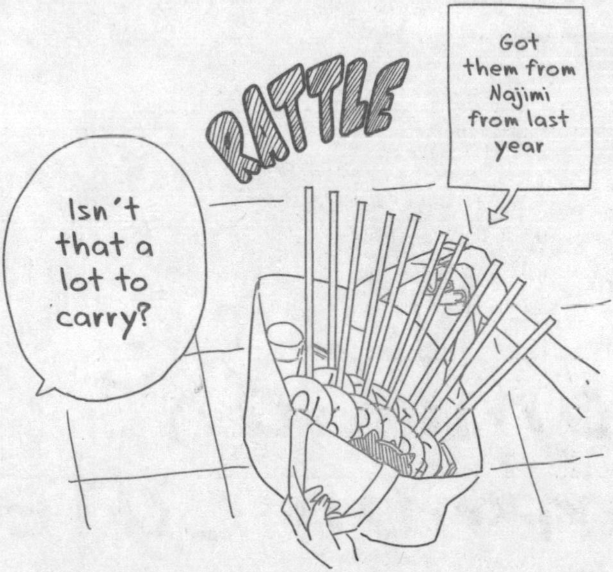
Got them from Najimi from last year
RATTLE
Isn't that a lot to carry?

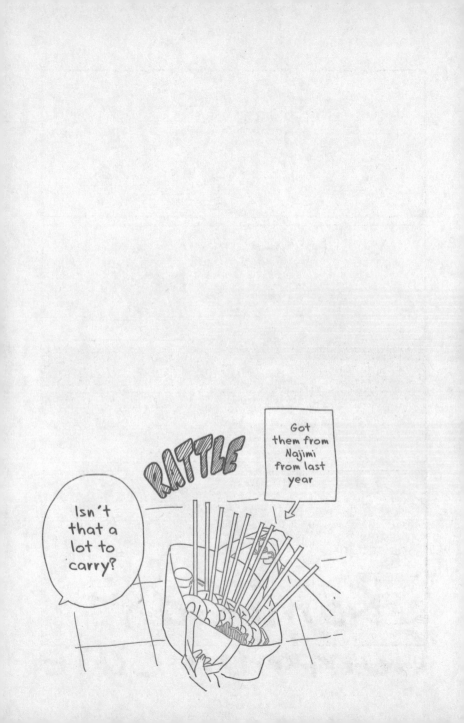

Komi Can't Communicate

Komi Can't Communicate

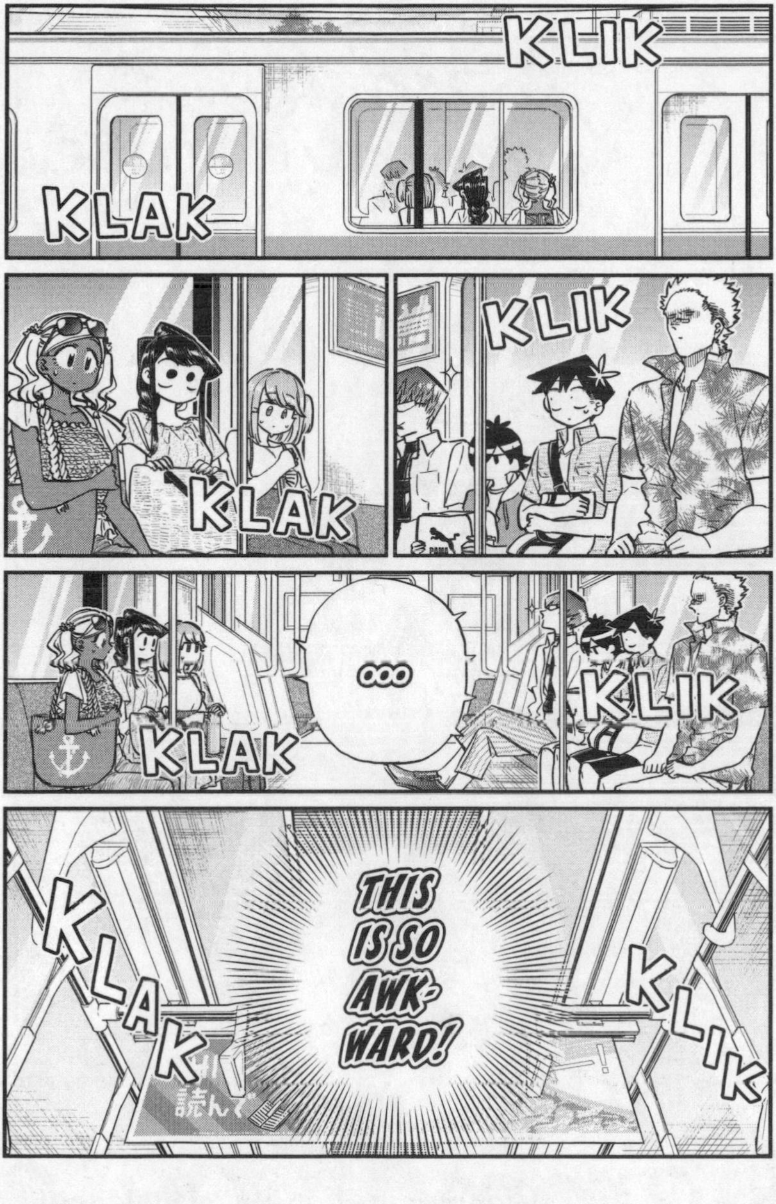
KLIK
KLAK
KLIK
KLAK
KLIK
...
KLAK
KLIK
THIS IS SO AWK-WARD!
KLAK

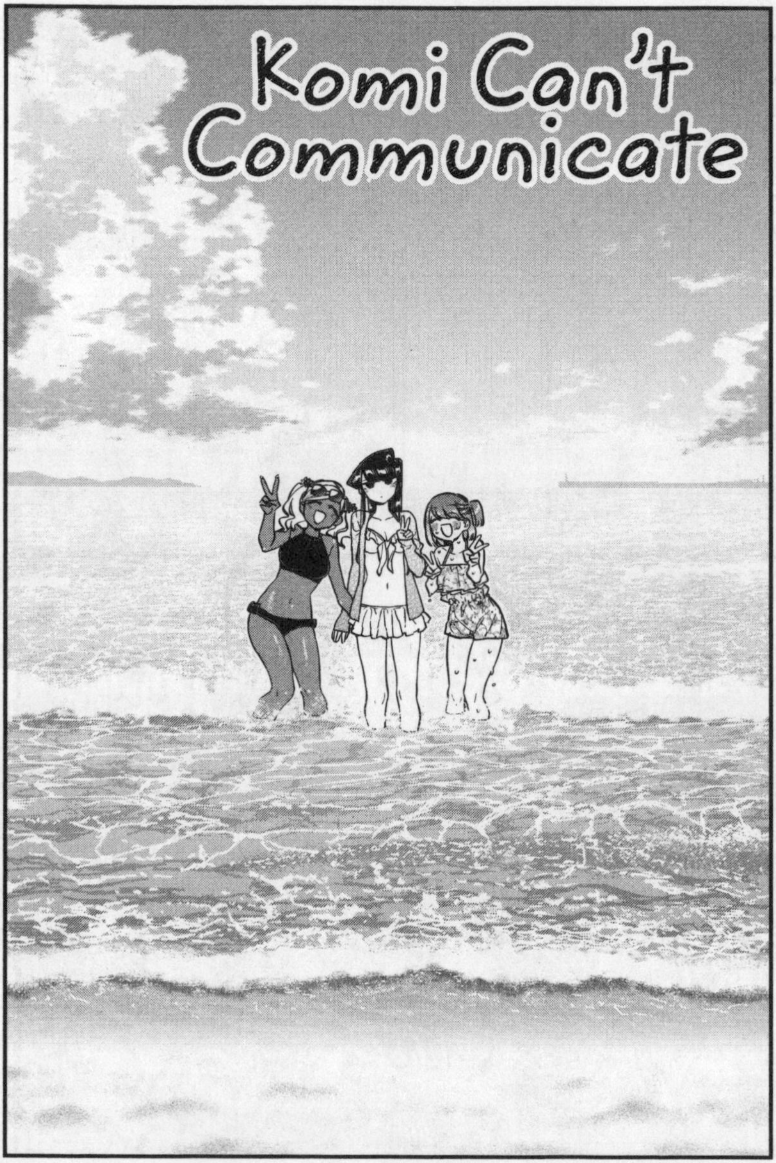
Komi Can't
Communicate

Communication 164: The Ocean!

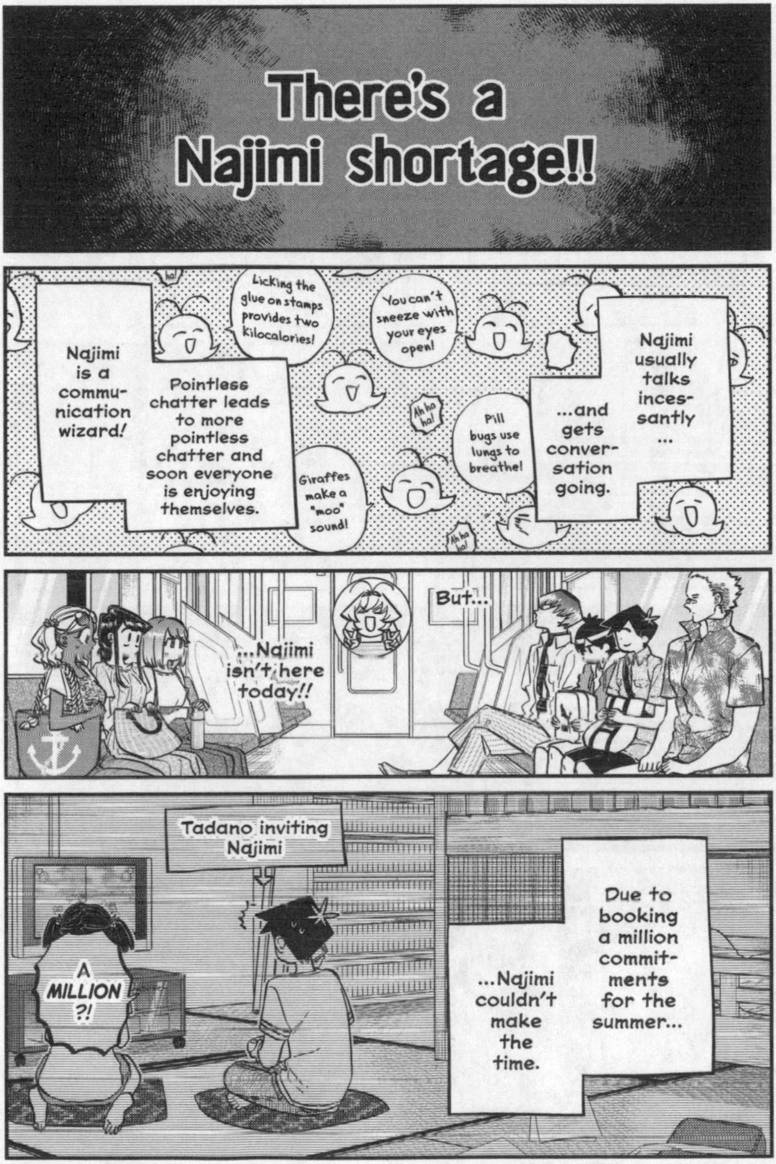
There's a Najimi shortage!!
Najimi usually talks incessantly...
...and gets conversation going.
Ah ha ha!
Pill bugs use lungs to breathe!
You can't sneeze with your eyes open!
Ah ha ha!
Giraffes make a "moo" sound!
Licking the glue on stamps provides two kilocalories!
ha!
Najimi is a communication wizard!
Pointless chatter leads to more pointless chatter and soon everyone is enjoying themselves.
But...
...Najimi isn't here today!!
Due to booking a million commitments for the summer...
...Najimi couldn't make the time.
Tadano inviting Najimi
A MILLION?!

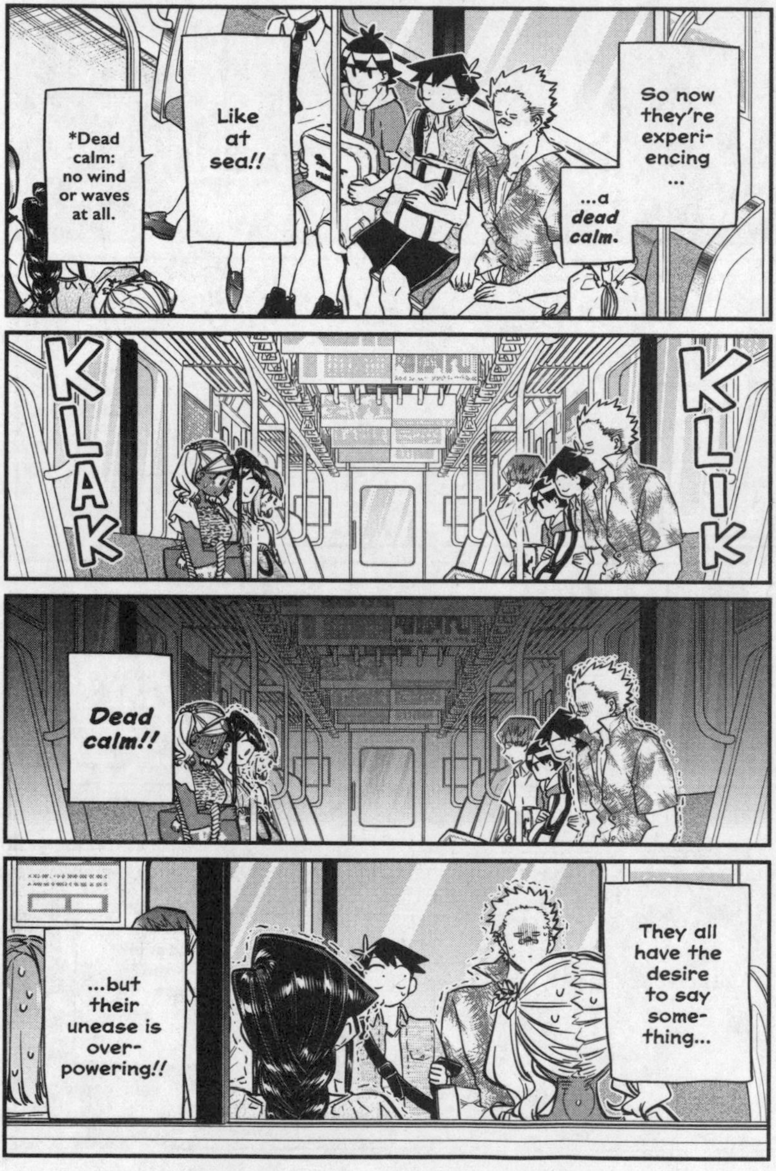
So now they're experiencing ...
...a *dead calm.*
Like at sea!!
*Dead calm: no wind or waves at all.
KLIK
KLAK
Dead calm!!
They all have the desire to say something...
...but their unease is overpowering!!

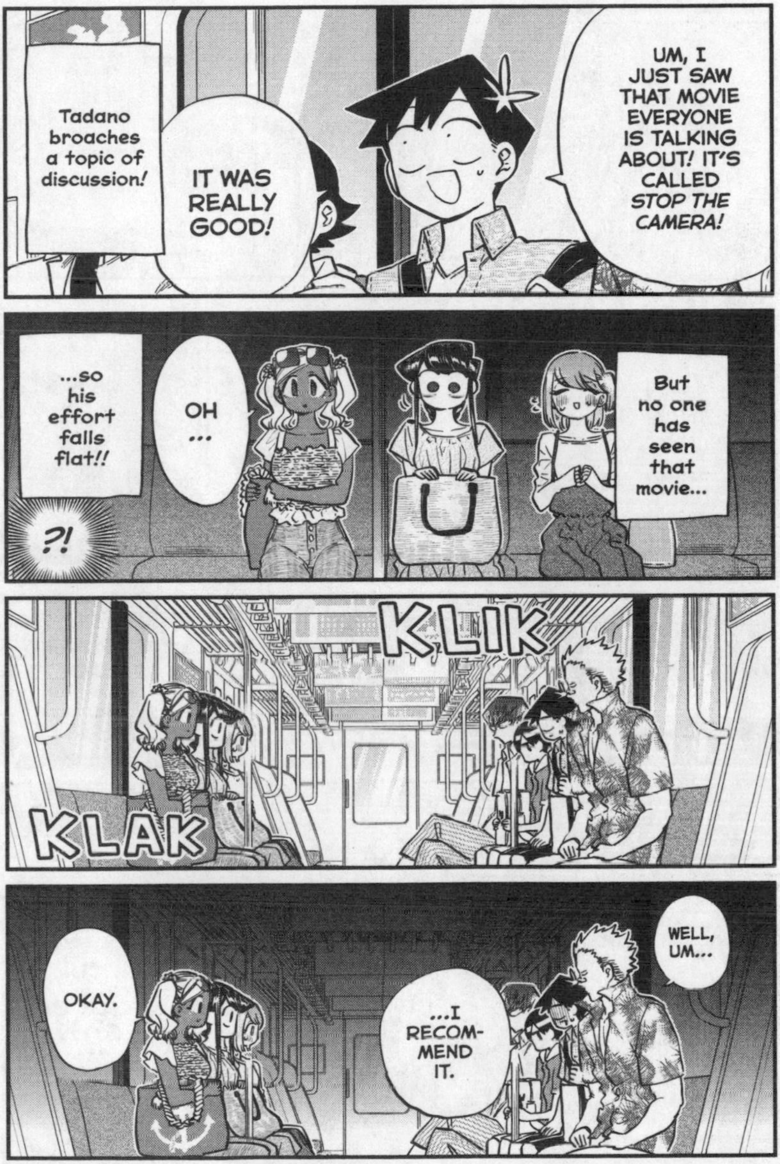
UM, I JUST SAW THAT MOVIE EVERYONE IS TALKING ABOUT! IT'S CALLED *STOP THE CAMERA!*
IT WAS REALLY GOOD!
Tadano broaches a topic of discussion!
But no one has seen that movie...
OH ...
...so his effort falls flat!!
?!
KLIK
KLAK
WELL, UM...
...I RECOM-MEND IT.
OKAY.

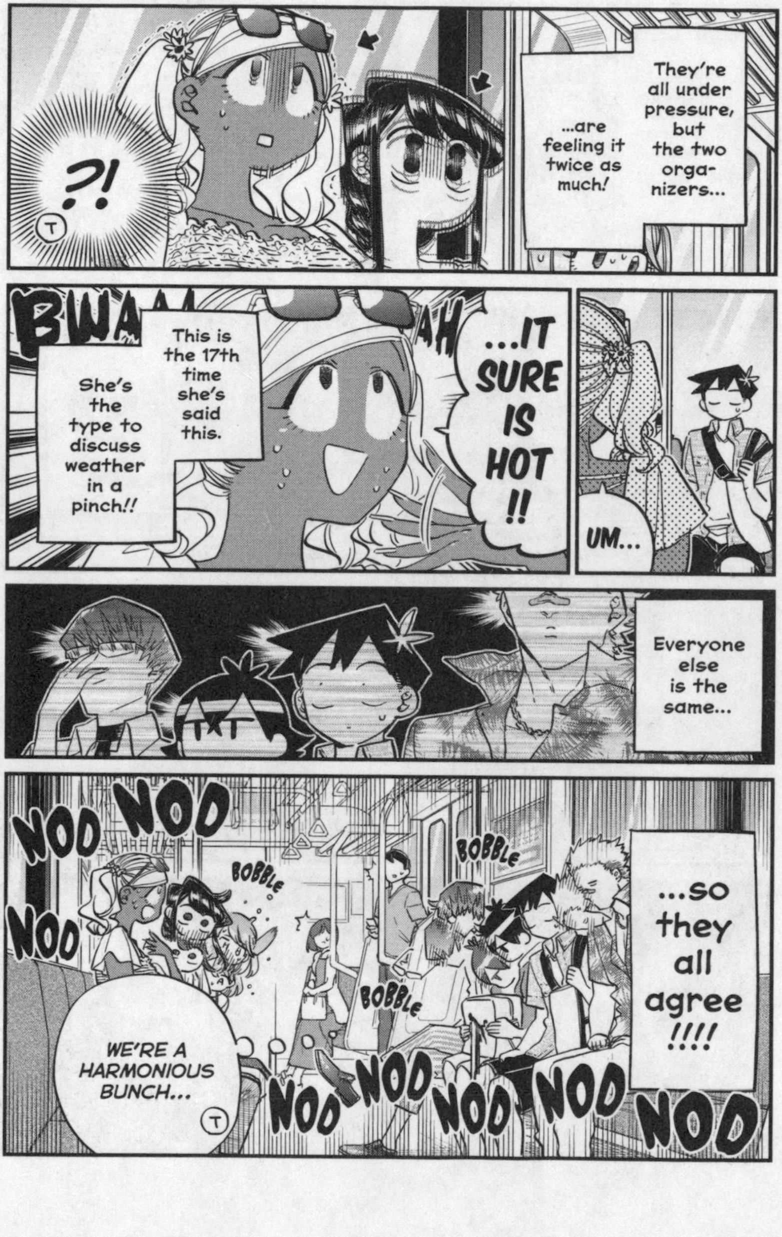
They're all under pressure, but the two organizers...
...are feeling it twice as much!
?!
UM...
...IT SURE IS HOT!!
This is the 17th time she's said this.
She's the type to discuss weather in a pinch!!
Everyone else is the same...
...so they all agree!!!!
BOBBLE
NOD NOD
NOD
BOBBLE
BOBBLE
NOD NOD NOD NOD NOD
WE'RE A HARMONIOUS BUNCH...

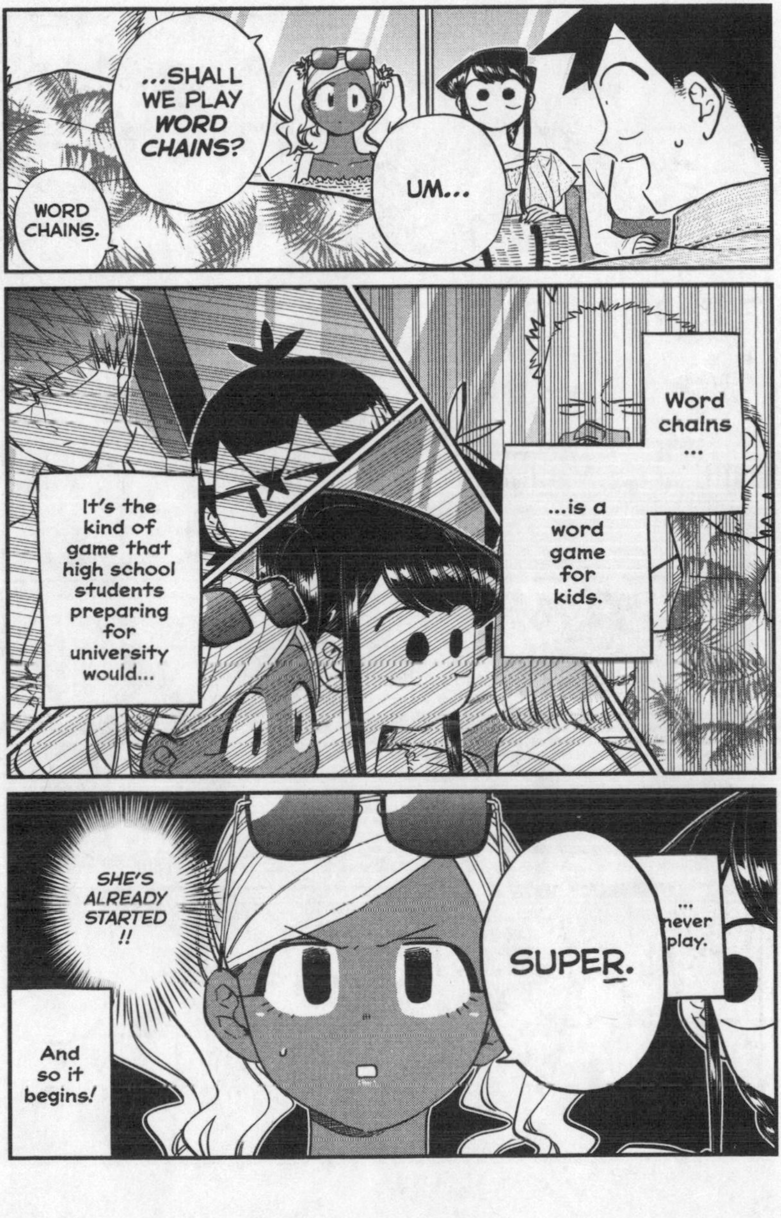
...SHALL WE PLAY WORD CHAINS?
UM...
WORD CHAINS.
Word chains...
...is a word game for kids.
It's the kind of game that high school students preparing for university would...
...never play.
SUPER.
SHE'S ALREADY STARTED!!
And so it begins!

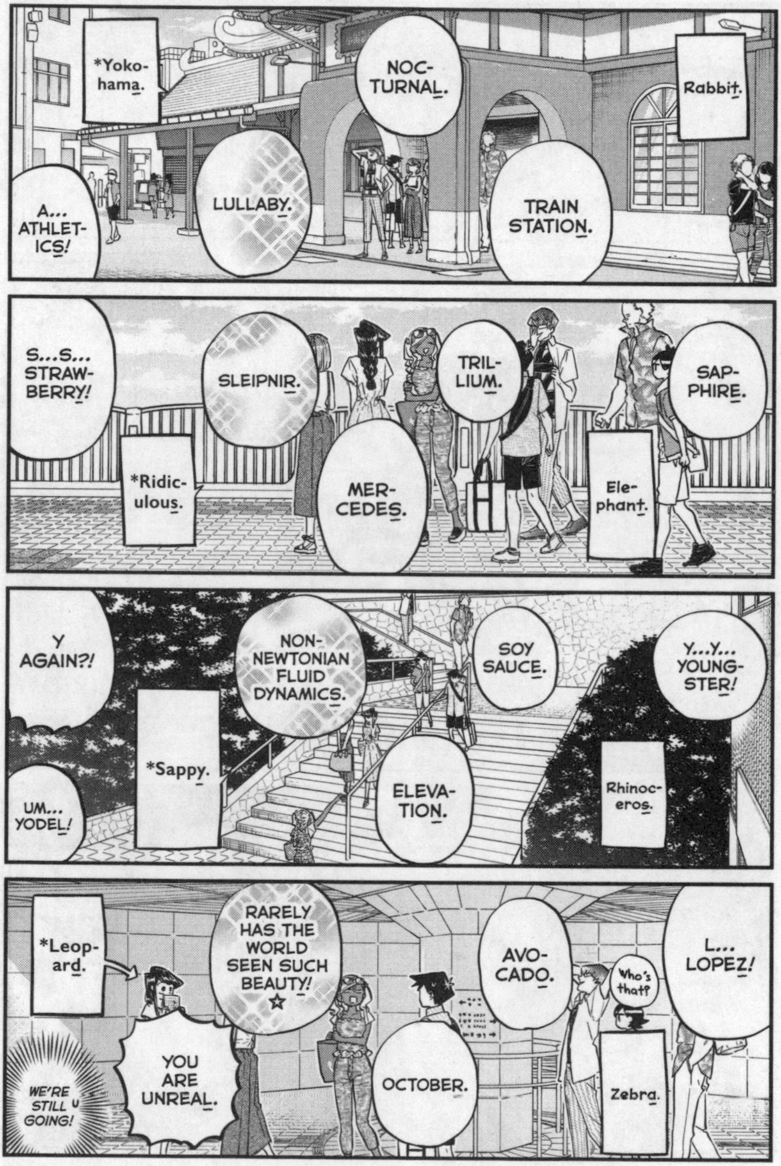
Rabbit.
NOCTURNAL.
*Yokohama.
TRAIN STATION.
LULLABY.
A... ATHLETICS!
SAPPHIRE.
Elephant.
TRILLIUM.
MERCEDES.
SLEIPNIR.
S...S... STRAWBERRY!
*Ridiculous.
Y...Y... YOUNGSTER!
SOY SAUCE.
Rhinoceros.
NON-NEWTONIAN FLUID DYNAMICS.
ELEVATION.
Y AGAIN?!
*Sappy.
UM... YODEL!
L... LOPEZ!
Who's that?
AVOCADO.
Zebra.
RARELY HAS THE WORLD SEEN SUCH BEAUTY! ☆
OCTOBER.
*Leopard.
YOU ARE UNREAL.
WE'RE STILL GOING!

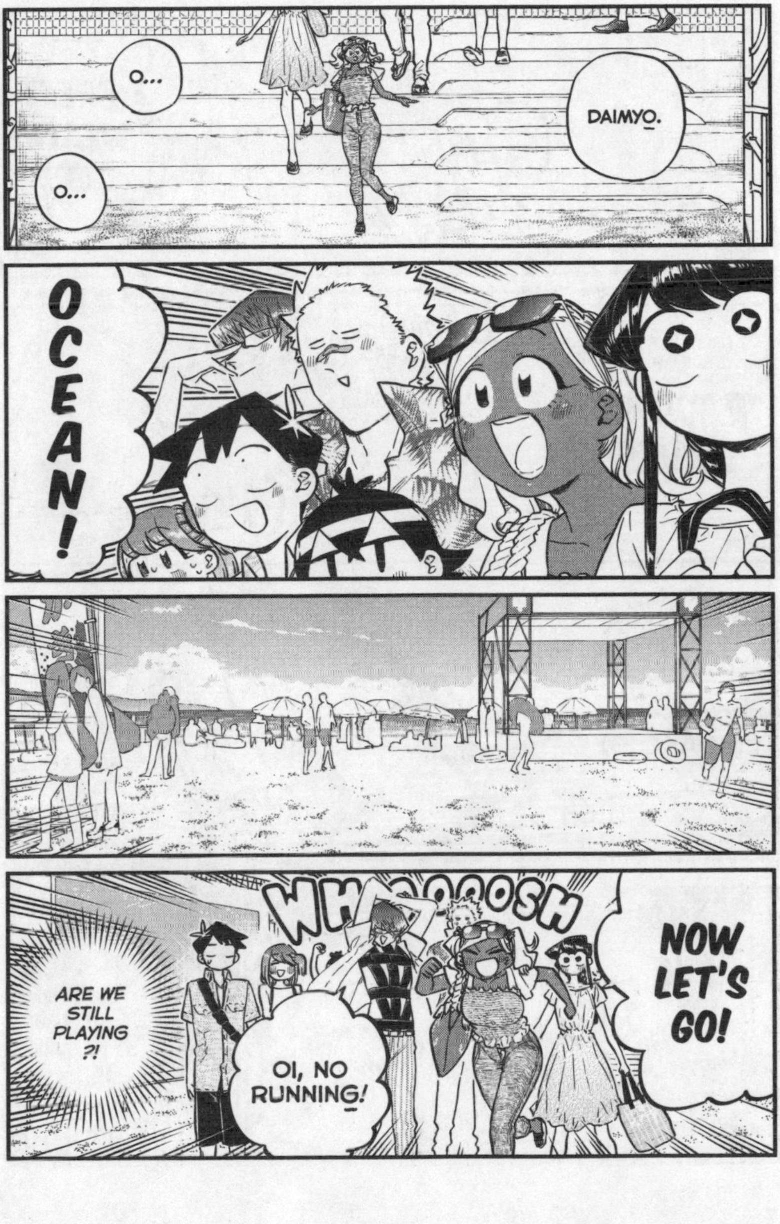
DAIMYO.
O...
O...
OCEAN!
WHOOOOSH
NOW LET'S GO!
OI, NO RUNNING!
ARE WE STILL PLAYING?!

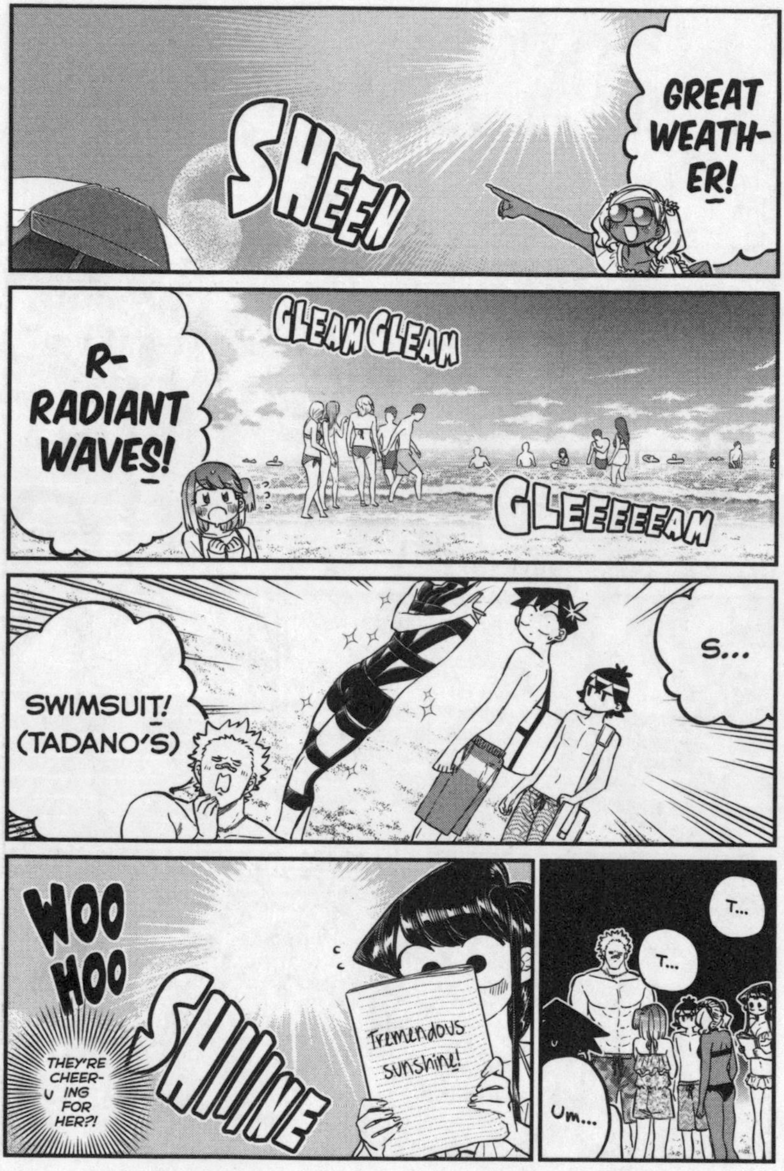
GREAT WEATH-ER!
SHEEN
GLEAM GLEAM
R-RADIANT WAVES!
GLEEEEEAM
S...
SWIMSUIT! (TADANO'S)
T...
T...
Um...
WOO HOO
SHIINE
Tremendous sunshine!
THEY'RE CHEER-ING FOR HER?!

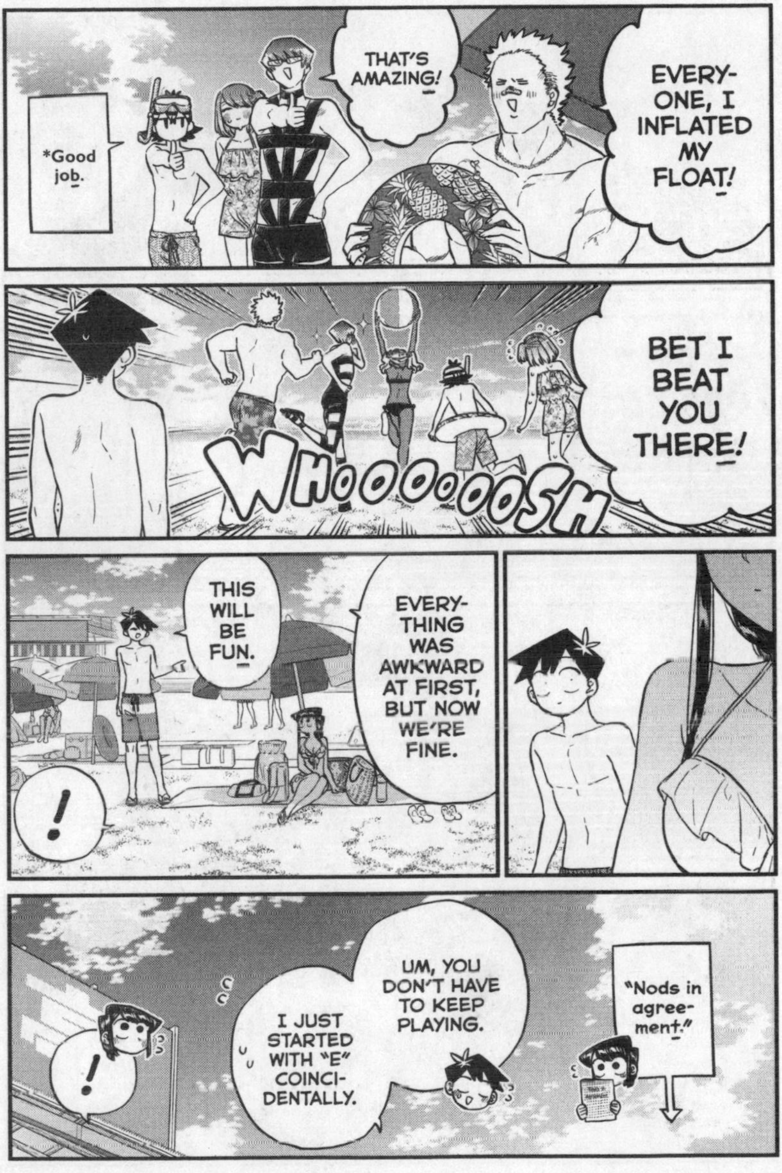
EVERYONE, I INFLATED MY FLOAT!
THAT'S AMAZING!
*Good job.
BET I BEAT YOU THERE!
WHOOOOOOSH
EVERYTHING WAS AWKWARD AT FIRST, BUT NOW WE'RE FINE.
THIS WILL BE FUN.
!
Nods in agreement.
UM, YOU DON'T HAVE TO KEEP PLAYING.
I JUST STARTED WITH "E" COINCIDENTALLY.
!

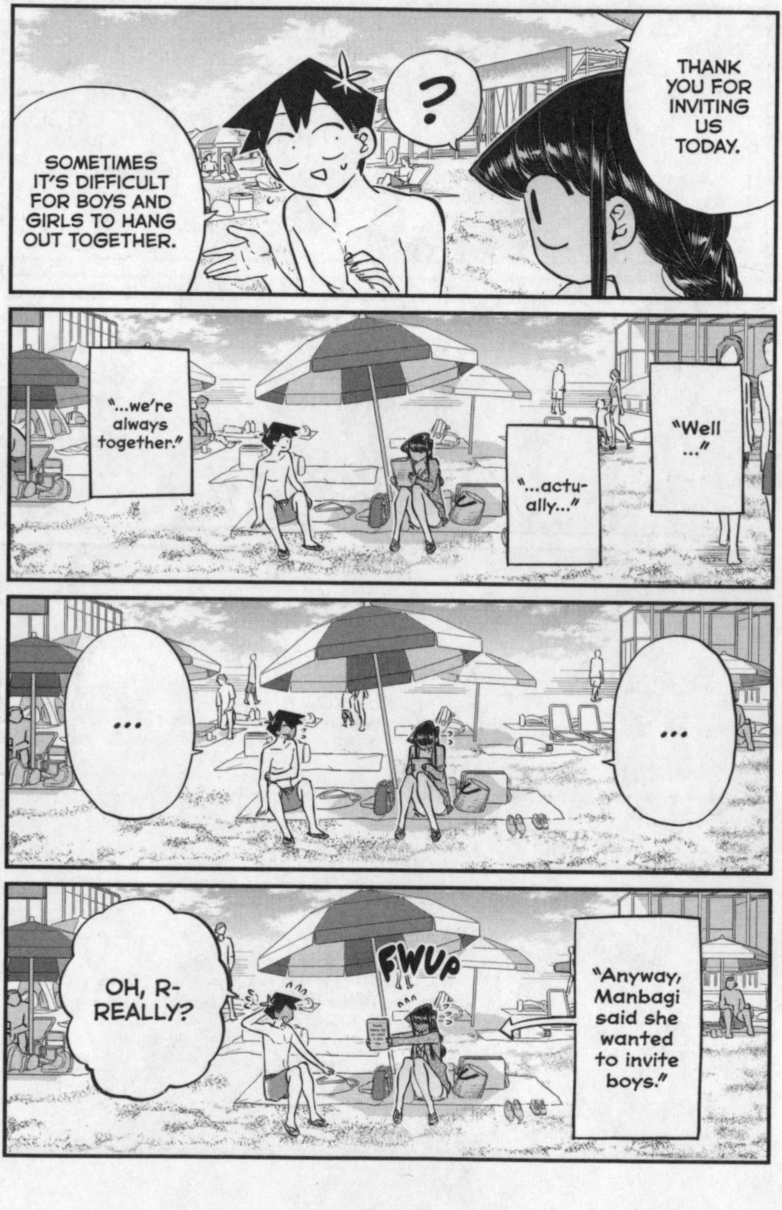
THANK YOU FOR INVITING US TODAY.
?
SOMETIMES IT'S DIFFICULT FOR BOYS AND GIRLS TO HANG OUT TOGETHER.
"Well ..."
"...actu-ally..."
"...we're always together."
...
...
"Anyway, Manbagi said she wanted to invite boys."
FWUP
OH, R-REALLY?

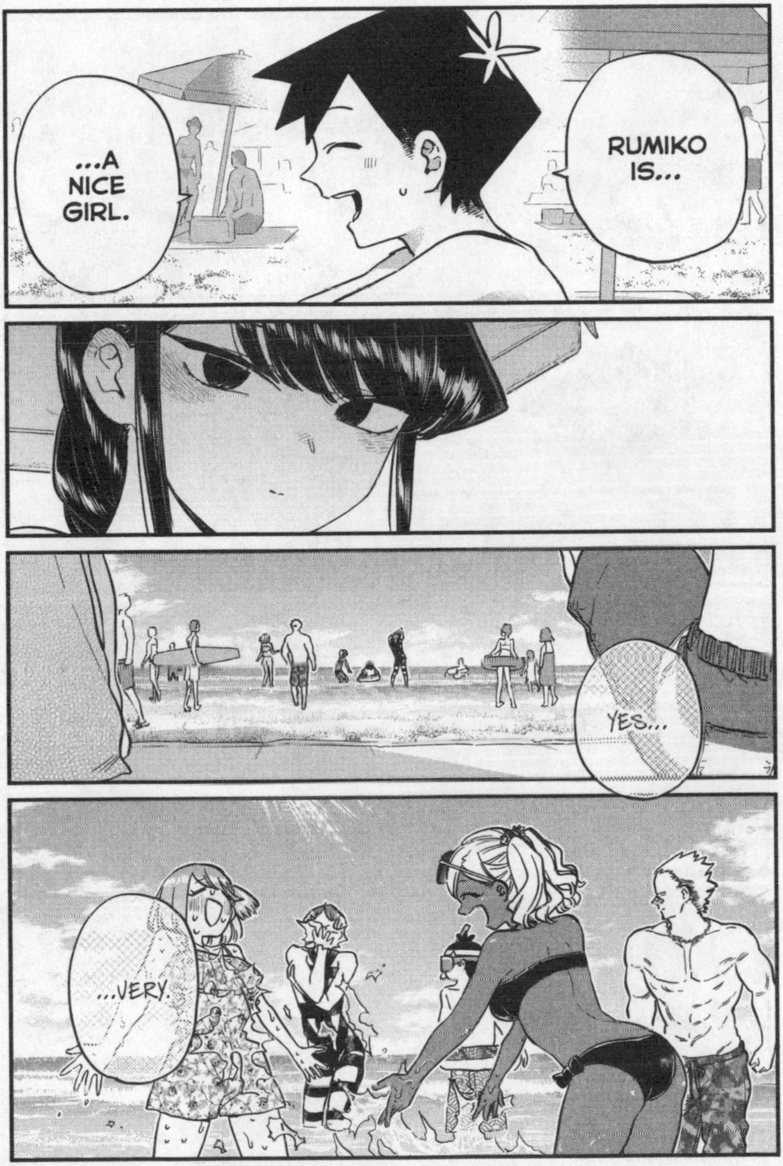
RUMIKO IS...
...A NICE GIRL.
YES...
...VERY.

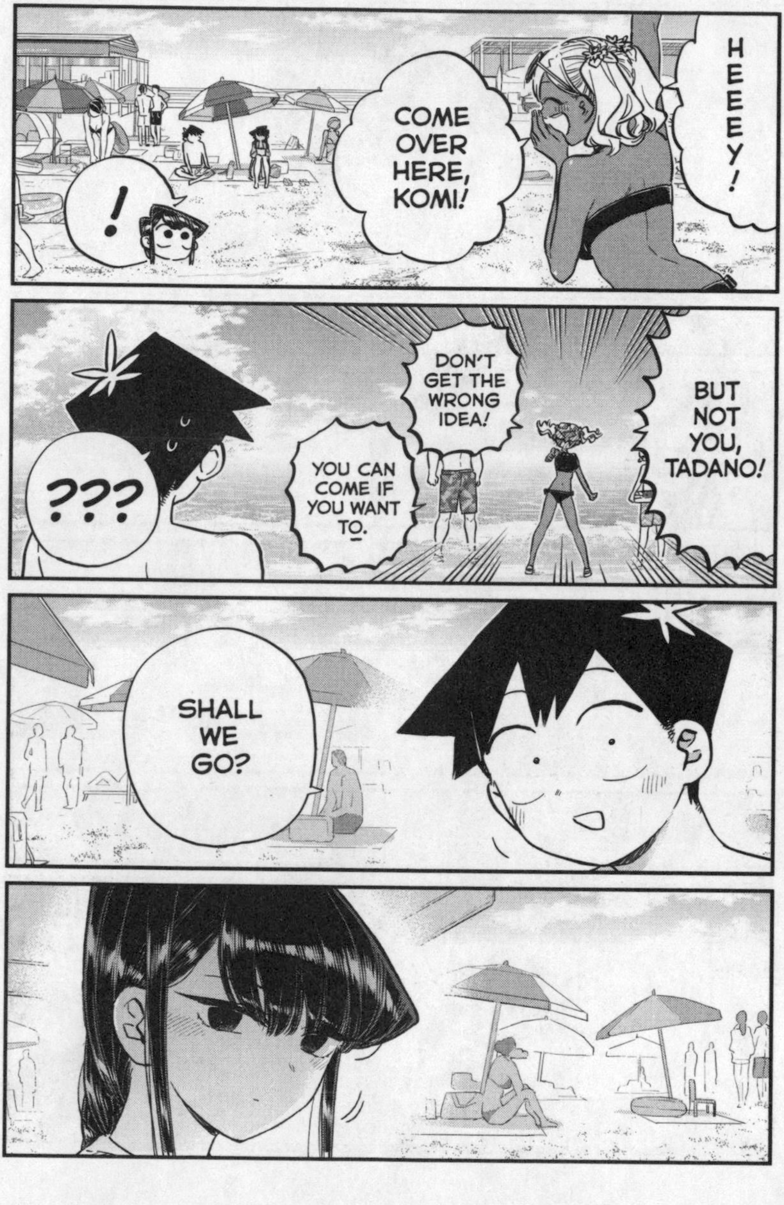
HEEEY!
COME OVER HERE, KOMI!
!
BUT NOT YOU, TADANO!
DON'T GET THE WRONG IDEA!
YOU CAN COME IF YOU WANT TO.
???
SHALL WE GO?

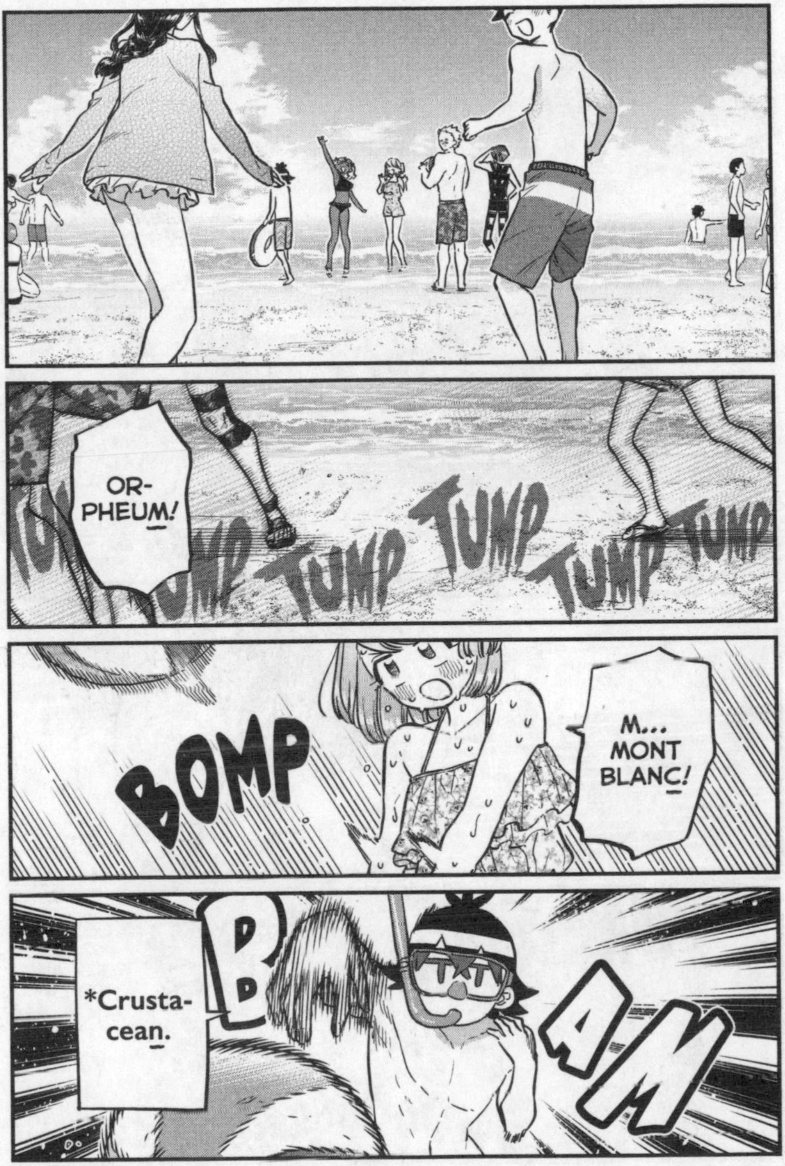
TUMP TUMP
TUMP
TUMP
ORPHEUM!
M... MONT BLANC!
BOMP
BAM
*Crustacean.

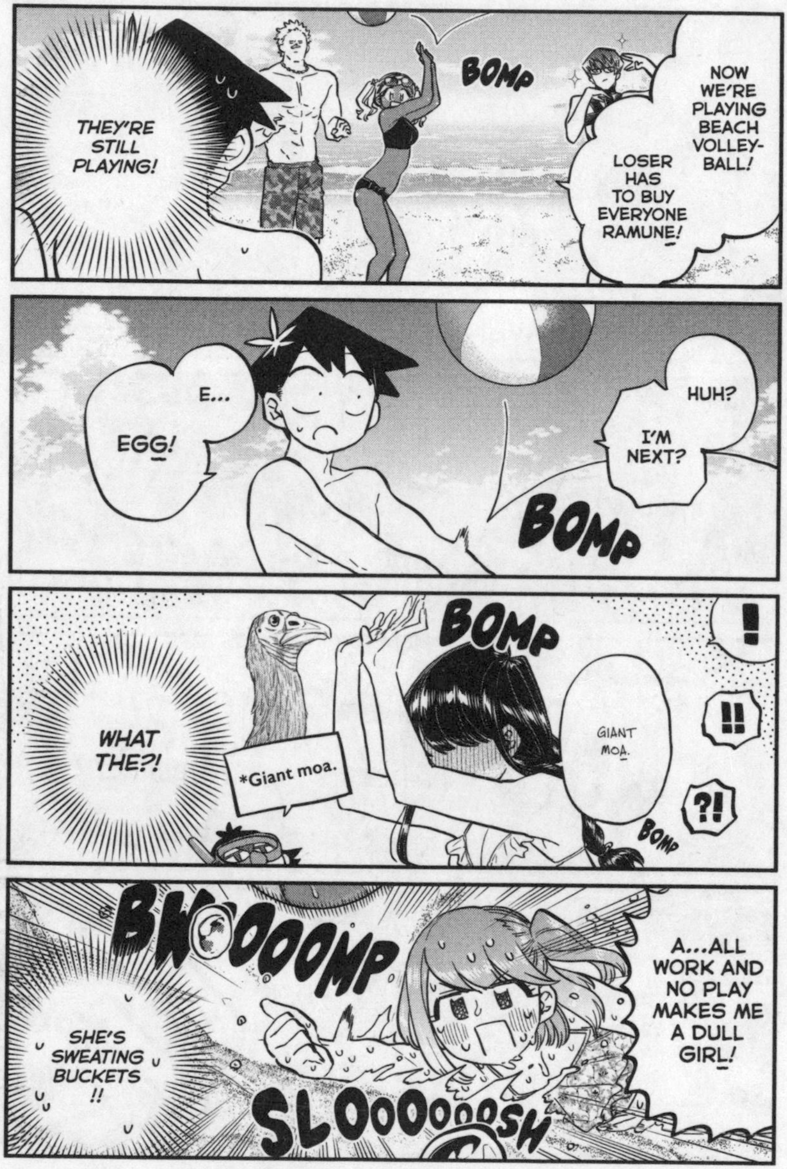
NOW WE'RE PLAYING BEACH VOLLEY-BALL!
LOSER HAS TO BUY EVERYONE RAMUNE!
BOMP
THEY'RE STILL PLAYING!
HUH? I'M NEXT?
BOMP
E... EGG!
!
BOMP
!!
GIANT MOA.
?!
BOMP
*Giant moa.
WHAT THE?!
A...ALL WORK AND NO PLAY MAKES ME A DULL GIRL!
BWOOOOMP
SLOOOOooosh
SHE'S SWEATING BUCKETS!!

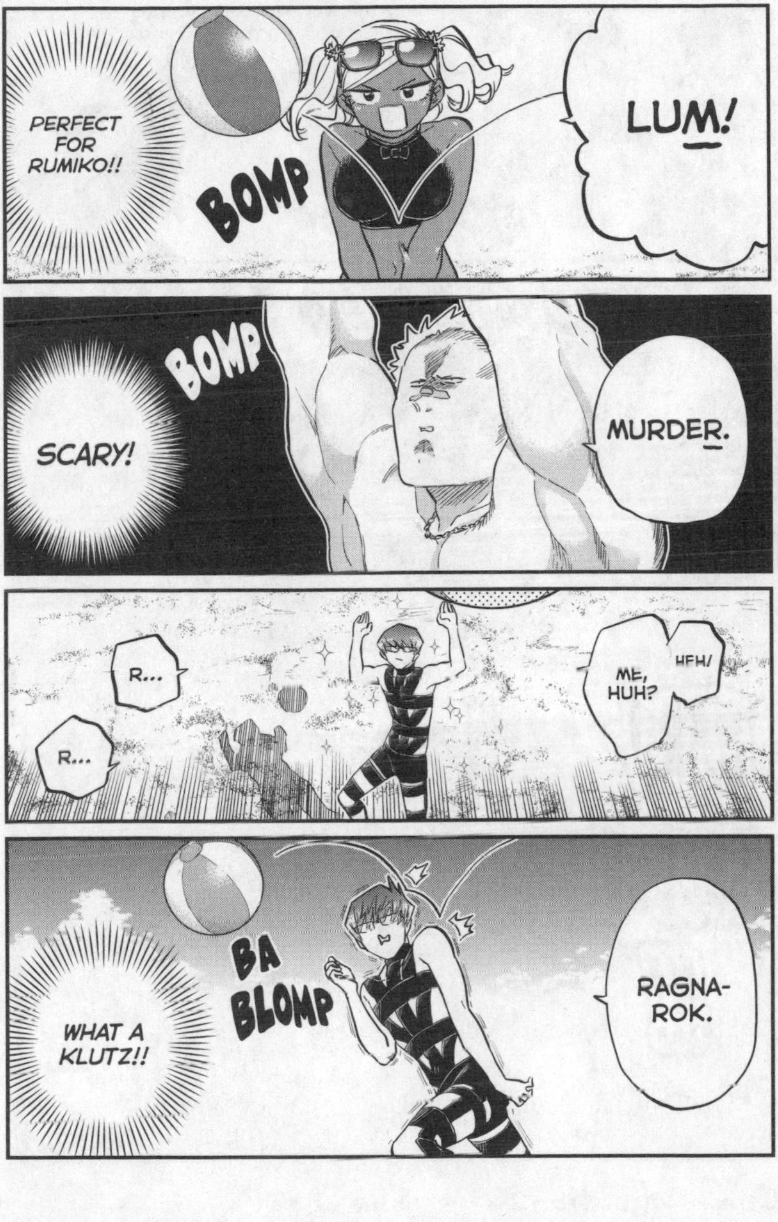
LUM!
BOMP
PERFECT FOR RUMIKO!!
MURDER.
BOMP
SCARY!
HEH!
ME, HUH?
R...
R...
RAGNA-ROK.
BA BLOMP
WHAT A KLUTZ!!

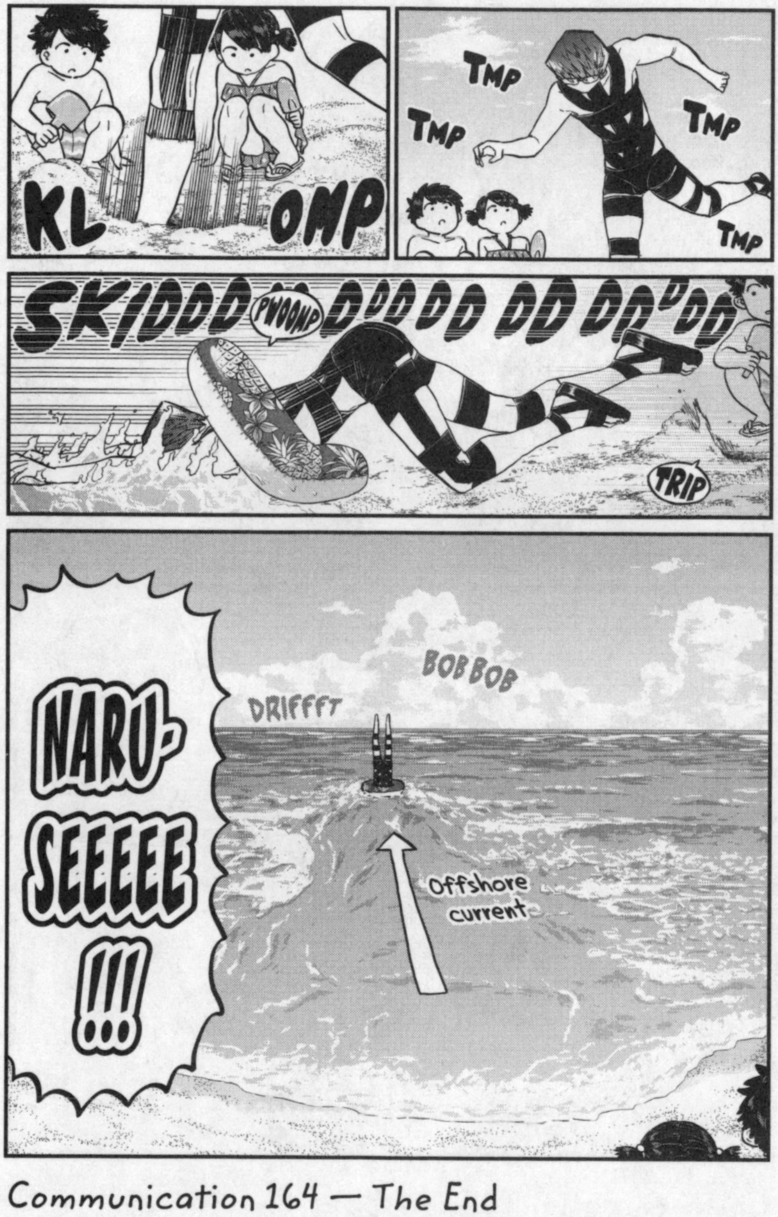
TMP
TMP
TMP
TMP
KL
OMP
SKIDDDDDDDD DD DDDDD
PWOOMP
TRIP
NARU-SEEEEE!!!
BOB BOB
DRIFFFT
Offshore current

Communication 164 — The End

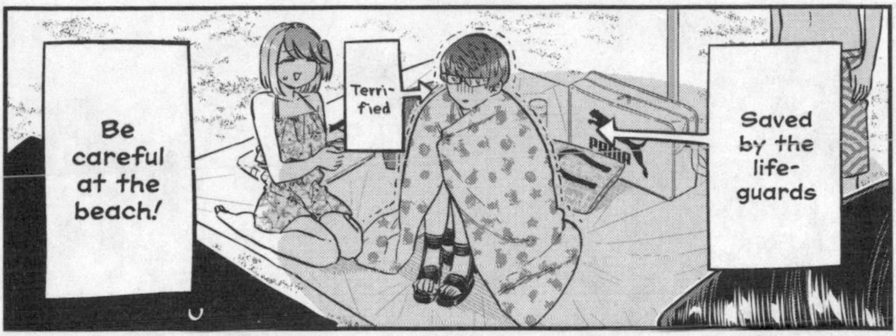
Saved by the life-guards
Terri-fied
Be careful at the beach!

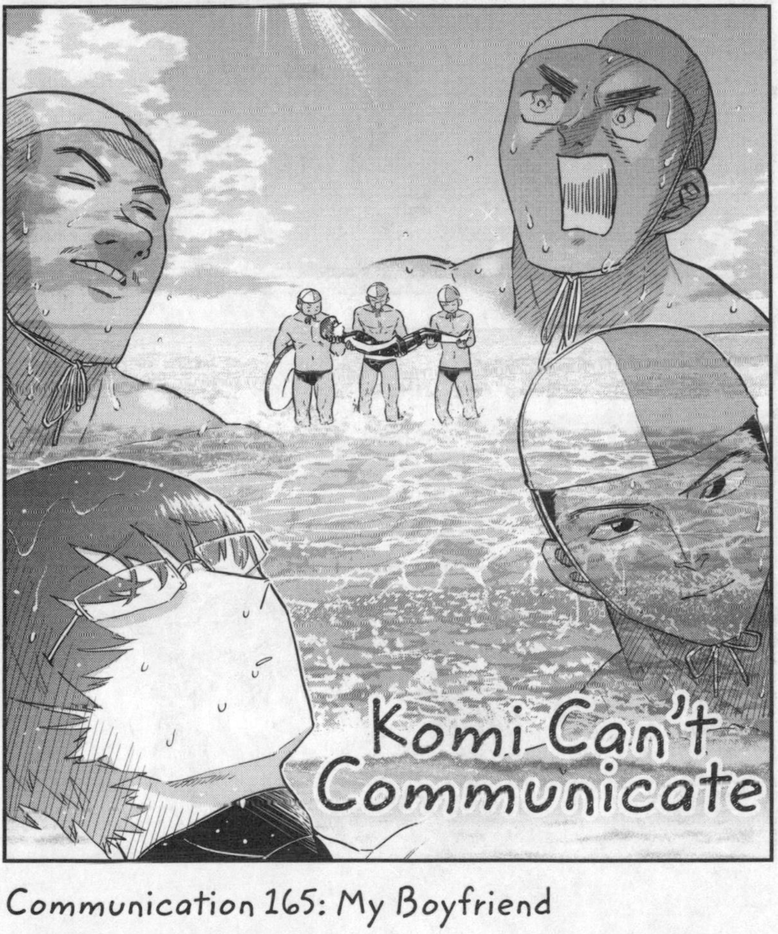
Komi Can't Communicate

Communication 165: My Boyfriend

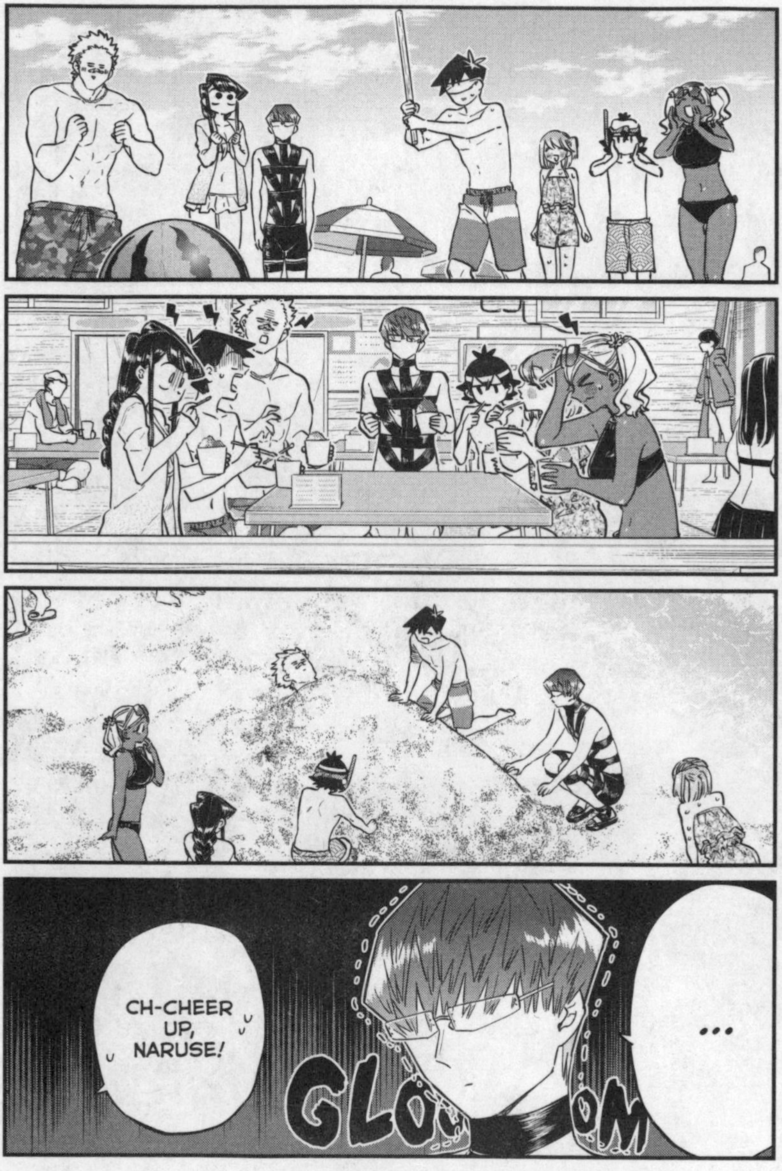
...
CH-CHEER UP, NARUSE!

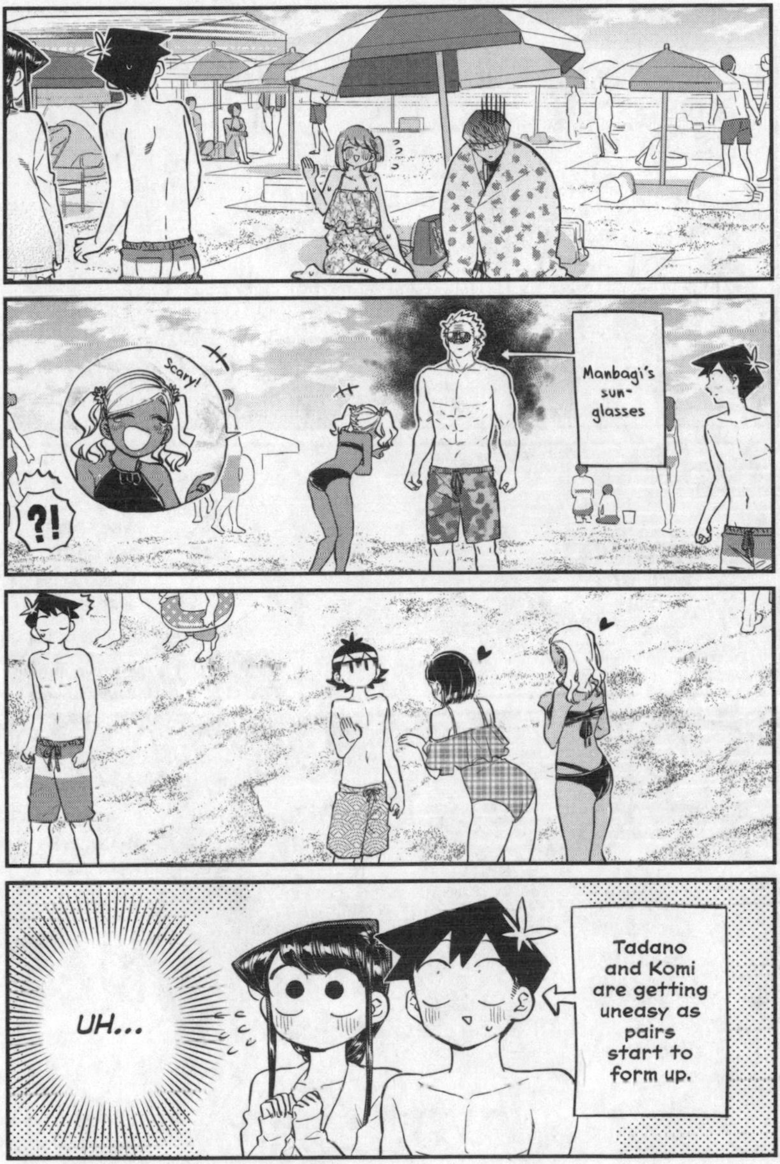
Manbagi's sun-glasses
Scary!
?!
Tadano and Komi are getting uneasy as pairs start to form up.
UH...

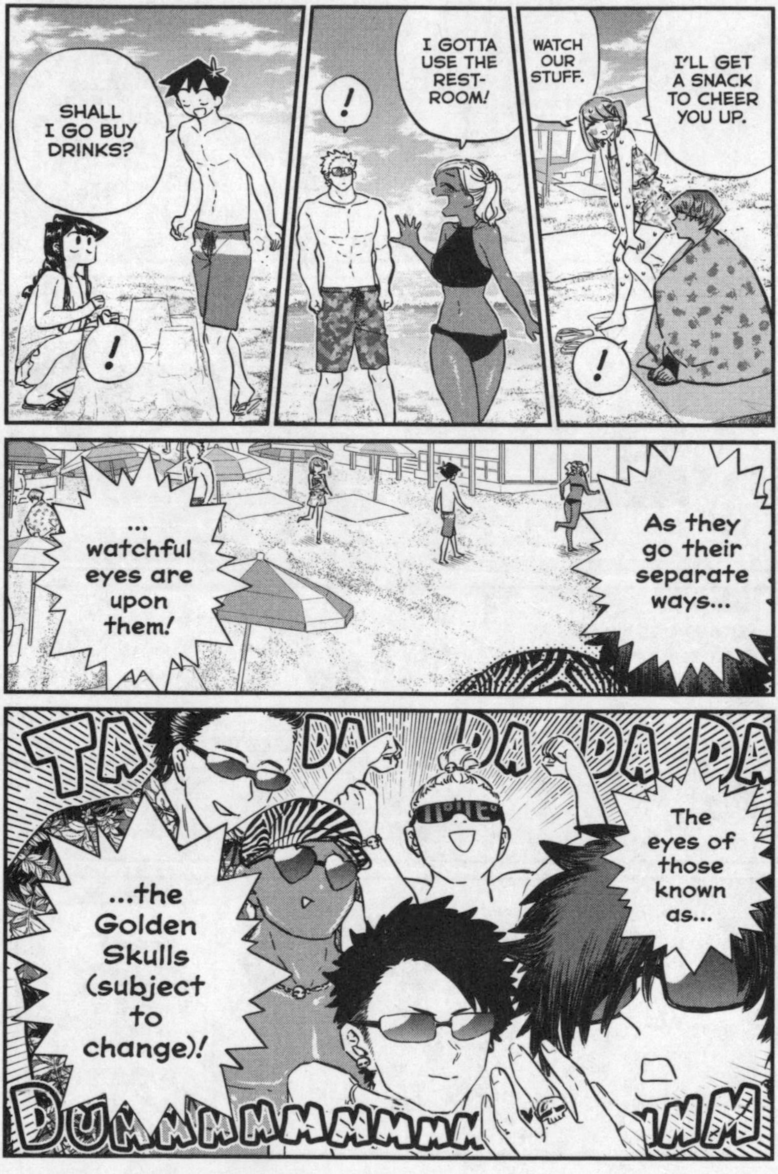
I'LL GET A SNACK TO CHEER YOU UP.
WATCH OUR STUFF.
!
I GOTTA USE THE REST-ROOM!
!
SHALL I GO BUY DRINKS?
!
As they go their separate ways...
...watchful eyes are upon them!
TA DA DA DA DA
The eyes of those known as...
...the Golden Skulls (subject to change)!
DUMMMMMMMMMM MM

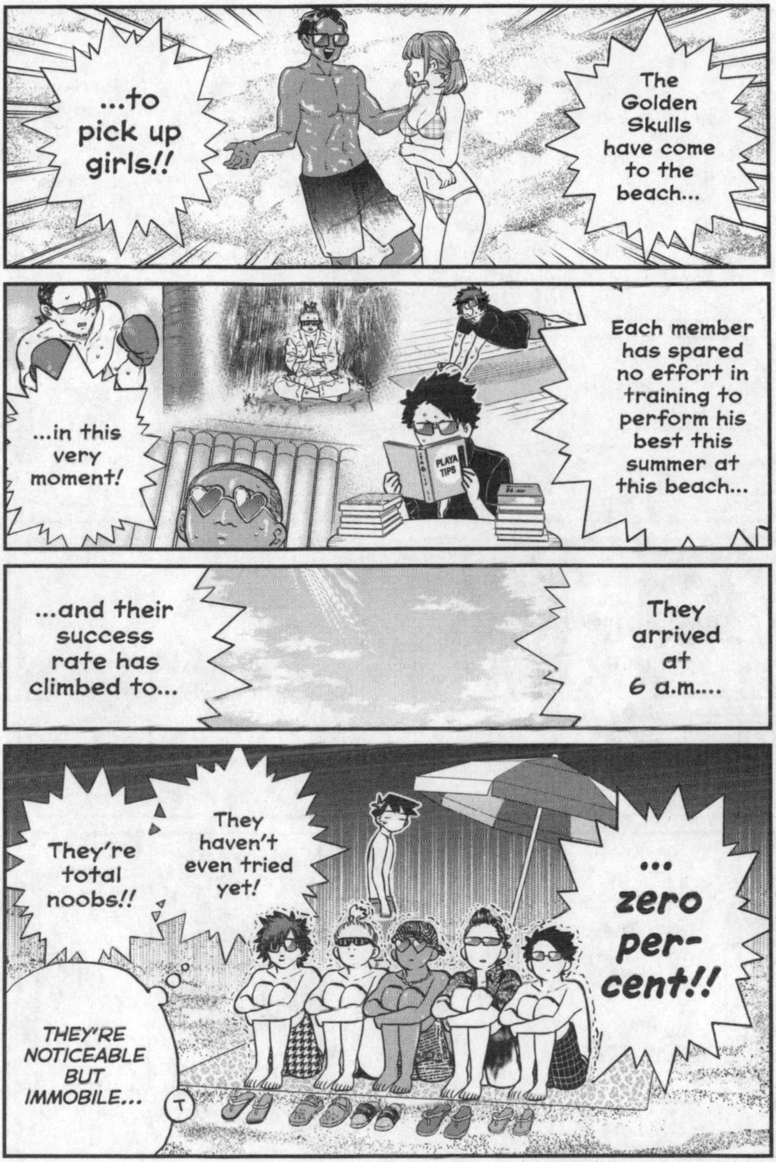
The Golden Skulls have come to the beach...
...to pick up girls!!
Each member has spared no effort in training to perform his best this summer at this beach...
PLAYA TIPS
...in this very moment!
They arrived at 6 a.m....
...and their success rate has climbed to...
... zero per-cent!!
They haven't even tried yet!
They're total noobs!!
THEY'RE NOTICEABLE BUT IMMOBILE...
T

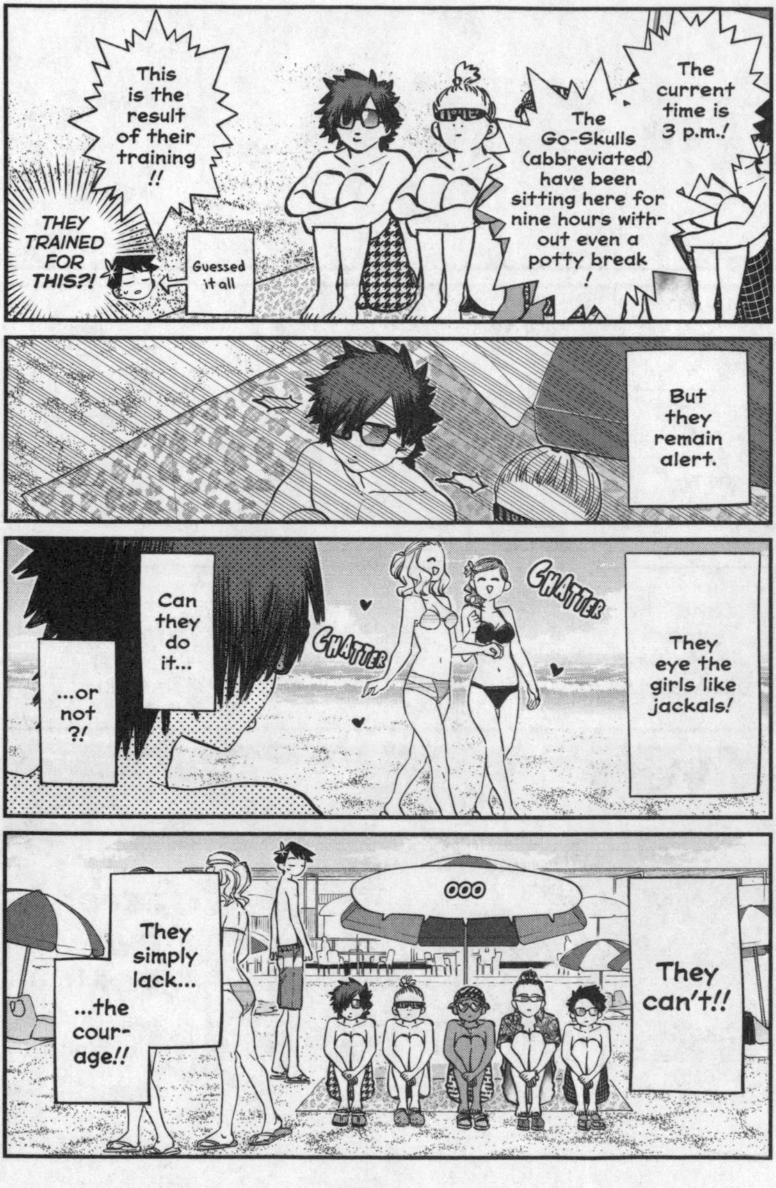

The current time is 3 p.m.!
The Go-Skulls (abbreviated) have been sitting here for nine hours with-out even a potty break!
This is the result of their training!!
Guessed it all
THEY TRAINED FOR THIS?!
But they remain alert.
They eye the girls like jackals!
CHATTER
CHATTER
Can they do it...
...or not?!
They can't!!
ooo
They simply lack...
...the cour-age!!

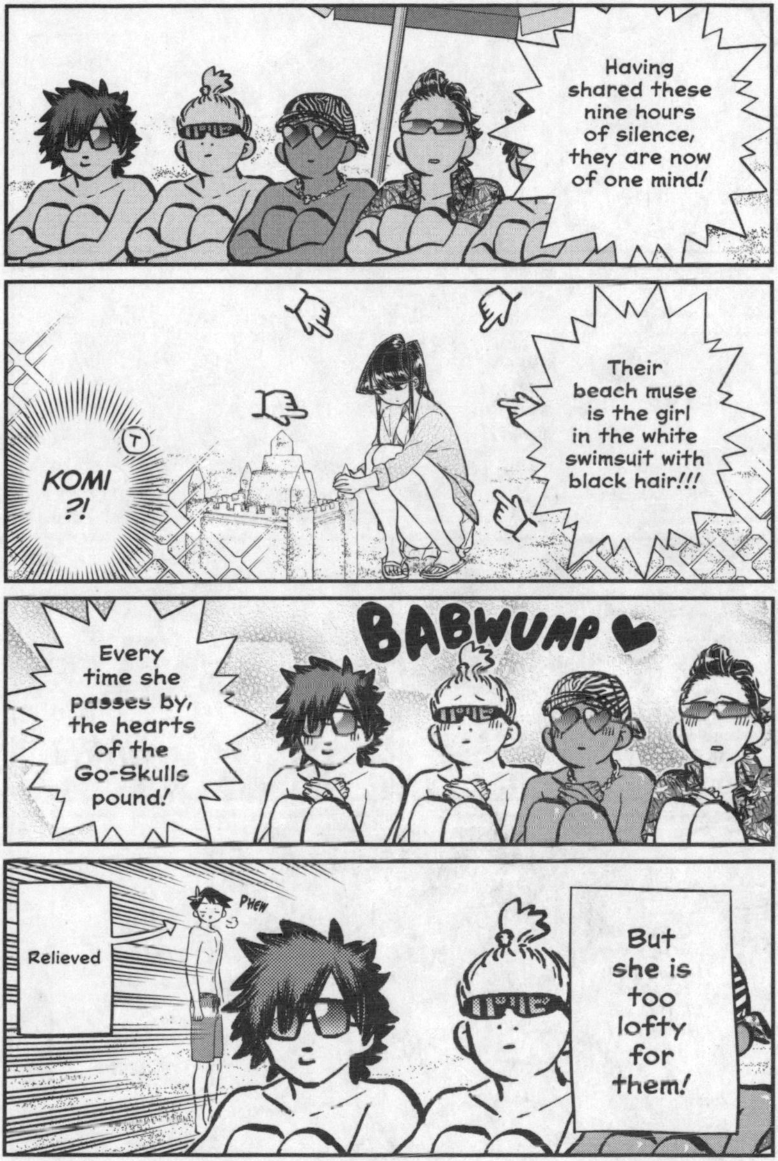
Having shared these nine hours of silence, they are now of one mind!
Their beach muse is the girl in the white swimsuit with black hair!!!
T
KOMI ?!
BABWUMP
Every time she passes by, the hearts of the Go-Skulls pound!
But she is too lofty for them!
PHEW
Relieved

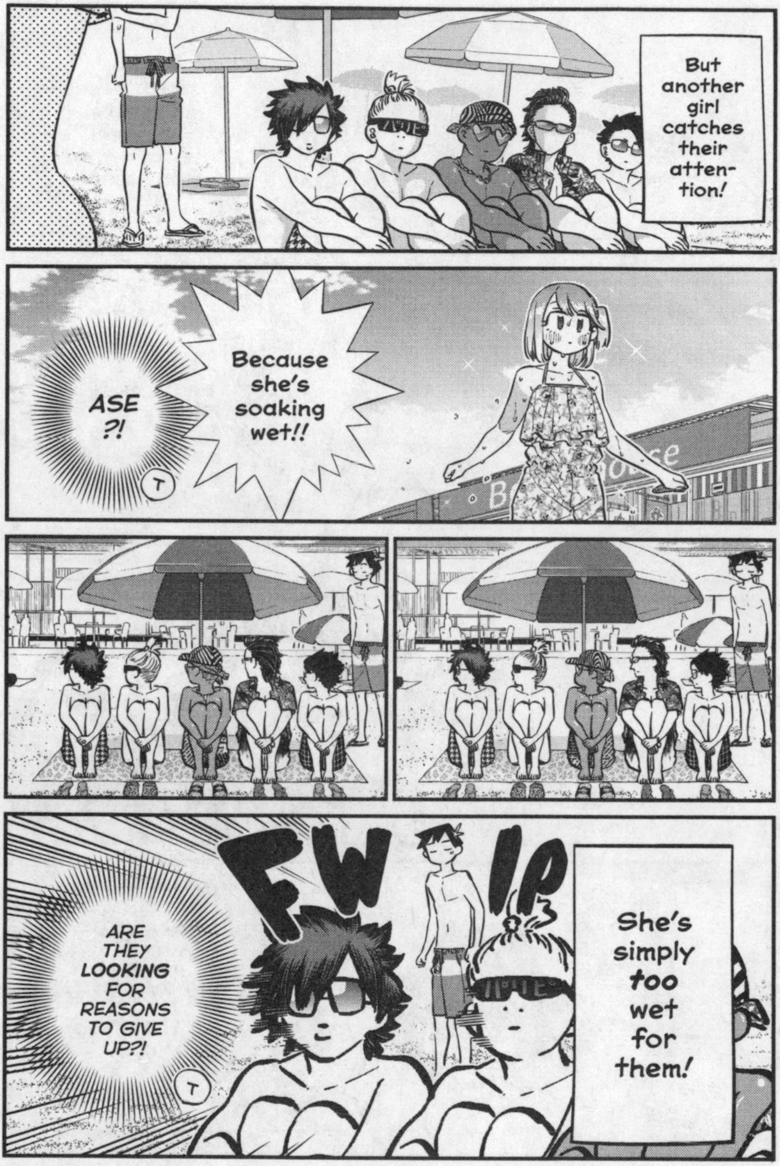
But another girl catches their atten-tion!
Because she's soaking wet!!
ASE ?!
She's simply *too* wet for them!
FWIP
ARE THEY LOOKING FOR REASONS TO GIVE UP?!

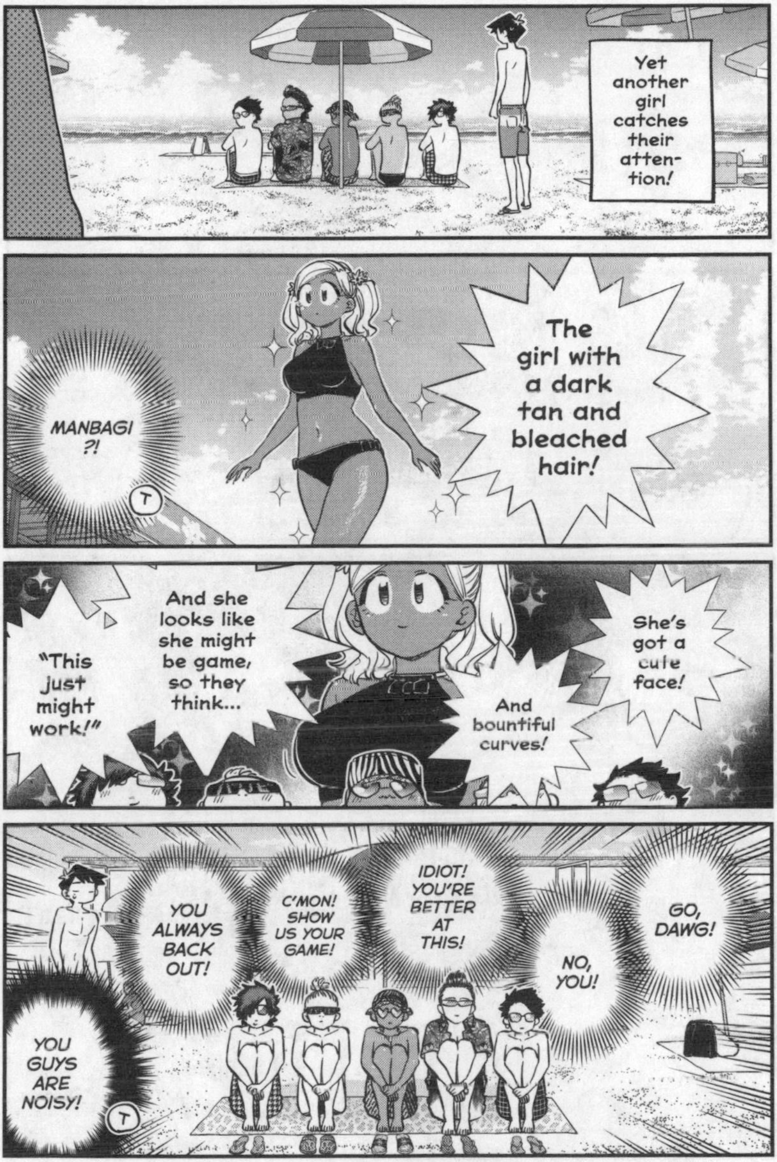
Yet another girl catches their attention!
The girl with a dark tan and bleached hair!
MANBAGI ?!
She's got a cute face!
And bountiful curves!
And she looks like she might be game, so they think...
"This just might work!"
GO, DAWG!
NO, YOU!
IDIOT! YOU'RE BETTER AT THIS!
C'MON! SHOW US YOUR GAME!
YOU ALWAYS BACK OUT!
YOU GUYS ARE NOISY!

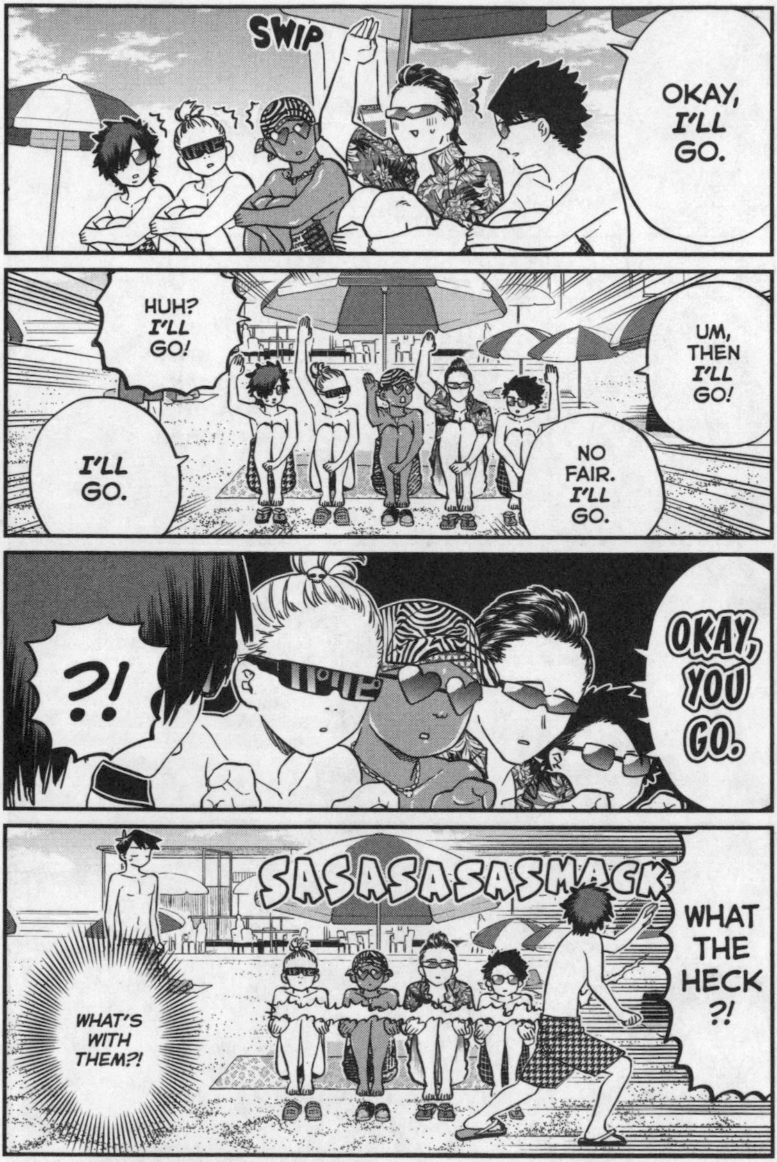
OKAY, I'LL GO.
SWIP
UM, THEN I'LL GO!
HUH? I'LL GO!
NO FAIR. I'LL GO.
I'LL GO.
OKAY, YOU GO.
?!
WHAT THE HECK?!
SASASASASMACK
WHAT'S WITH THEM?!

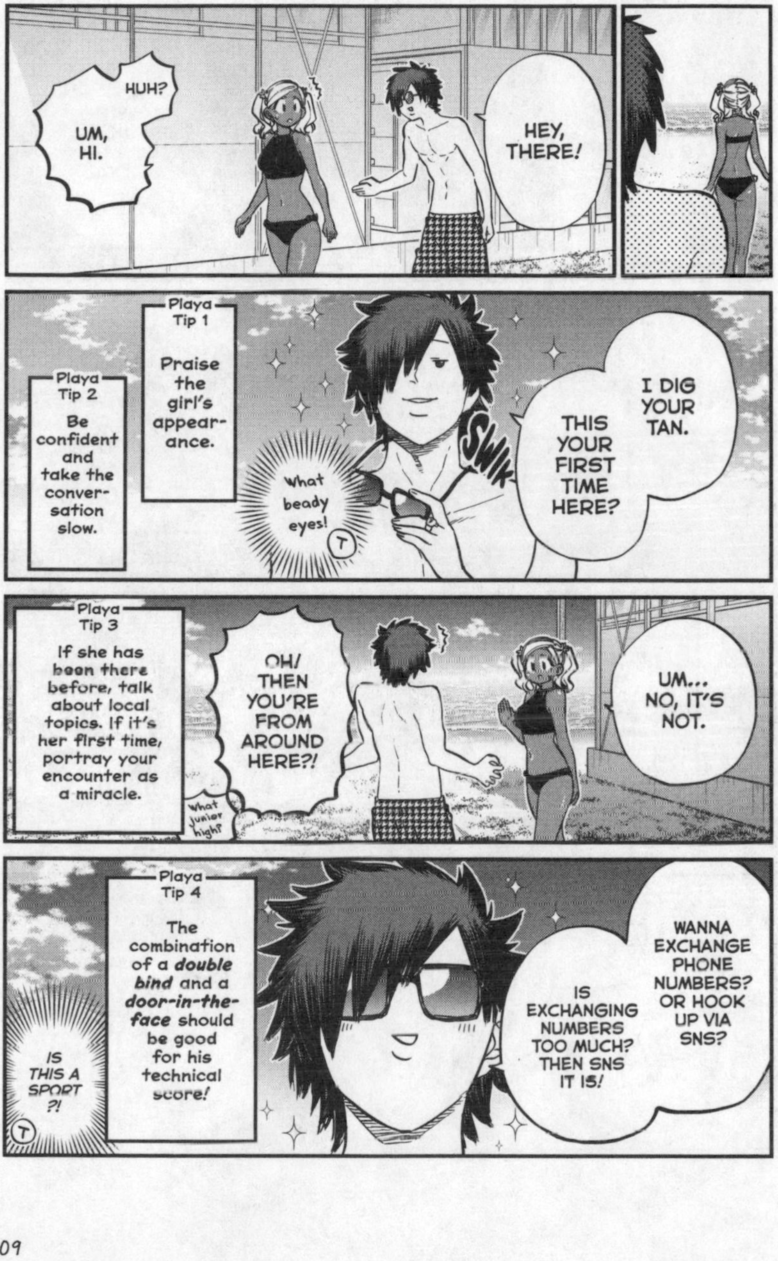
HEY, THERE!
HUH?
UM, HI.
I DIG YOUR TAN.
THIS YOUR FIRST TIME HERE?
SWIK
Playa Tip 1 Praise the girl's appearance.
What beady eyes!
Playa Tip 2 Be confident and take the conversation slow.
UM... NO, IT'S NOT.
OH! THEN YOU'RE FROM AROUND HERE?!
What junior high?
Playa Tip 3 If she has been there before, talk about local topics. If it's her first time, portray your encounter as a miracle.
WANNA EXCHANGE PHONE NUMBERS? OR HOOK UP VIA SNS?
IS EXCHANGING NUMBERS TOO MUCH? THEN SNS IT IS!
Playa Tip 4 The combination of a double bind and a door-in-the-face should be good for his technical score!
IS THIS A SPORT?!

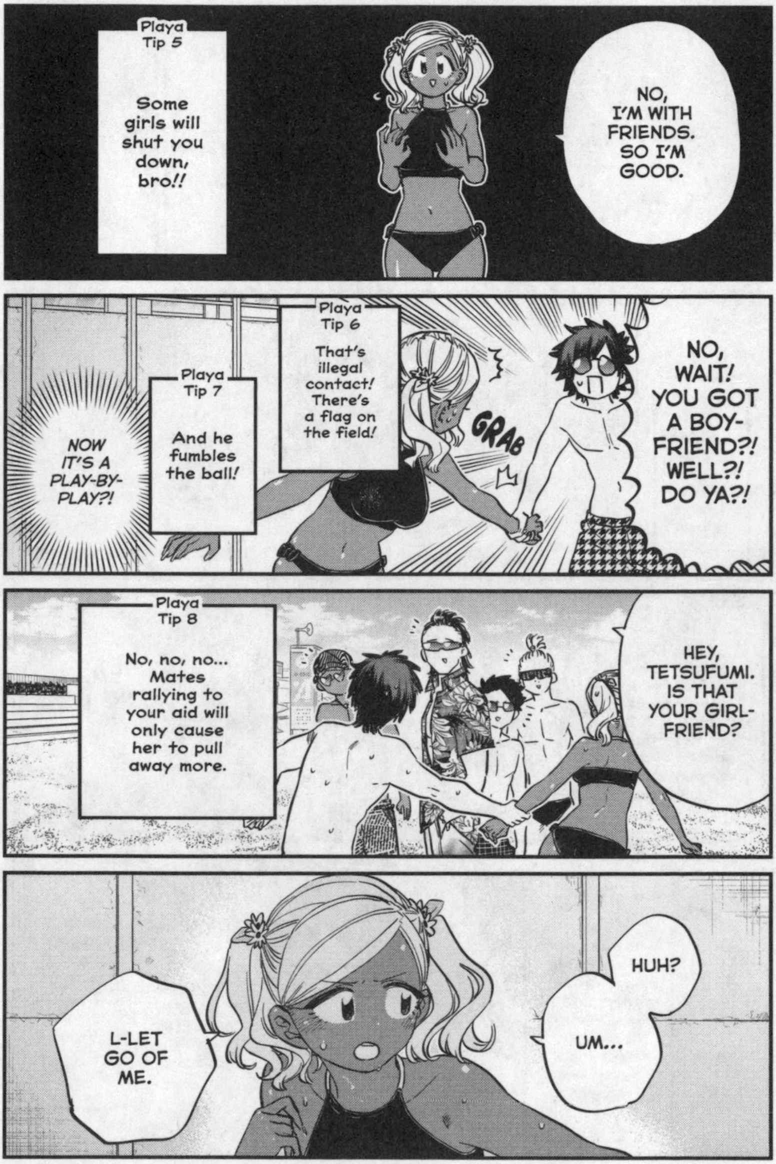
NO, I'M WITH FRIENDS. SO I'M GOOD.
Playa Tip 5
Some girls will shut you down, bro!!
NO, WAIT! YOU GOT A BOY-FRIEND?! WELL?! DO YA?!
GRAB
Playa Tip 6
That's illegal contact! There's a flag on the field!
Playa Tip 7
And he fumbles the ball!
NOW IT'S A PLAY-BY-PLAY?!
HEY, TETSUFUMI. IS THAT YOUR GIRL-FRIEND?
Playa Tip 8
No, no, no... Mates rallying to your aid will only cause her to pull away more.
HUH?
UM...
L-LET GO OF ME.

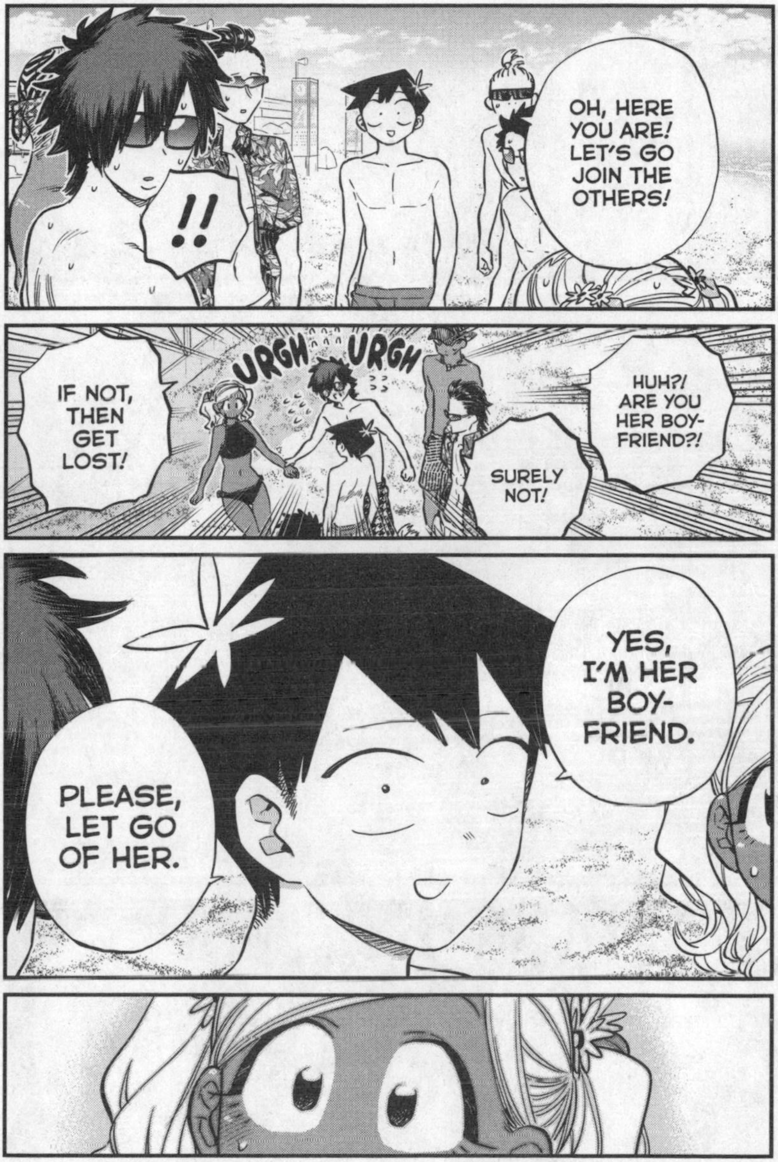
OH, HERE YOU ARE! LET'S GO JOIN THE OTHERS!
!!
HUH?! ARE YOU HER BOY-FRIEND?!
SURELY NOT!
URGH URGH
IF NOT, THEN GET LOST!
YES, I'M HER BOY-FRIEND.
PLEASE, LET GO OF HER.

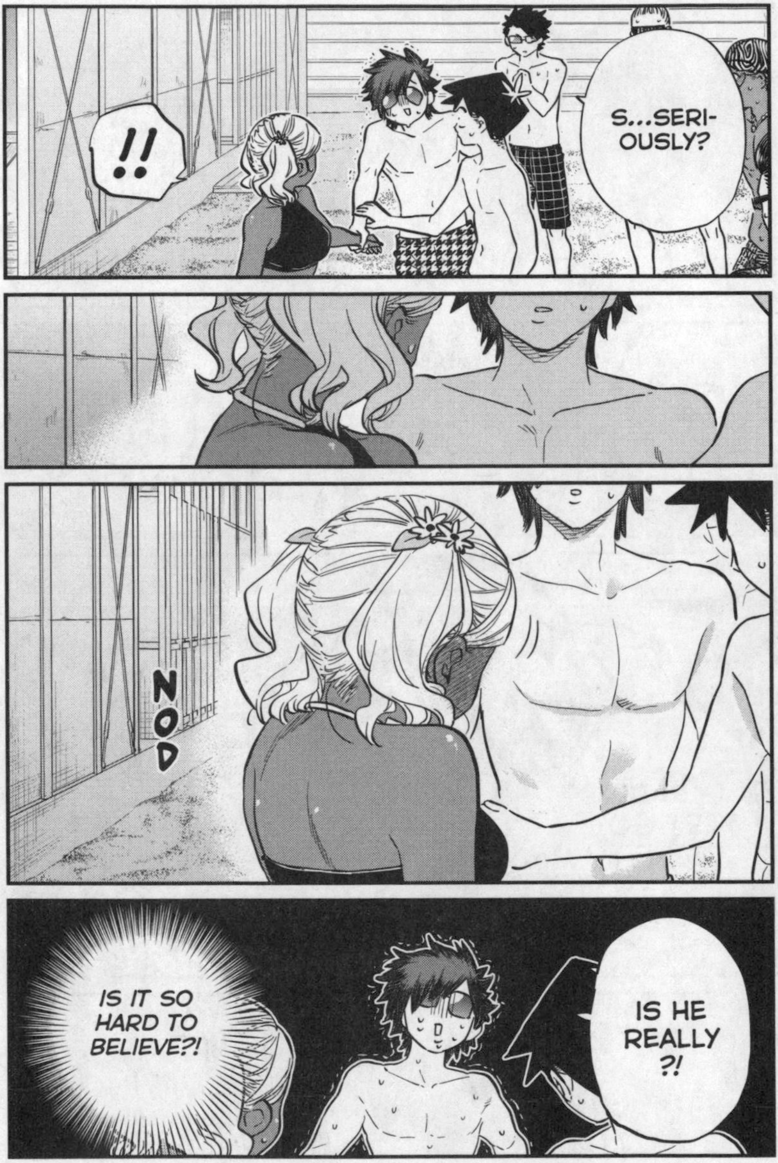
S...SERI-OUSLY?
!!
NOD
IS HE REALLY ?!
IS IT SO HARD TO BELIEVE?!

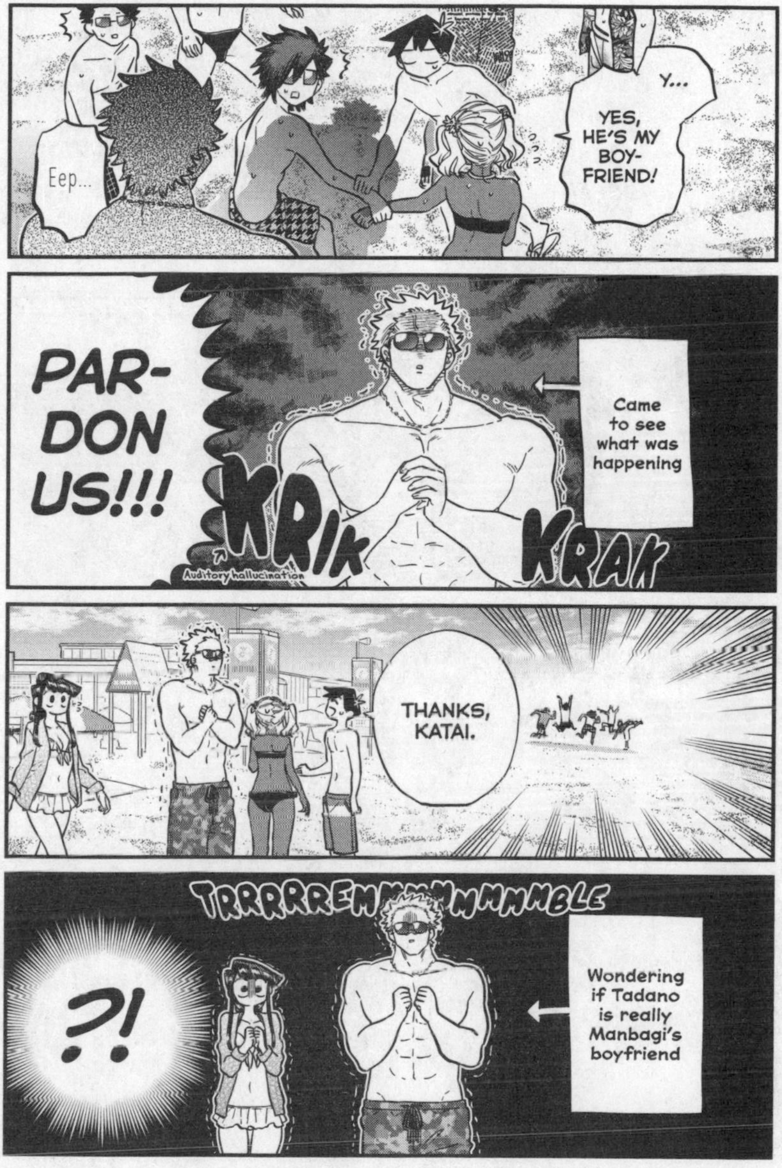
Y...
YES, HE'S MY BOY-FRIEND!
Eep...
Came to see what was happening
KRIK KRAK
Auditory hallucination
PAR-DON US!!!
THANKS, KATAI.
TRRRRREMMMMMMMMMBLE
Wondering if Tadano is really Manbagi's boyfriend
?!

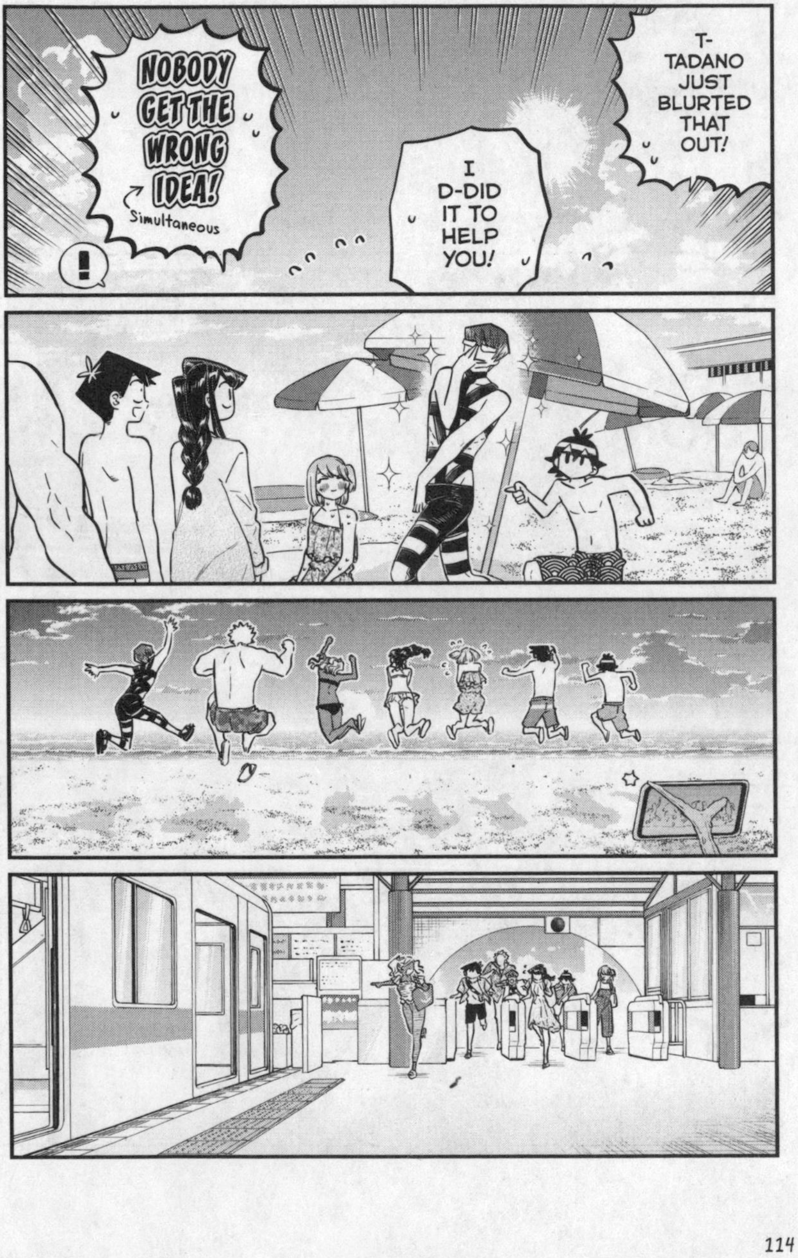
T-TADANO JUST BLURTED THAT OUT!
I D-DID IT TO HELP YOU!
NOBODY GET THE WRONG IDEA!
Simultaneous
!

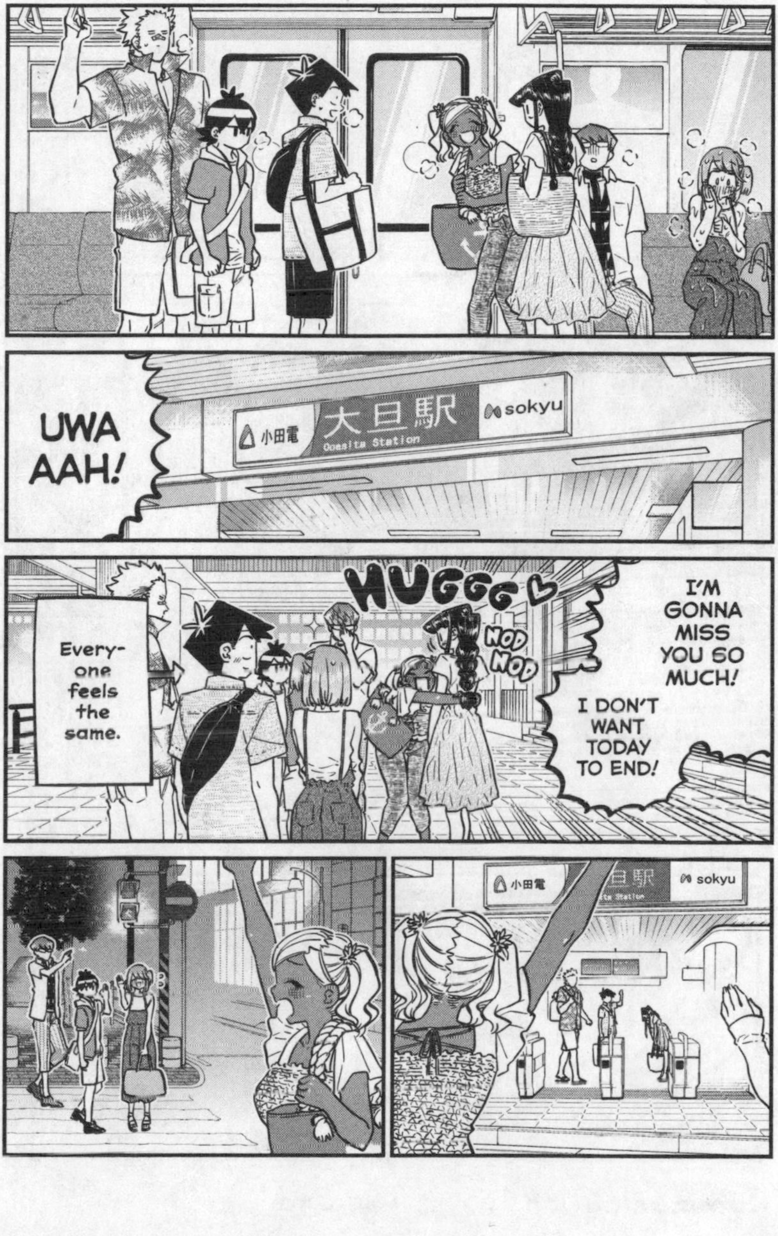
小田電
大旦駅
sokyu
UWA AAH!
I'M GONNA MISS YOU SO MUCH!
I DON'T WANT TODAY TO END!
NOD NOD
HUGGG
Every-one feels the same.
小田電
sokyu

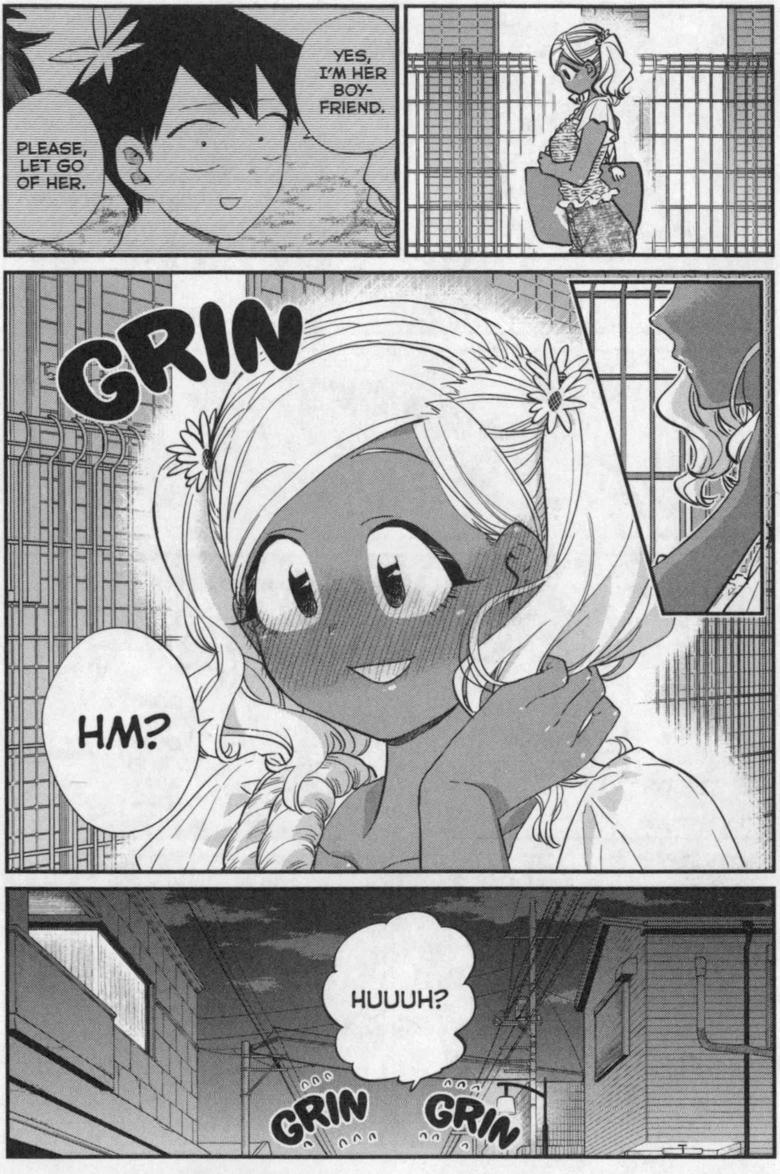
YES, I'M HER BOY-FRIEND.
PLEASE, LET GO OF HER.
GRIN
HM?
HUUUH?
GRIN
GRIN

Communication 165 — The End

Komi Can't Communicate

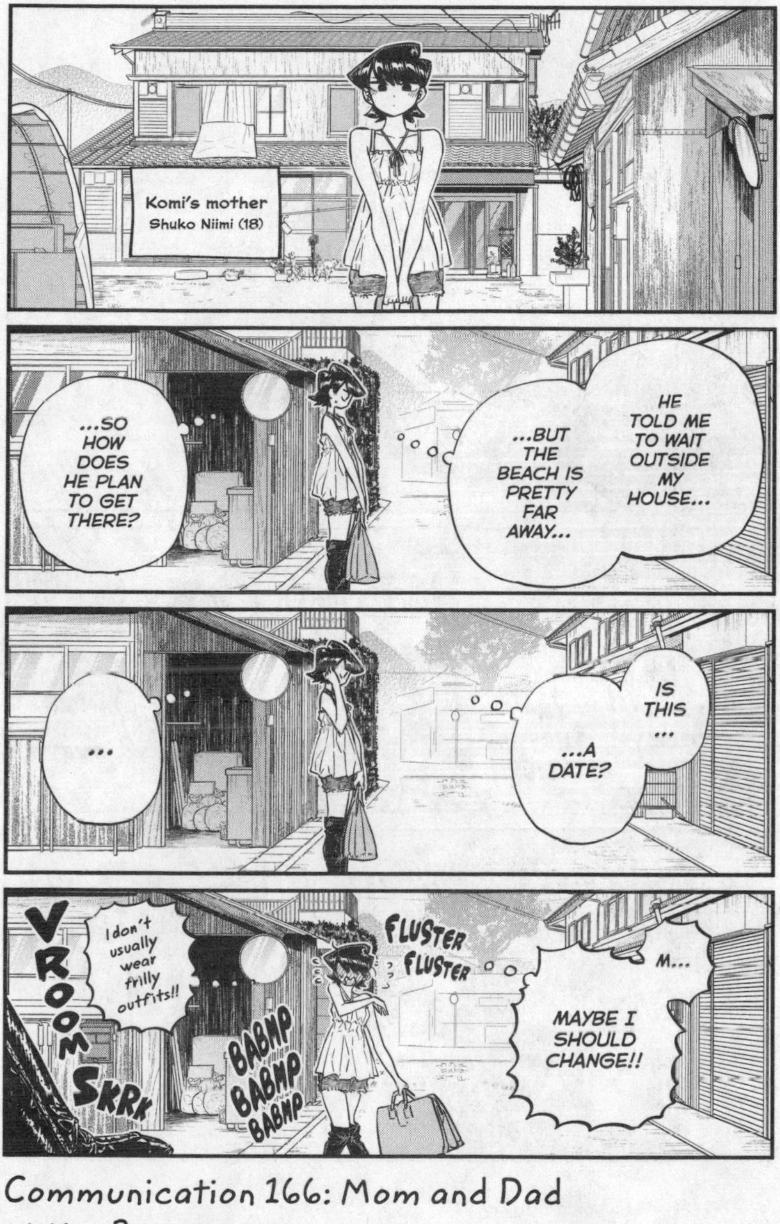
Komi's mother
Shuko Niimi (18)
HE TOLD ME TO WAIT OUTSIDE MY HOUSE...
...BUT THE BEACH IS PRETTY FAR AWAY...
...SO HOW DOES HE PLAN TO GET THERE?
IS THIS ...
...A DATE?
...
M...
MAYBE I SHOULD CHANGE!!
FLUSTER FLUSTER
BABMP BABMP BABMP
I don't usually wear frilly outfits!!
VROOM
SKRK

Communication 166: Mom and Dad at the Beach

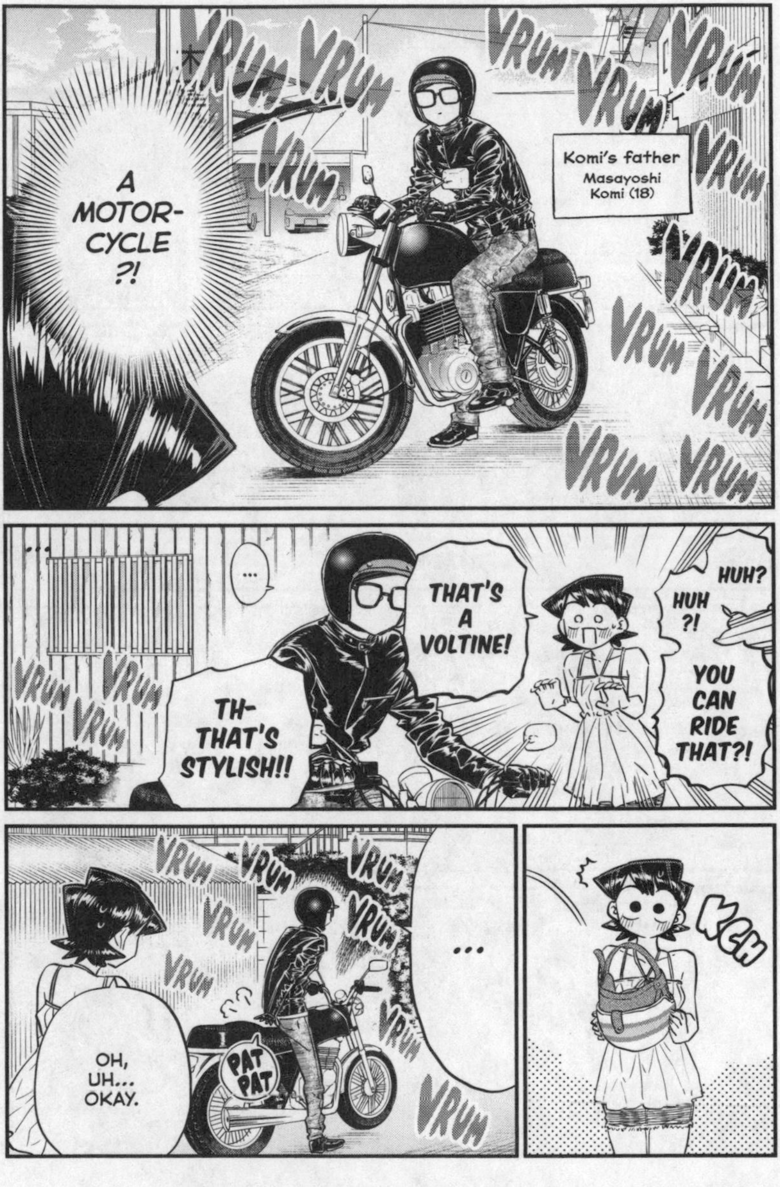
VRUM VRUM
VRUM VRUM
Komi's father
Masayoshi Komi (18)
VRUM VRUM VRUM VRUM VRUM
VRUM VRUM VRUM
A MOTOR-CYCLE ?!
HUH?
HUH ?!
YOU CAN RIDE THAT?!
THAT'S A VOLTINE!
...
TH- THAT'S STYLISH!!
VRUM VRUM VRUM
...
KCH
...
VRUM VRUM VRUM VRUM VRUM VRUM
PAT PAT
OH, UH... OKAY.

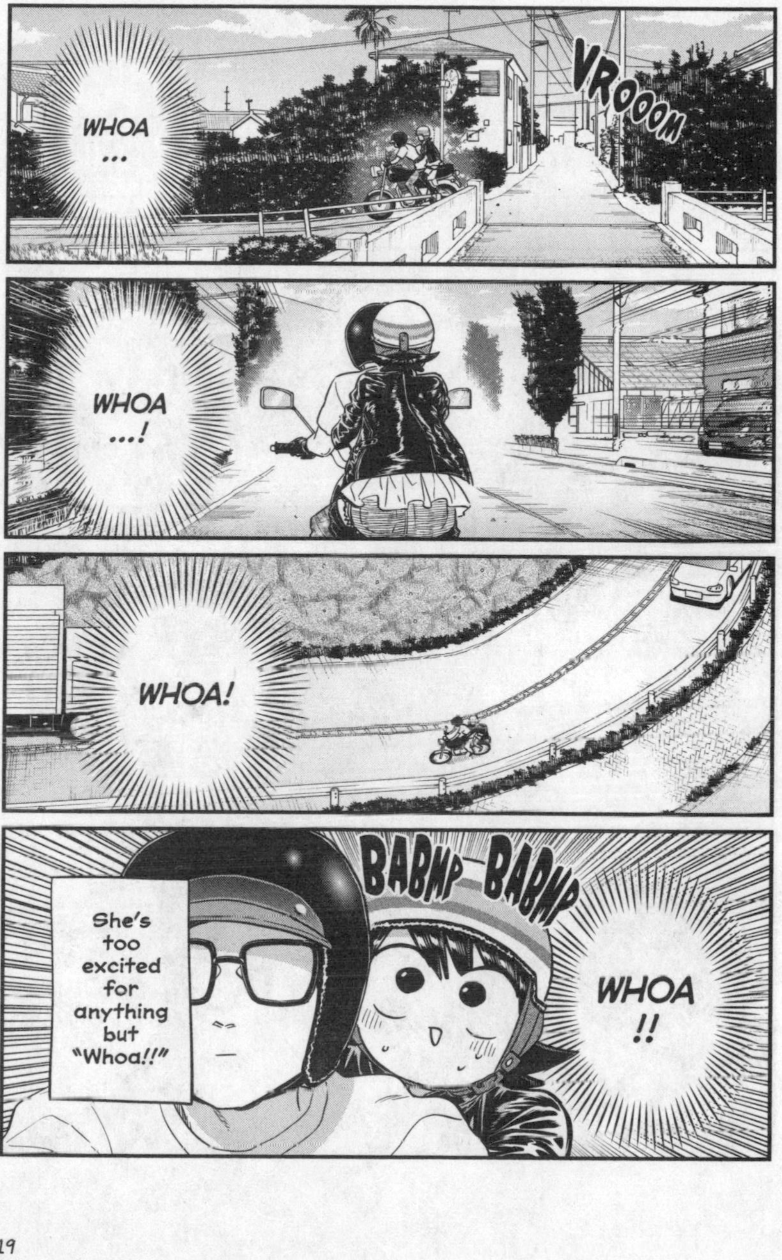
VROOOM
WHOA ...
WHOA ...!
WHOA!
BABMP BABMP
WHOA !!
She's too excited for anything but "Whoa!!"

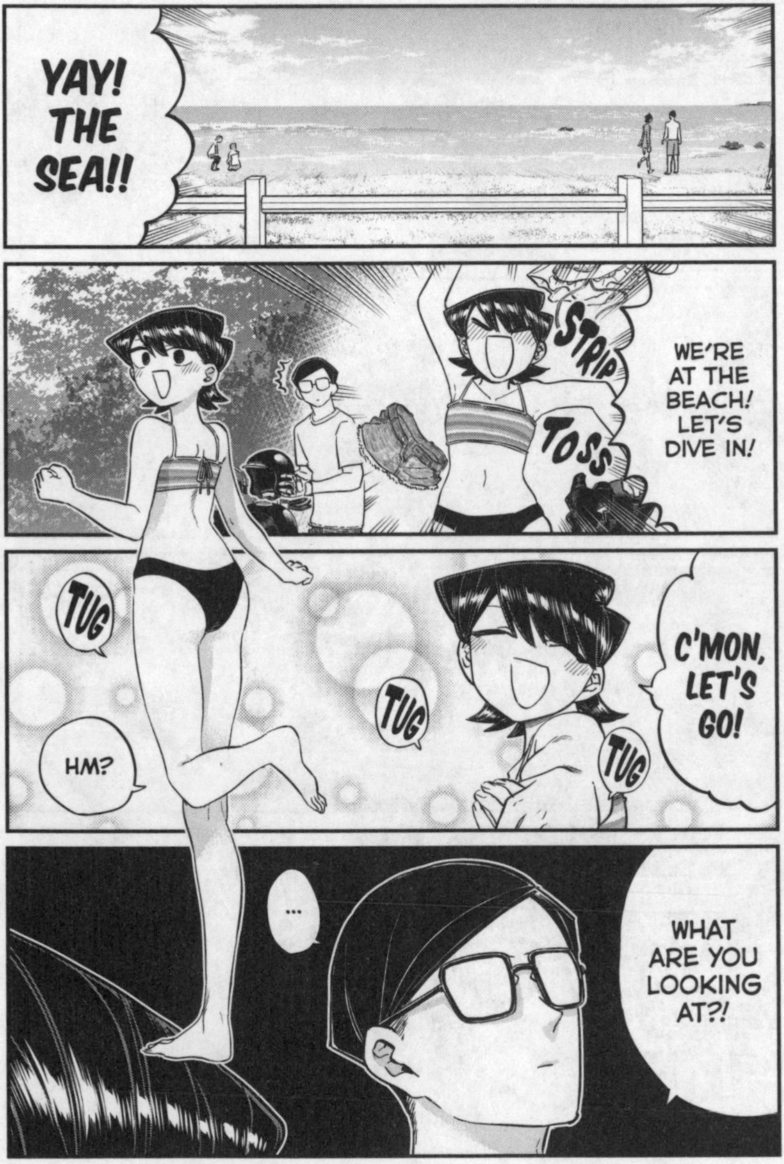

YAY! THE SEA!!
WE'RE AT THE BEACH! LET'S DIVE IN!
STRIP
TOSS
C'MON, LET'S GO!
TUG
TUG
TUG
HM?
WHAT ARE YOU LOOKING AT?!
...

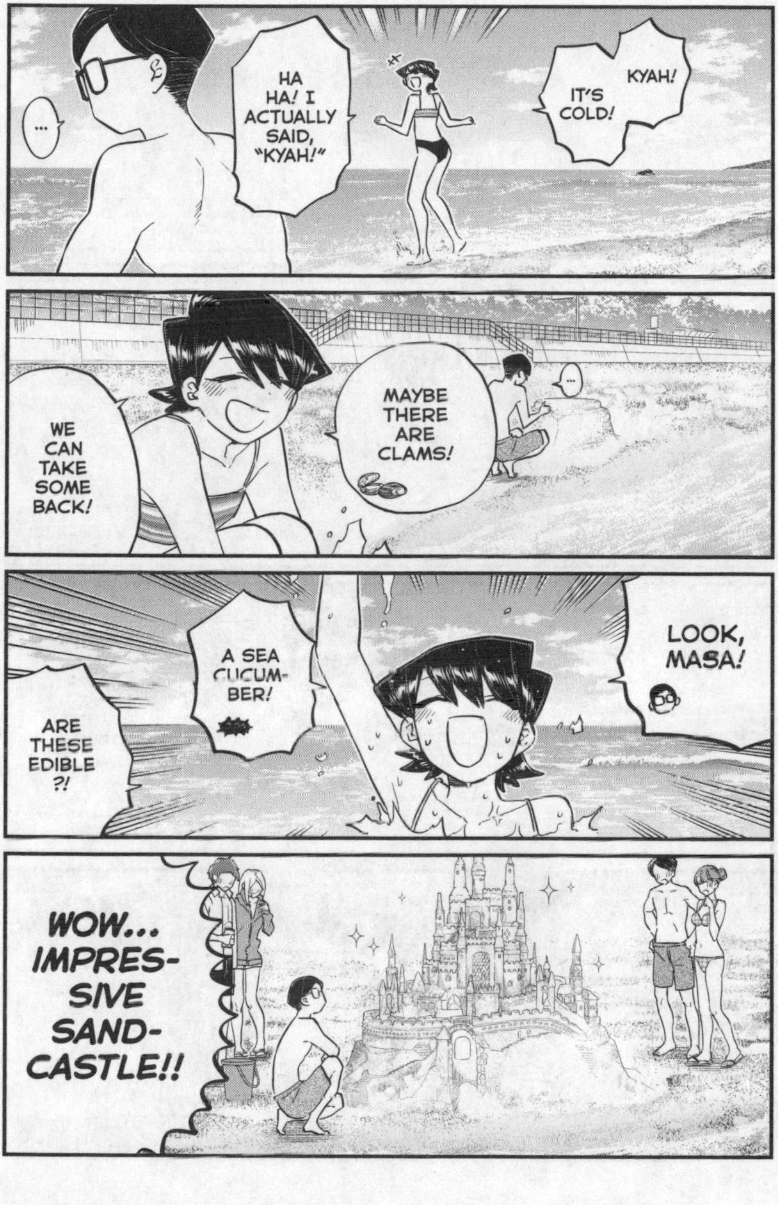
KYAH! IT'S COLD!
HA HA! I ACTUALLY SAID, "KYAH!"
...
...
MAYBE THERE ARE CLAMS!
WE CAN TAKE SOME BACK!
LOOK, MASA!
A SEA CUCUMBER!
ARE THESE EDIBLE?!
WOW... IMPRESSIVE SANDCASTLE!!

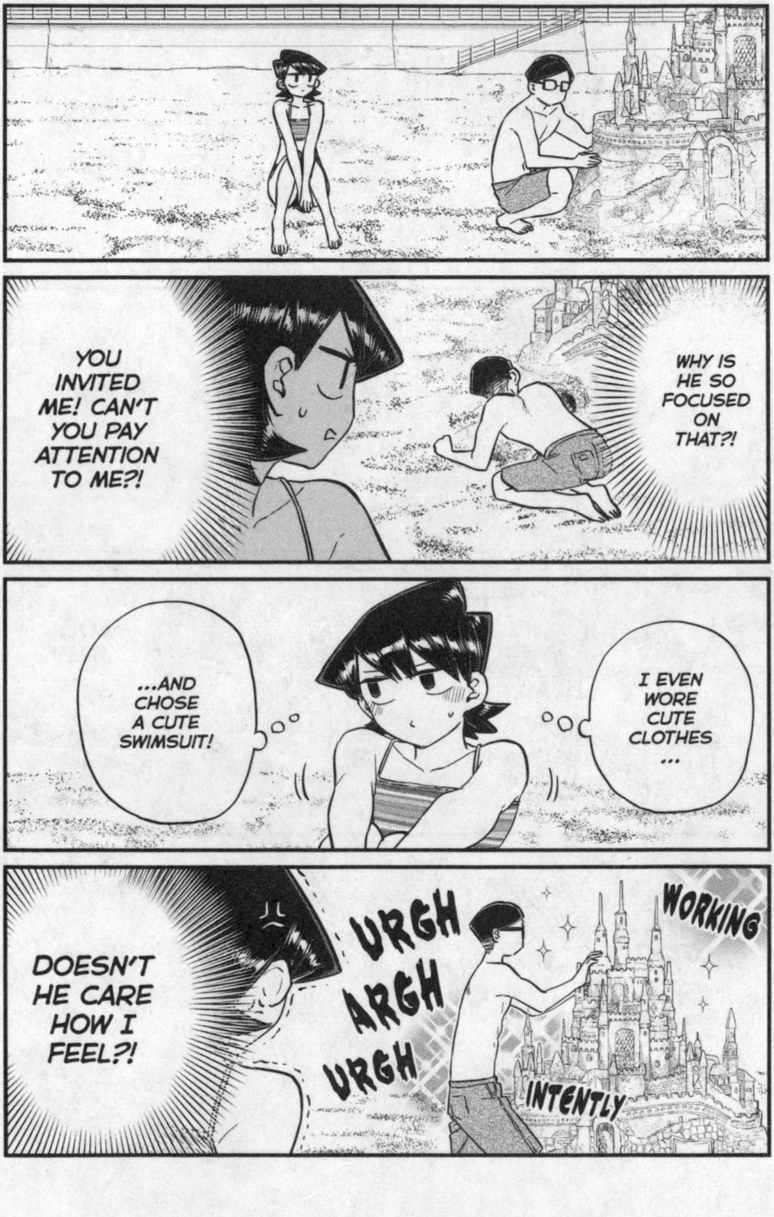
WHY IS HE SO FOCUSED ON THAT?!
YOU INVITED ME! CAN'T YOU PAY ATTENTION TO ME?!
I EVEN WORE CUTE CLOTHES ...
...AND CHOSE A CUTE SWIMSUIT!
WORKING
INTENTLY
URGH
ARGH
URGH
DOESN'T HE CARE HOW I FEEL?!

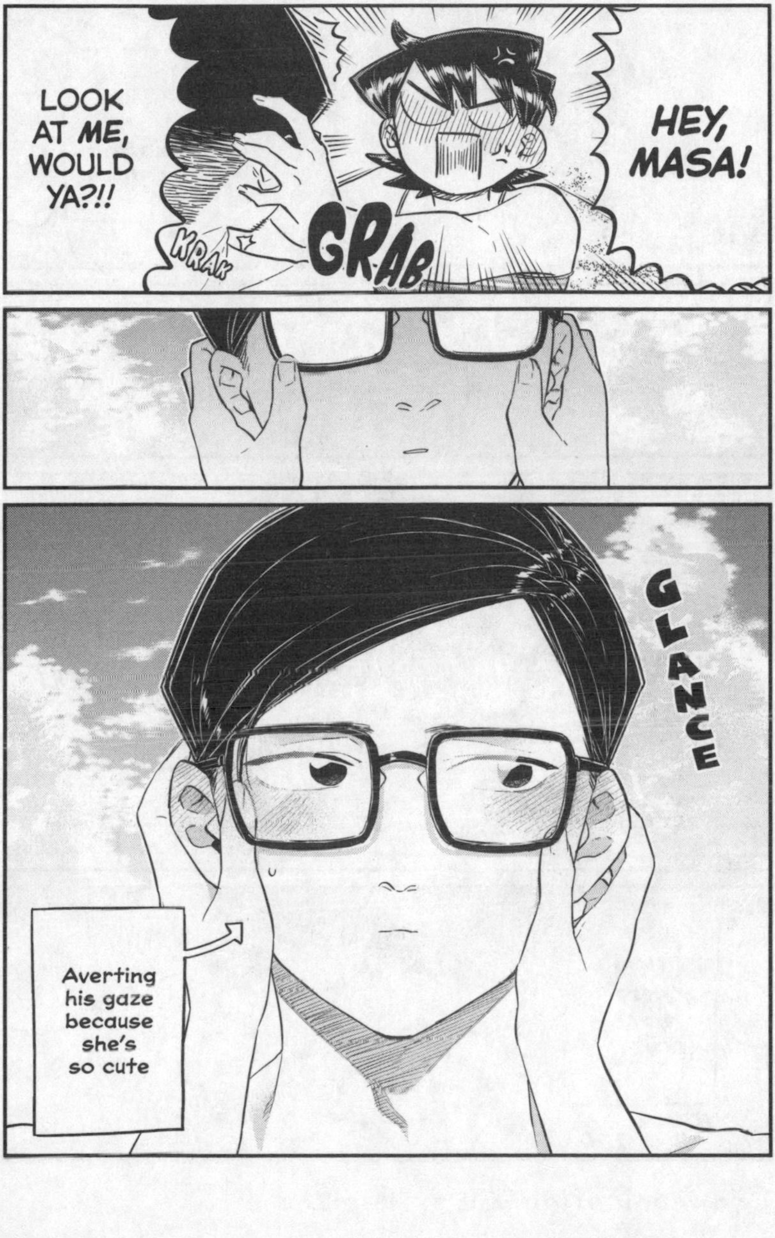
HEY, MASA!
LOOK AT ME, WOULD YA?!!
GRAB
KRAK
GLANCE
Averting his gaze because she's so cute

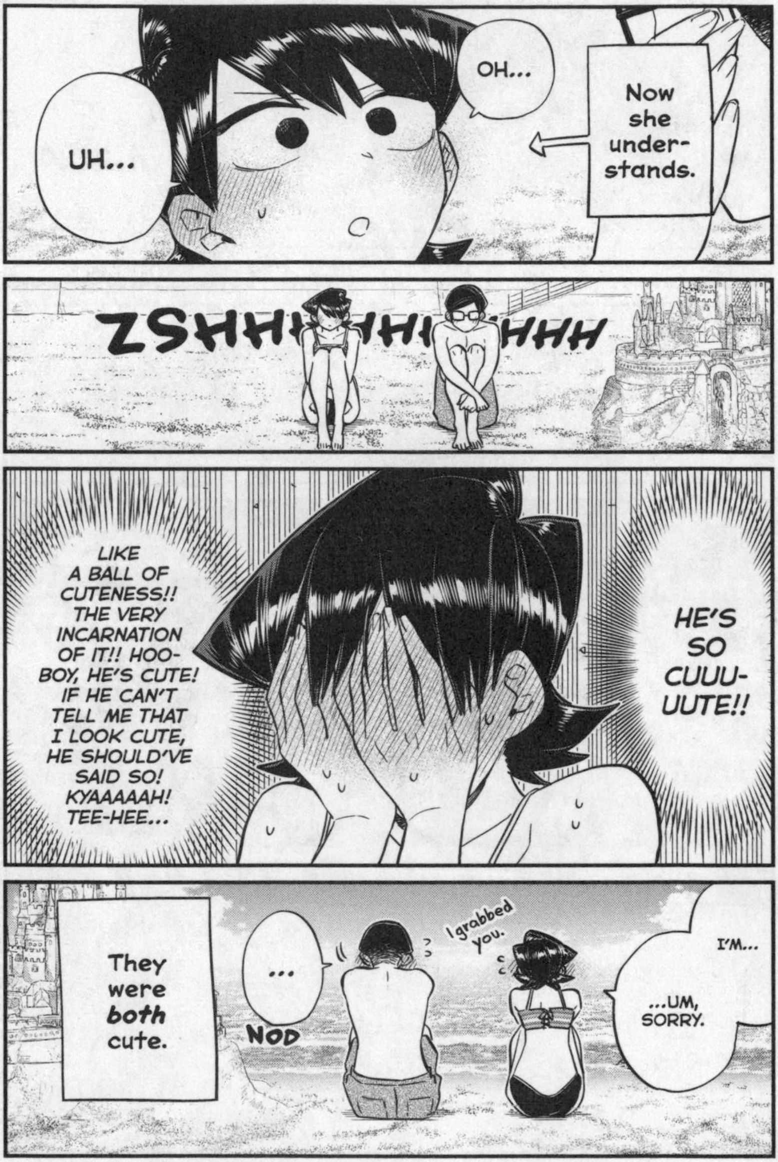
Now she under-stands.
OH...
UH...
ZSHHHHHHHHHH
HE'S SO CUUU-UUTE!!
LIKE A BALL OF CUTENESS!! THE VERY INCARNATION OF IT!! HOO-BOY, HE'S CUTE! IF HE CAN'T TELL ME THAT I LOOK CUTE, HE SHOULD'VE SAID SO! KYAAAAAH! TEE-HEE...
I'M... ...UM, SORRY.
I grabbed you.
...
NOD
They were **both** cute.

Communication 166 — The End

Komi Can't Communicate

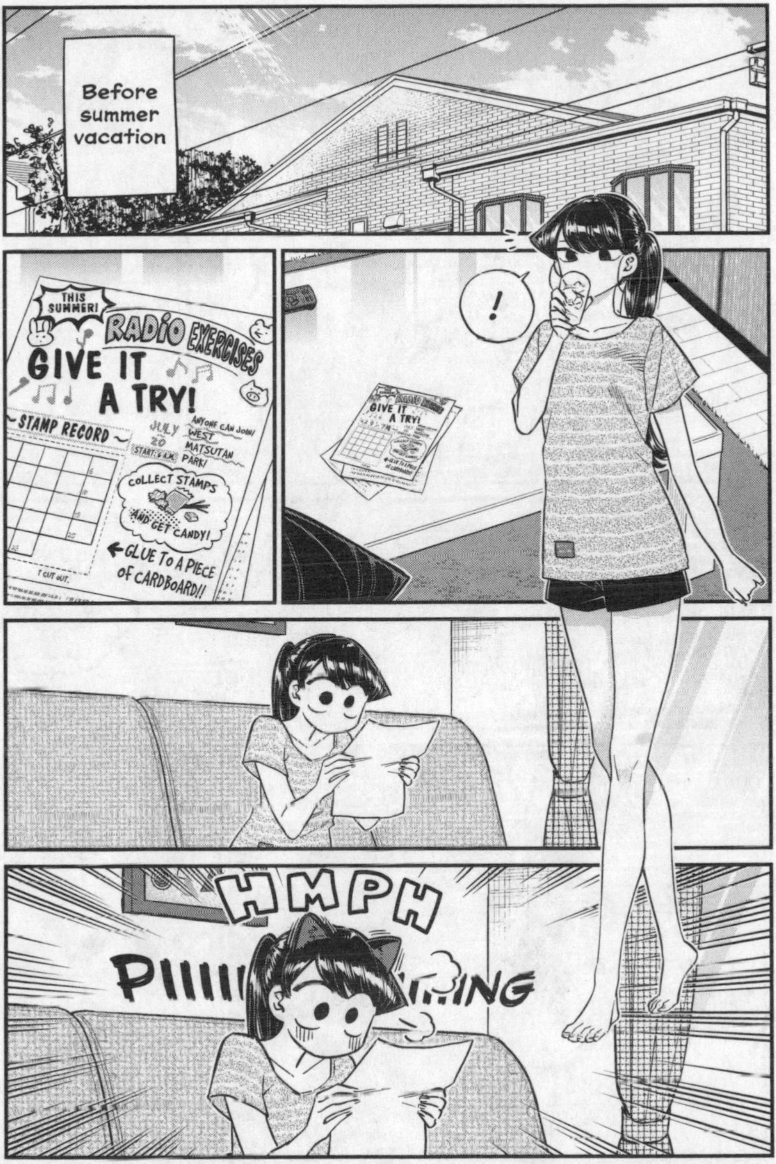
Before summer vacation
!
THIS SUMMER!
RADIO EXERCISES
GIVE IT A TRY!
STAMP RECORD
JULY 20
START: 6 A.M.
ANYONE CAN JOIN!
WEST MATSUTAN PARK!
COLLECT STAMPS AND GET CANDY!
CUT OUT.
GLUE TO A PIECE OF CARDBOARD!!
HMPH
PIIIII
ING

Communication 167: Radio Exercises

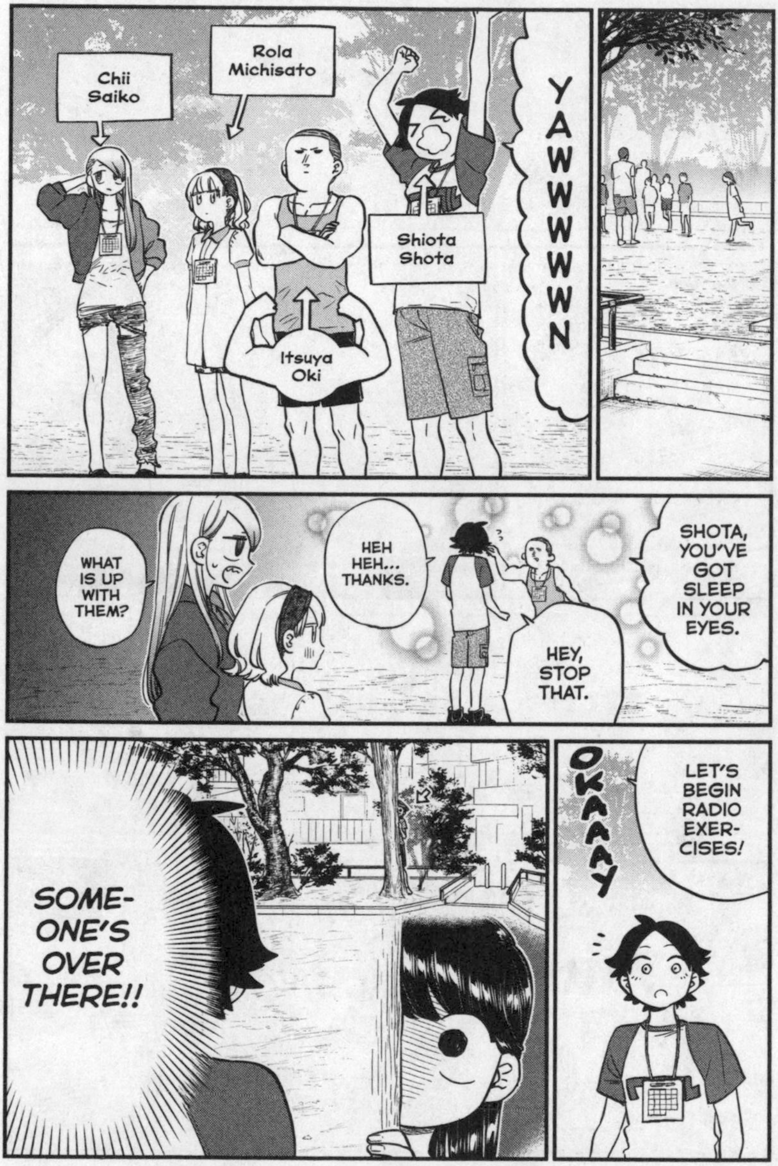
YAWWWWWWN
Rola Michisato
Chii Saiko
Shiota Shota
Itsuya Oki
SHOTA, YOU'VE GOT SLEEP IN YOUR EYES.
HEY, STOP THAT.
HEH HEH... THANKS.
WHAT IS UP WITH THEM?
LET'S BEGIN RADIO EXER-CISES!
OKAAAY
SOME-ONE'S OVER THERE!!

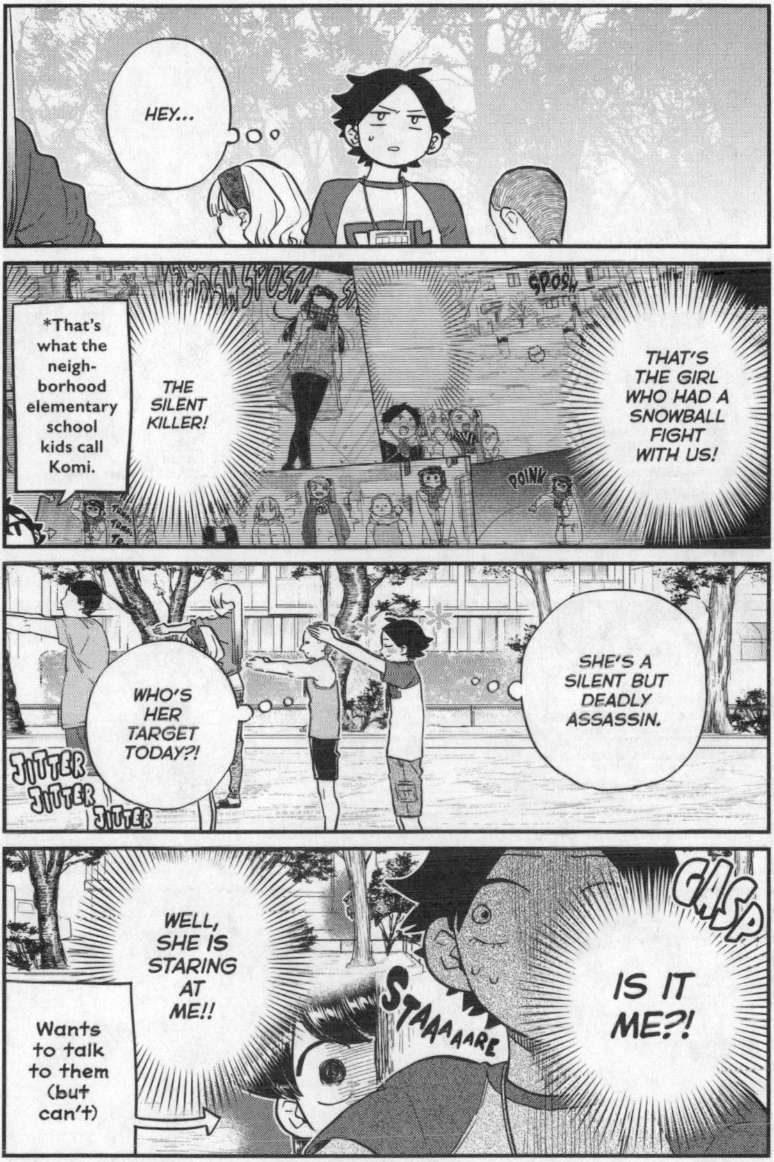
HEY...
SPOSH
THAT'S THE GIRL WHO HAD A SNOWBALL FIGHT WITH US!
POINK
SPOSH SPOSH
THE SILENT KILLER!
*That's what the neighborhood elementary school kids call Komi.
SHE'S A SILENT BUT DEADLY ASSASSIN.
WHO'S HER TARGET TODAY?!
JITTER JITTER JITTER
GASP
IS IT ME?!
STAAAAAARE
WELL, SHE IS STARING AT ME!!
Wants to talk to them (but can't)

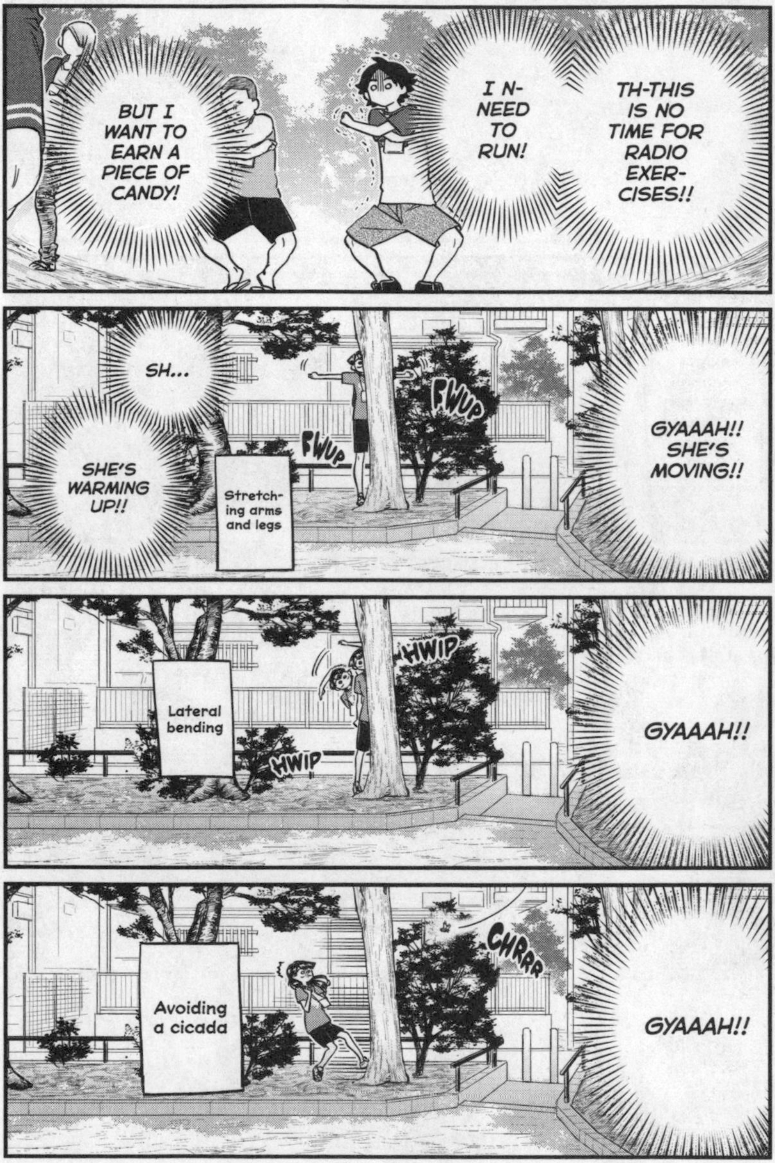
TH-THIS IS NO TIME FOR RADIO EXER-CISES!!
I N-NEED TO RUN!
BUT I WANT TO EARN A PIECE OF CANDY!
GYAAAH!! SHE'S MOVING!!
FWUP
FWUP
Stretch-ing arms and legs
SH...
SHE'S WARMING UP!!
GYAAAH!!
HWIP
HWIP
Lateral bending
GYAAAH!!
CHRRR
Avoiding a cicada

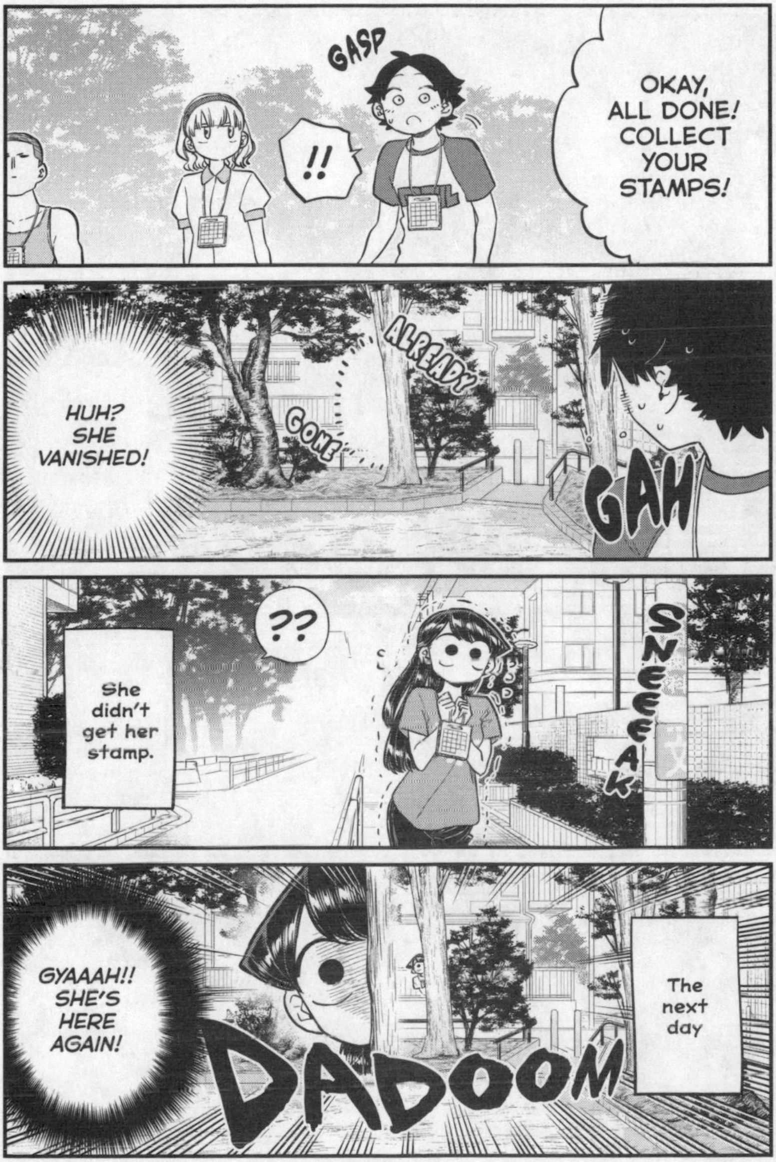
OKAY, ALL DONE! COLLECT YOUR STAMPS!
GASP
!!
ALREADY
GONE
GAH
HUH? SHE VANISHED!
SNEEEAK
??
She didn't get her stamp.
The next day
GYAAAH!! SHE'S HERE AGAIN!
DADOOM

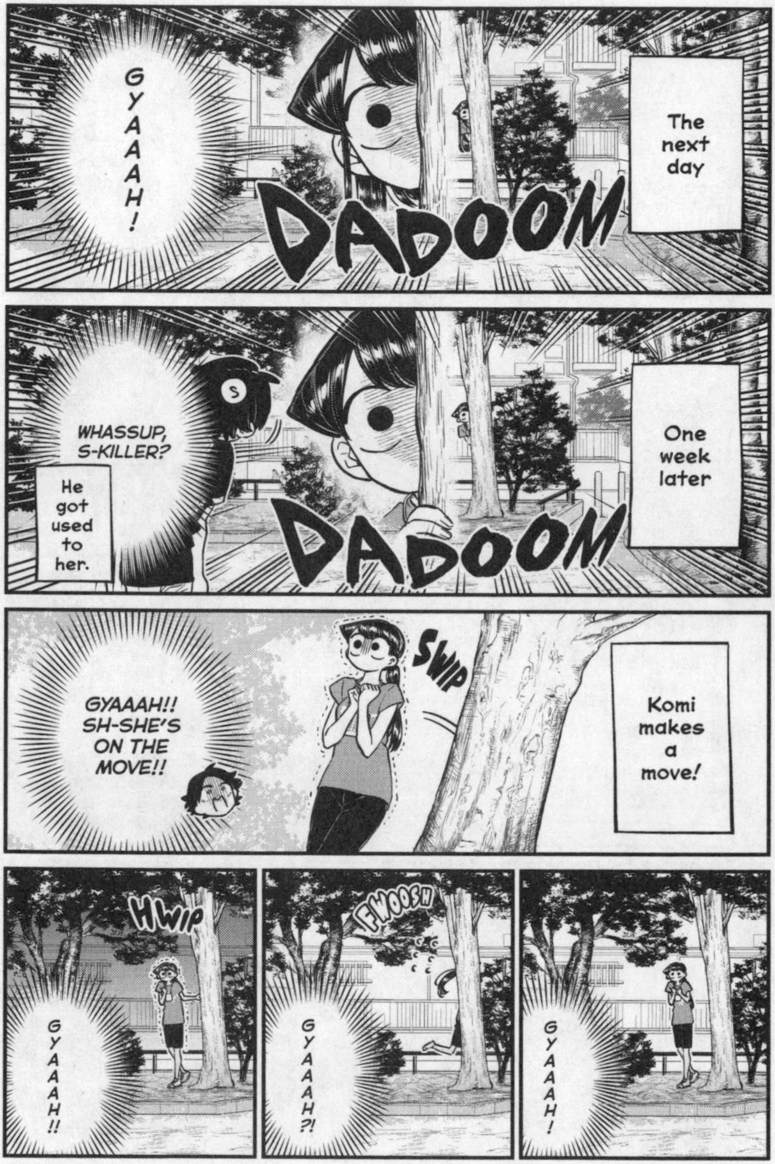
The next day
DADOOM
GYAAAH!
One week later
DADOOM
WHASSUP, S-KILLER?
He got used to her.
Komi makes a move!
SWIP
GYAAAH!! SH-SHE'S ON THE MOVE!!
GYAAAH!
FWOOSH
GYAAAH?!
HWIP
GYAAAH!!

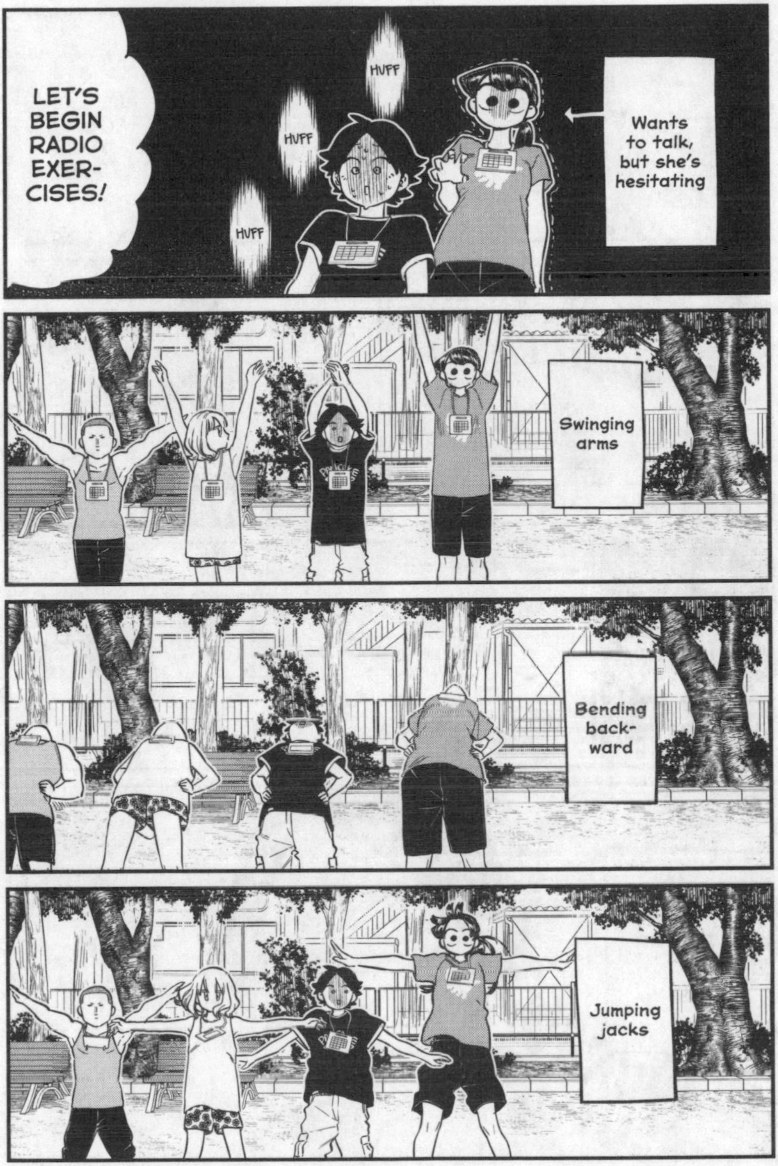
Wants to talk, but she's hesitating
HUFF
HUFF
HUFF
LET'S BEGIN RADIO EXER-CISES!
Swinging arms
Bending back-ward
Jumping jacks

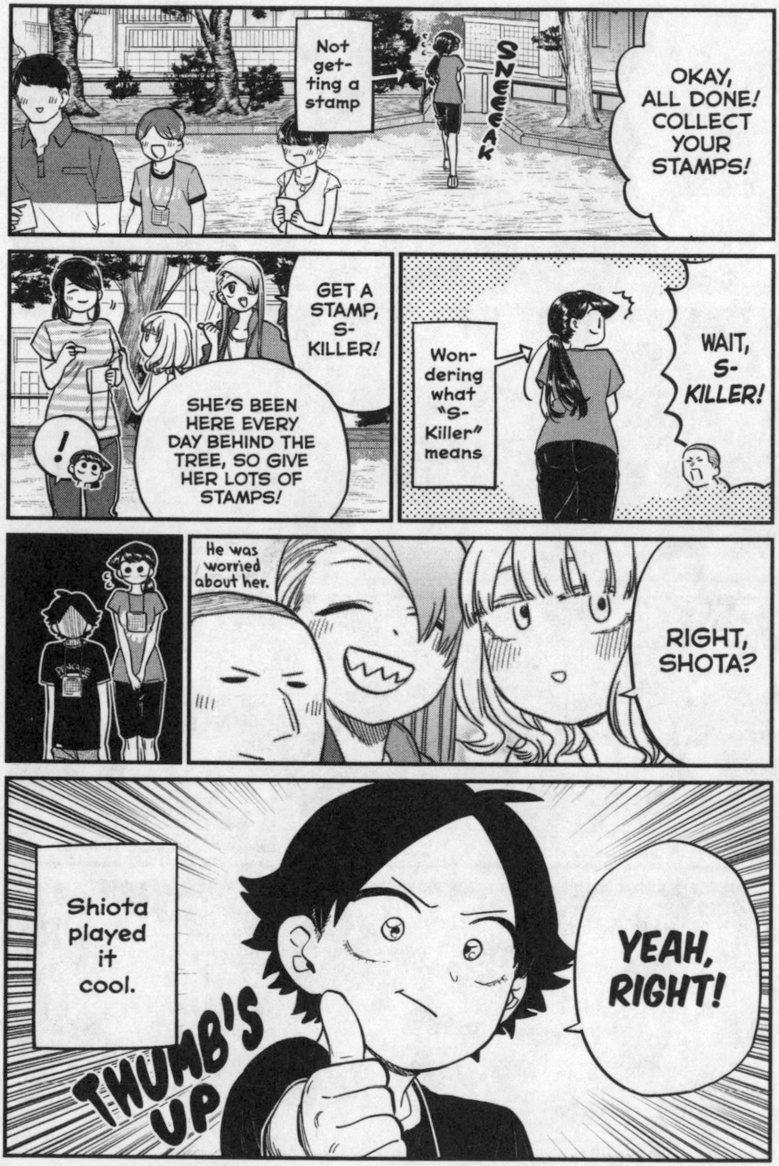
OKAY, ALL DONE! COLLECT YOUR STAMPS!
SNEEEAK
Not getting a stamp
WAIT, S-KILLER!
Wondering what "S-Killer" means
GET A STAMP, S-KILLER!
SHE'S BEEN HERE EVERY DAY BEHIND THE TREE, SO GIVE HER LOTS OF STAMPS!
!
RIGHT, SHOTA?
He was worried about her.
YEAH, RIGHT!
THUMB'S UP
Shiota played it cool.

Communication 167 — The End

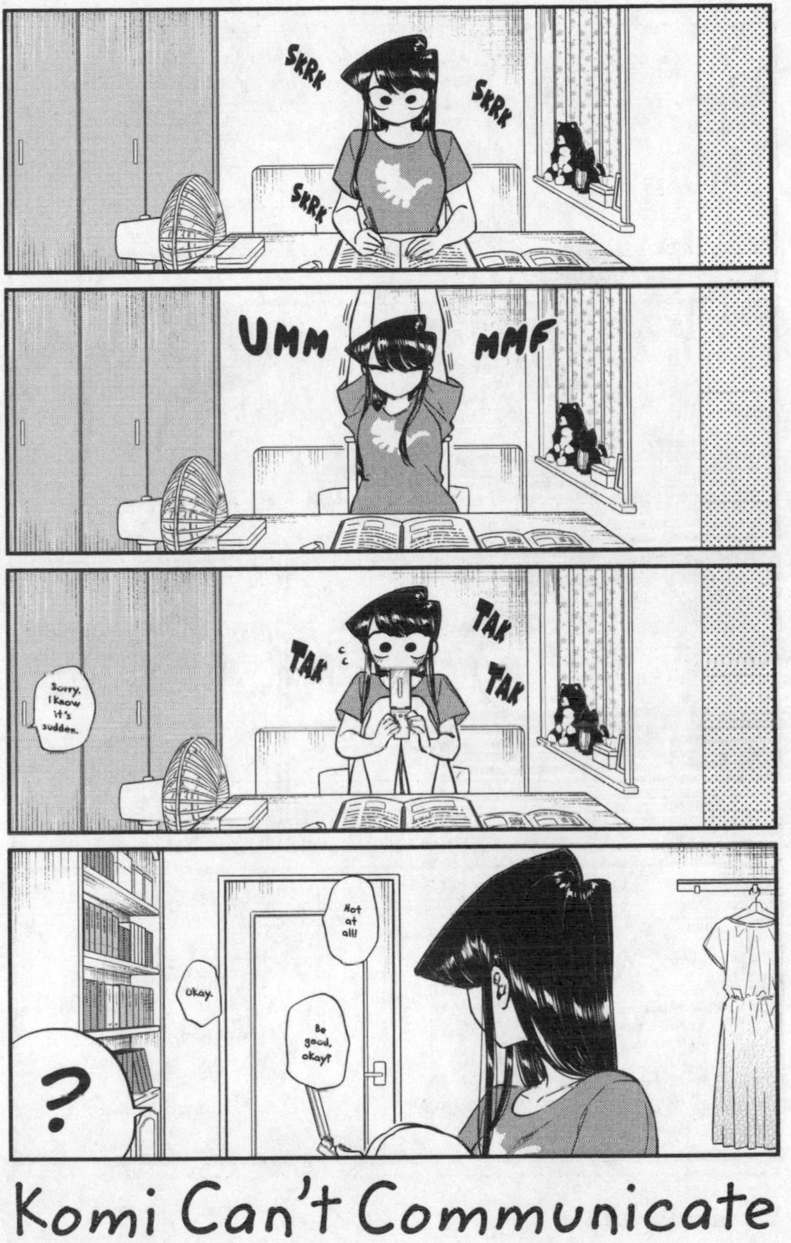
SKRK
SKRK
SKRK
MMF
UMM
TAK
TAK
TAK
Sorry. I know it's sudden.
Not at all!
Okay.
Be good, okay?
?

Komi Can't Communicate

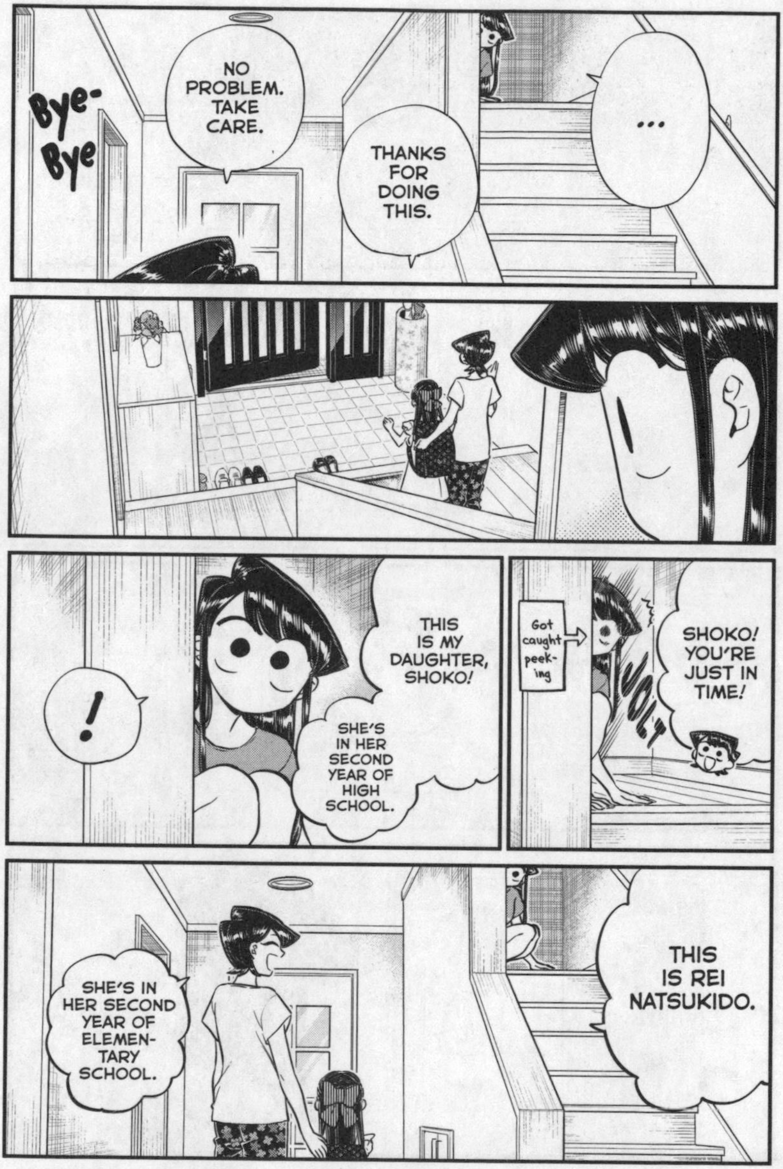
...
THANKS FOR DOING THIS.
NO PROBLEM. TAKE CARE.
Bye-Bye
SHOKO! YOU'RE JUST IN TIME!
JOLT
Got caught peek-ing
THIS IS MY DAUGHTER, SHOKO!
SHE'S IN HER SECOND YEAR OF HIGH SCHOOL.
!
THIS IS REI NATSUKIDO.
SHE'S IN HER SECOND YEAR OF ELEMENTARY SCHOOL.

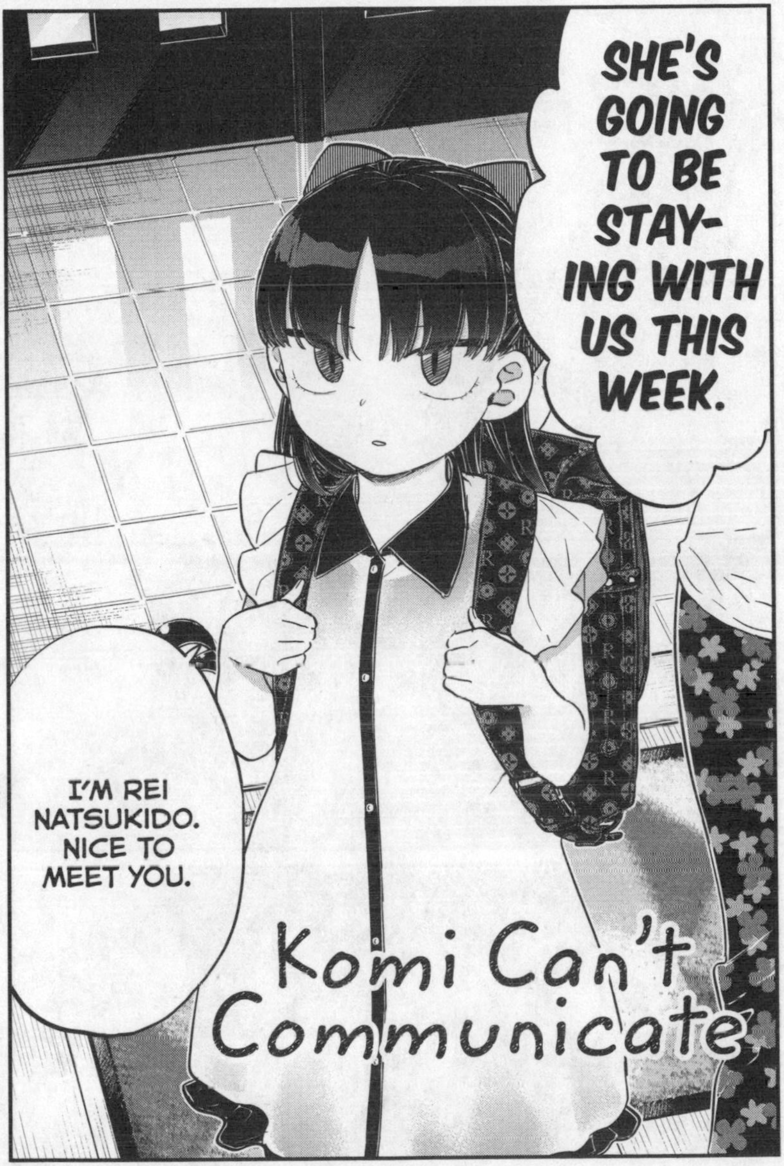
SHE'S GOING TO BE STAY-ING WITH US THIS WEEK.
I'M REI NATSUKIDO. NICE TO MEET YOU.
Komi Can't Communicate

Communication 168: Hot Milk

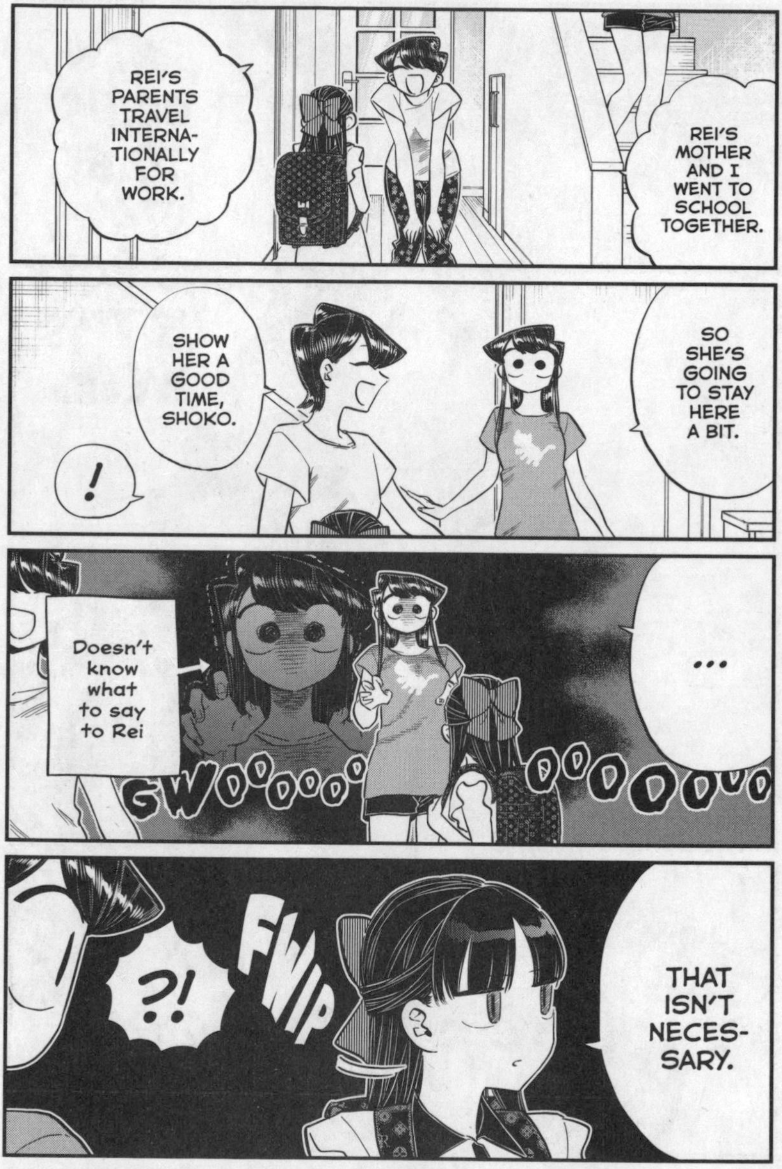
REI'S MOTHER AND I WENT TO SCHOOL TOGETHER.
REI'S PARENTS TRAVEL INTERNATIONALLY FOR WORK.
SO SHE'S GOING TO STAY HERE A BIT.
SHOW HER A GOOD TIME, SHOKO.
!
...
Doesn't know what to say to Rei
GWDDDDDDDDDDDDD
THAT ISN'T NECESSARY.
FWIP
?!

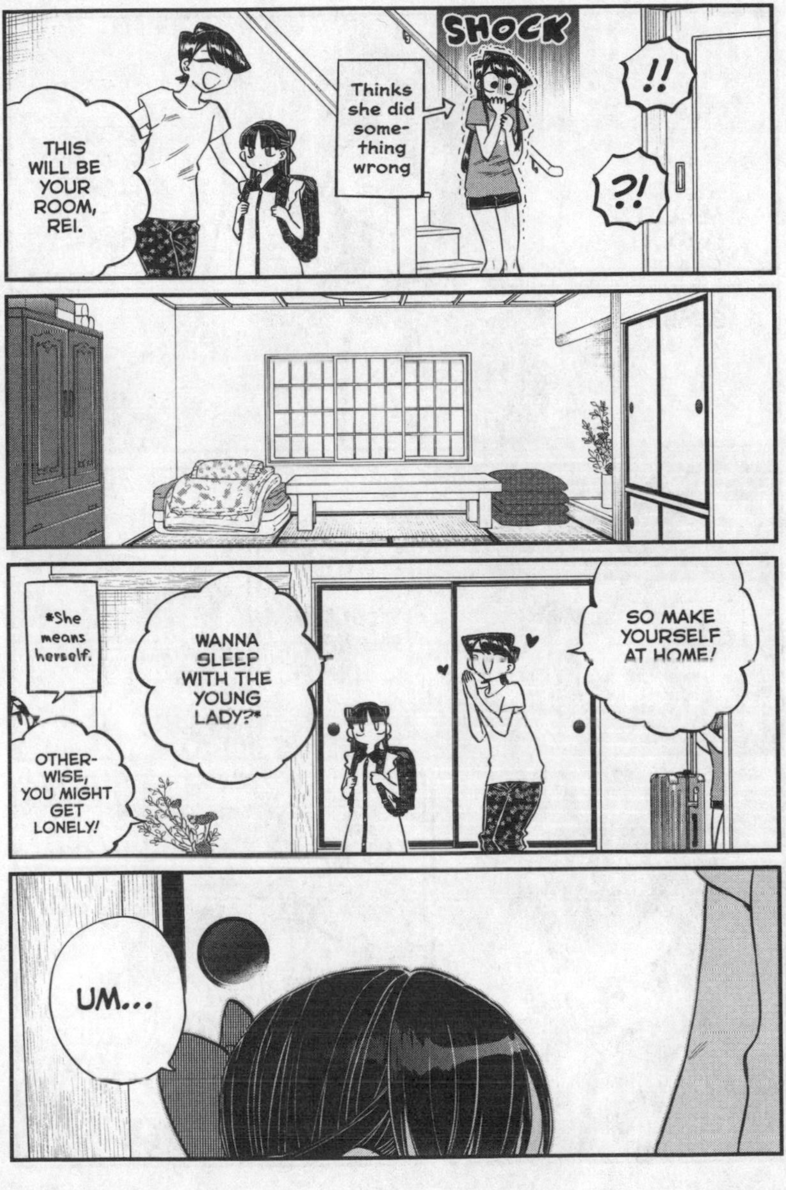
SHOCK
!!
Thinks she did some-thing wrong
?!
THIS WILL BE YOUR ROOM, REI.
SO MAKE YOURSELF AT HOME!
WANNA SLEEP WITH THE YOUNG LADY?*
*She means herself.
OTHER-WISE, YOU MIGHT GET LONELY!
UM...

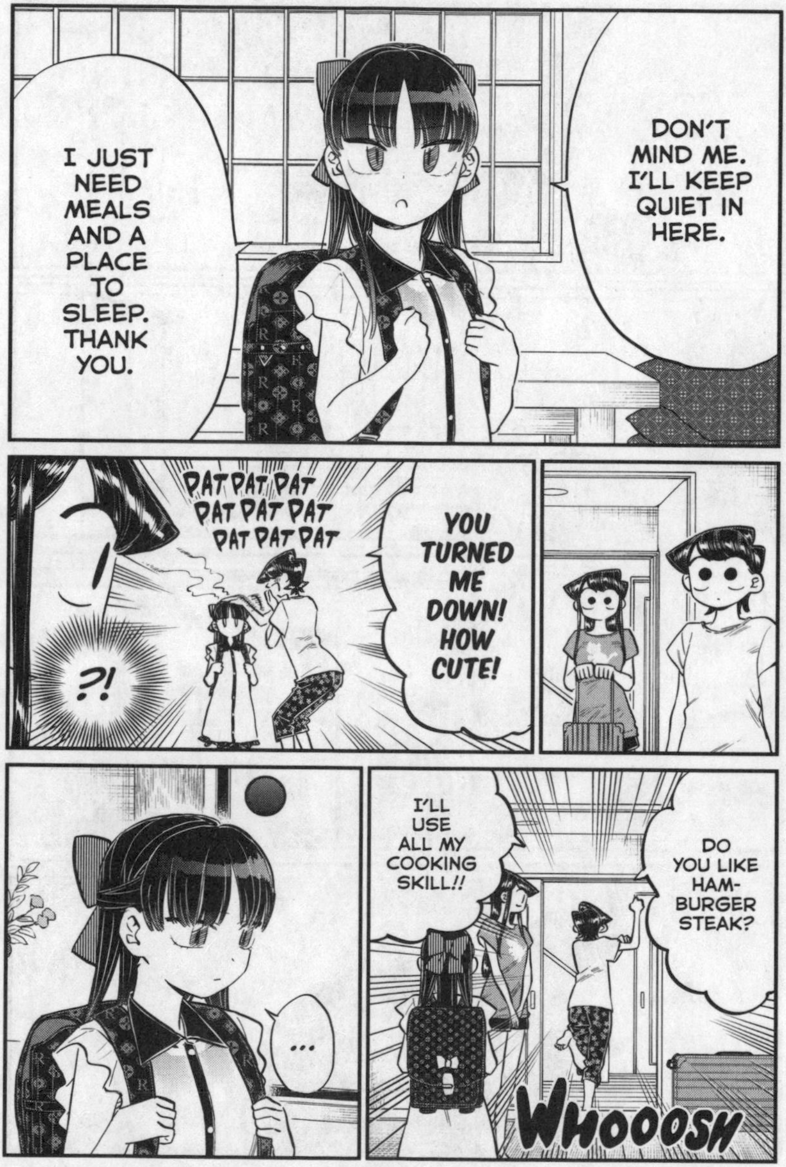
DON'T MIND ME. I'LL KEEP QUIET IN HERE.
I JUST NEED MEALS AND A PLACE TO SLEEP. THANK YOU.
YOU TURNED ME DOWN! HOW CUTE!
PAT PAT PAT PAT PAT PAT PAT PAT PAT
?!
DO YOU LIKE HAM-BURGER STEAK?
I'LL USE ALL MY COOKING SKILL!!
WHOOOSH
...

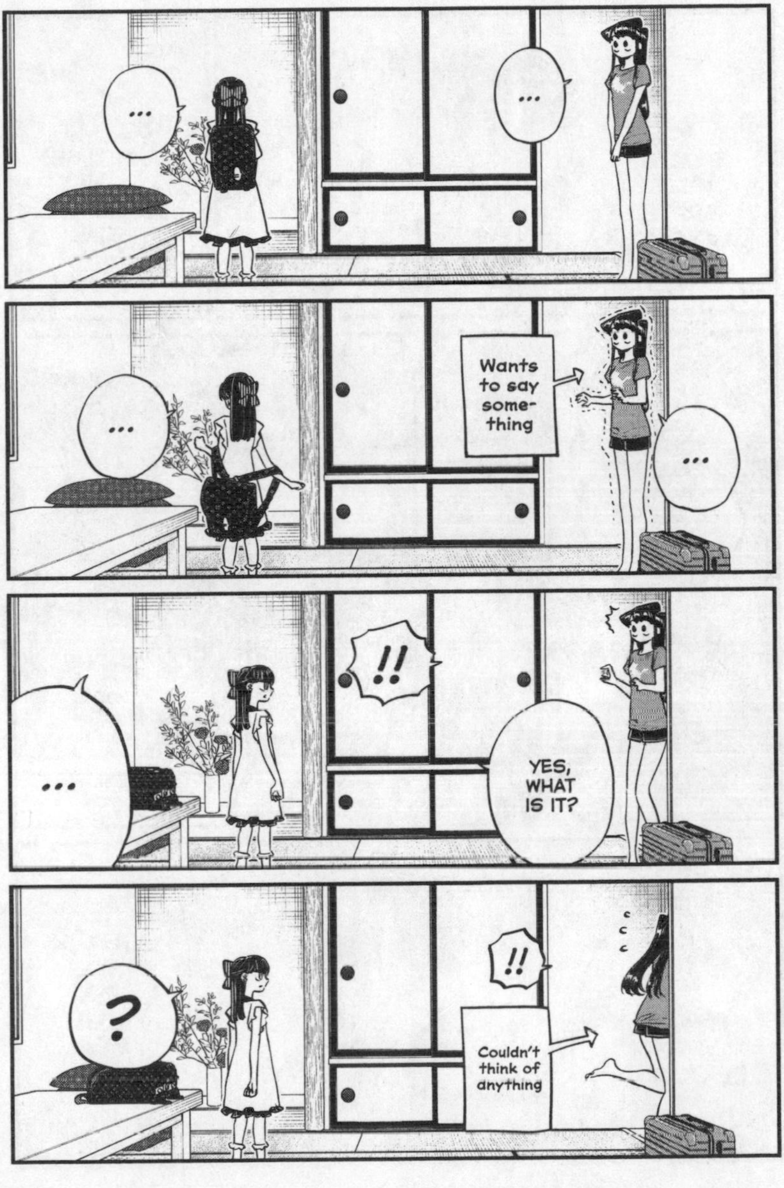
...
...
Wants to say some-thing
...
...
!!
YES, WHAT IS IT?
...
!!
Couldn't think of anything
?

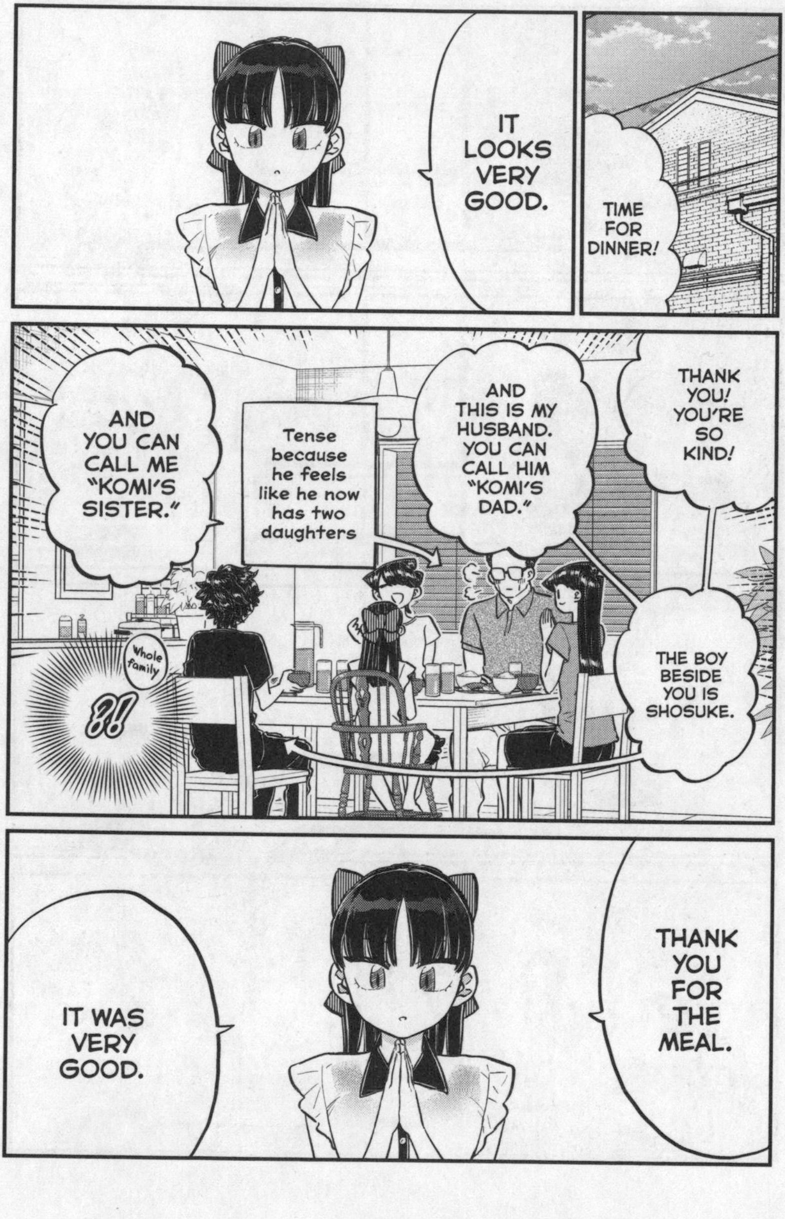
TIME FOR DINNER!
IT LOOKS VERY GOOD.
THANK YOU! YOU'RE SO KIND!
THE BOY BESIDE YOU IS SHOSUKE.
AND THIS IS MY HUSBAND. YOU CAN CALL HIM "KOMI'S DAD."
Tense because he feels like he now has two daughters
AND YOU CAN CALL ME "KOMI'S SISTER."
Whole family
?!
THANK YOU FOR THE MEAL.
IT WAS VERY GOOD.

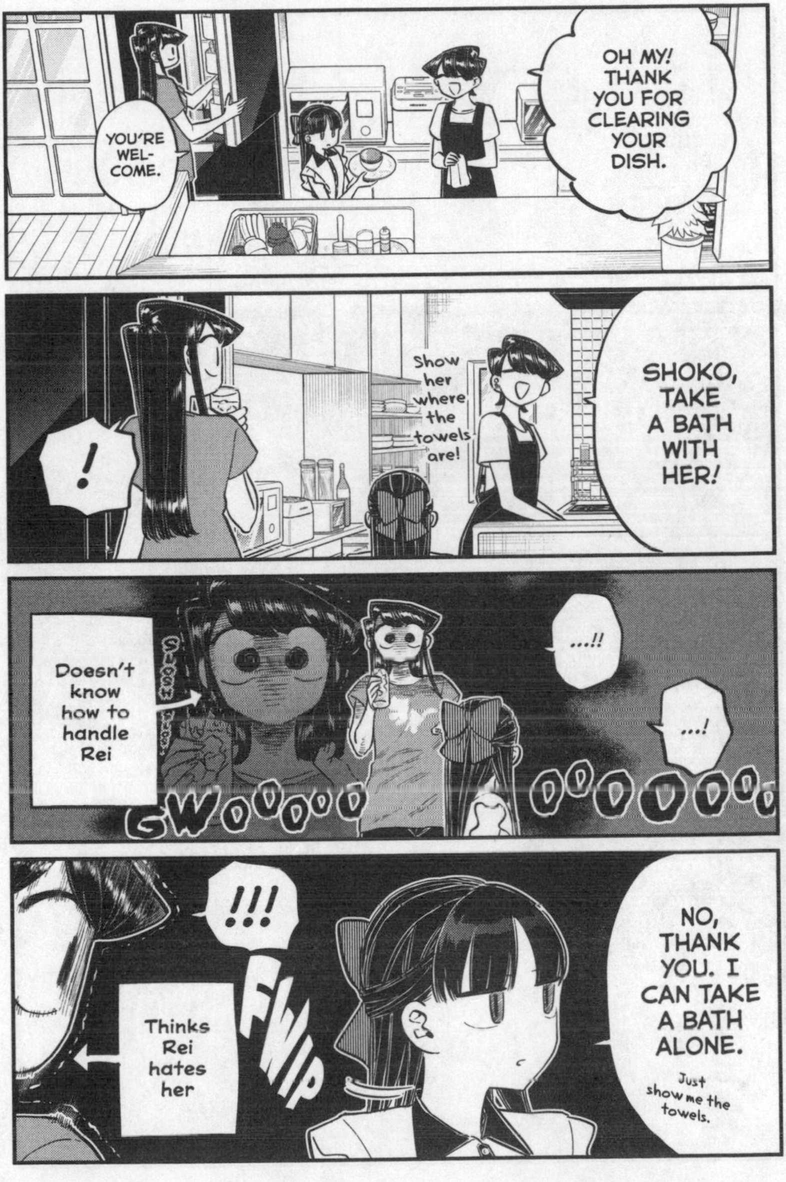
OH MY! THANK YOU FOR CLEARING YOUR DISH.
YOU'RE WEL-COME.
SHOKO, TAKE A BATH WITH HER!
Show her where the towels are!
!
...!!
...!
Doesn't know how to handle Rei
NO, THANK YOU. I CAN TAKE A BATH ALONE.
Just show me the towels.
FWIP
!!!
Thinks Rei hates her

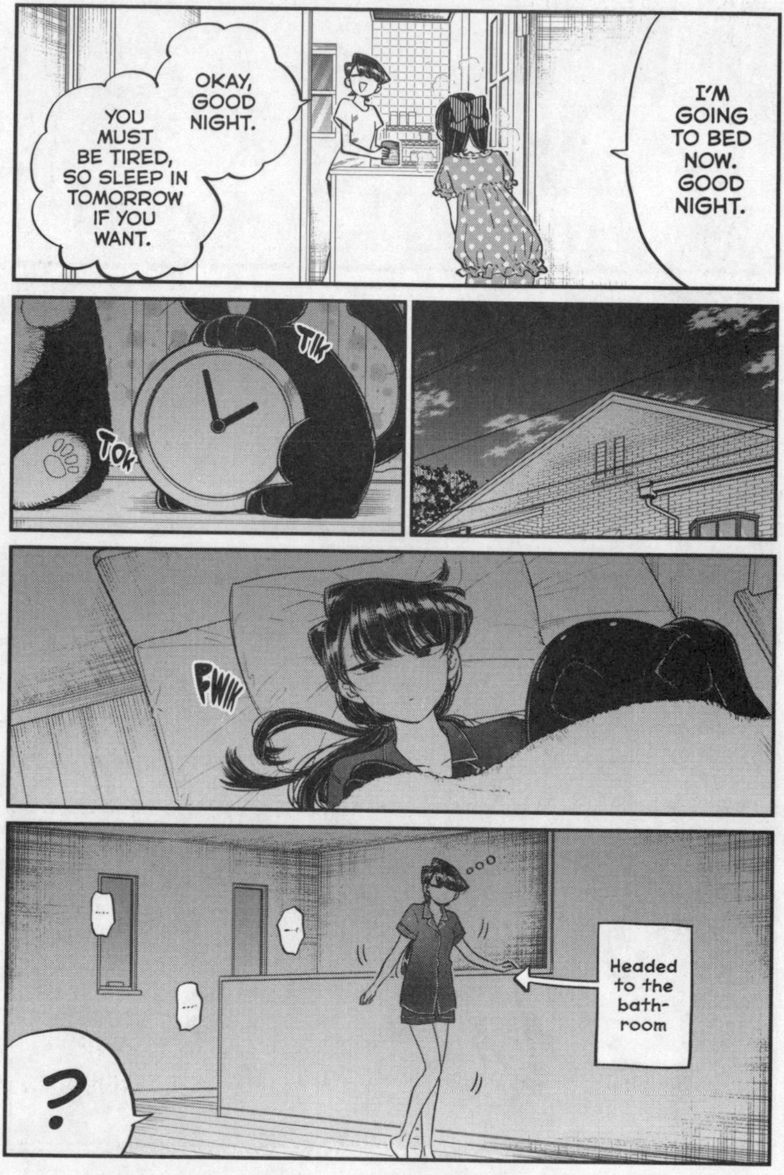
I'M GOING TO BED NOW. GOOD NIGHT.
OKAY, GOOD NIGHT.
YOU MUST BE TIRED, SO SLEEP IN TOMORROW IF YOU WANT.
TIK
TOK
FWIK
Headed to the bath-room
?

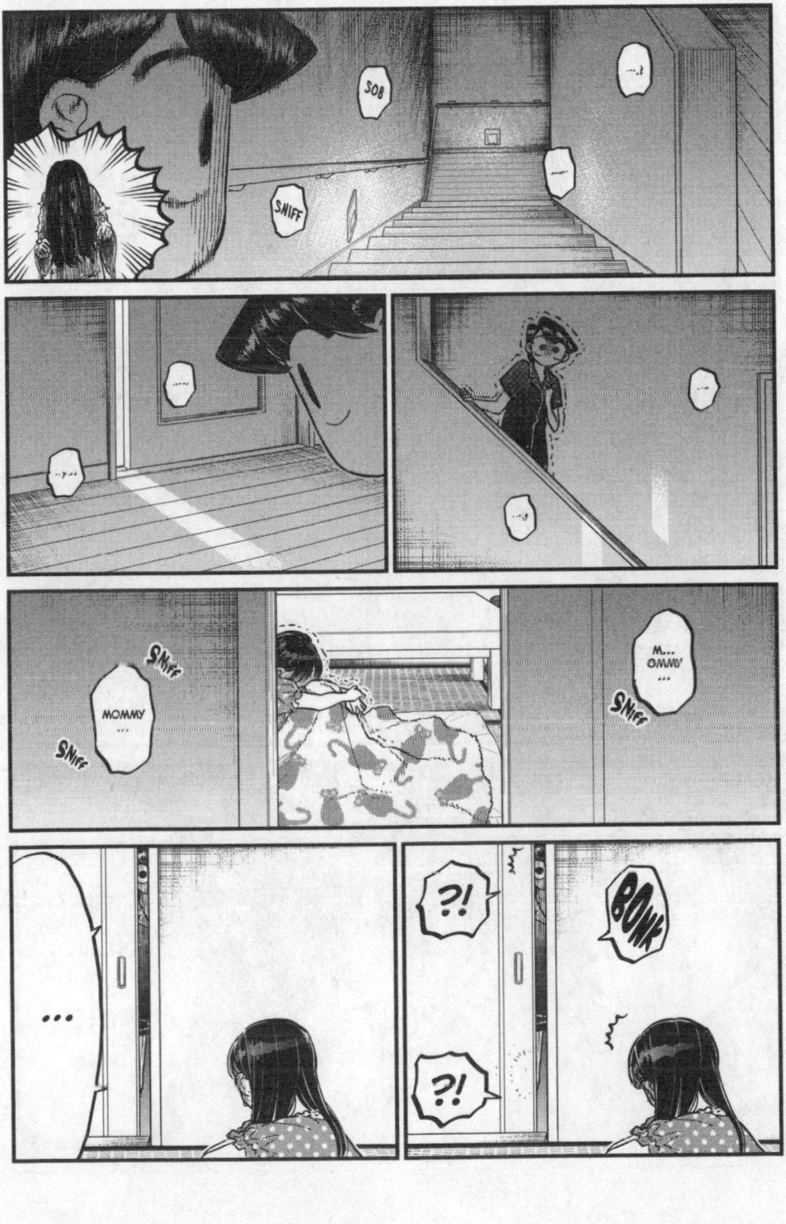
SOB
SNIFF
M... OMMY ...
SNIFF
SNIFF
MOMMY ...
SNIFF
BONK
?!
?!
...

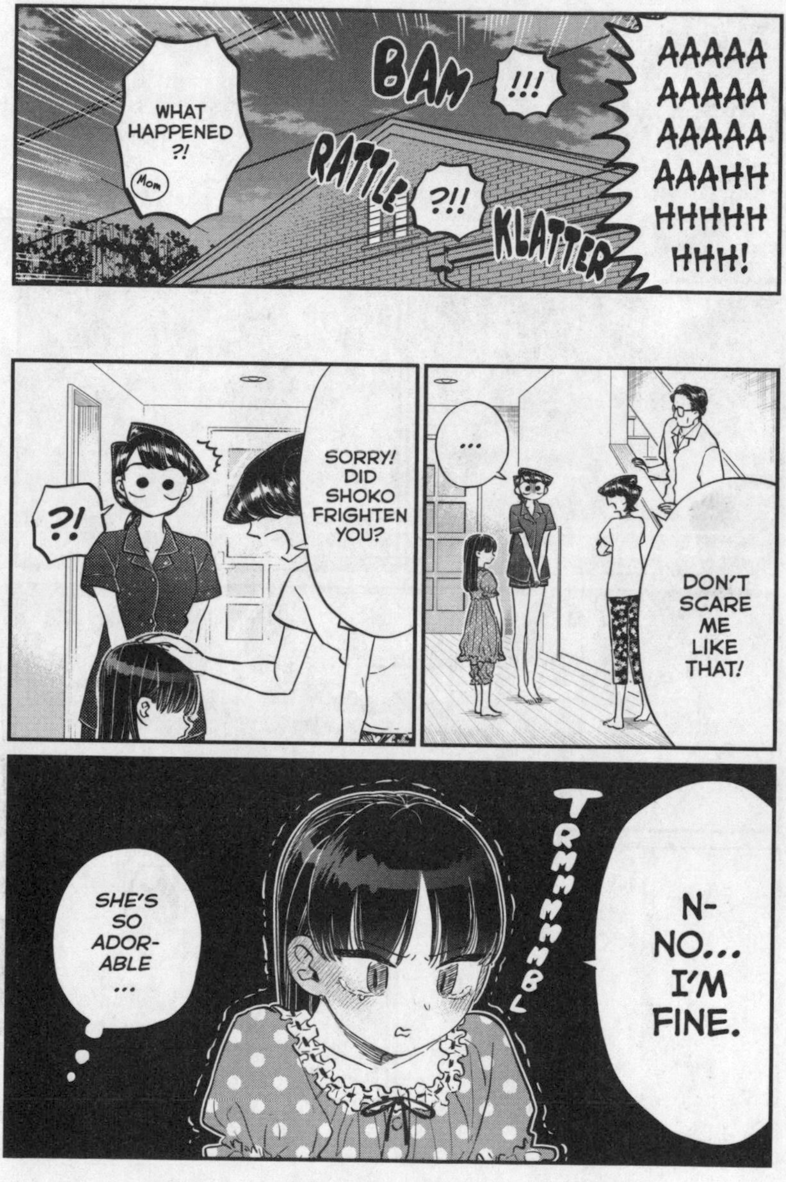
AAAAAAAAAAAAAAAAAAHHHHHHHHH!
BAM
!!!
KLATTER
?!!
RATTLE
WHAT HAPPENED ?!
Mom
...
DON'T SCARE ME LIKE THAT!
SORRY! DID SHOKO FRIGHTEN YOU?
?!
N-NO... I'M FINE.
TRMMMMBL
SHE'S SO ADOR-ABLE ...

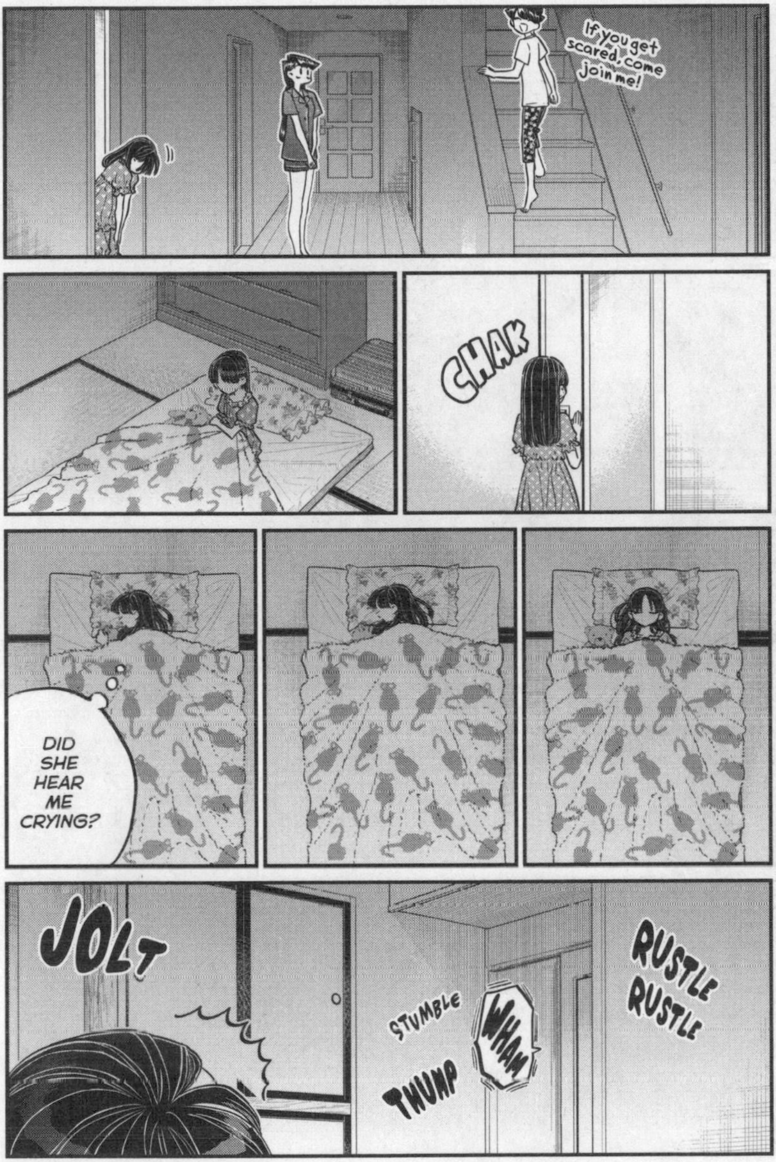
If you get scared, come join me!
CHAK
DID SHE HEAR ME CRYING?
RUSTLE RUSTLE
WHAM
STUMBLE
THUMP
JOLT

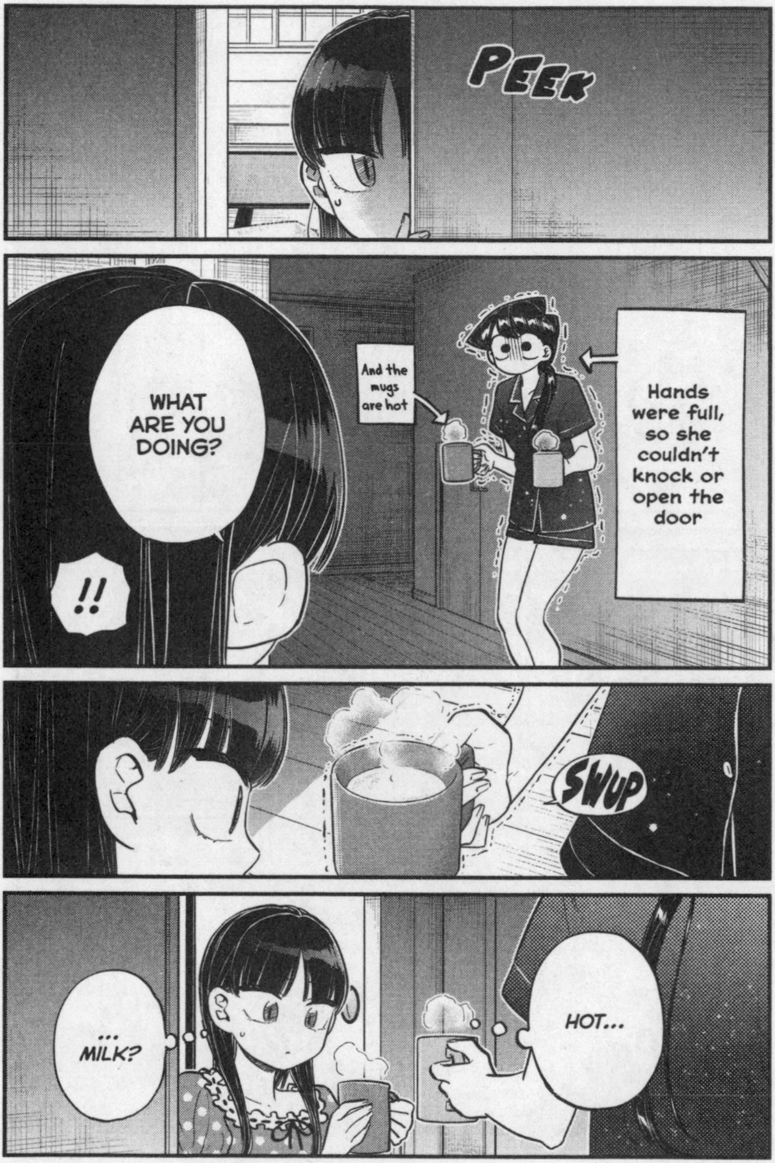
PEEK
Hands were full, so she couldn't knock or open the door
And the mugs are hot
WHAT ARE YOU DOING?
!!
SWUP
HOT...
... MILK?

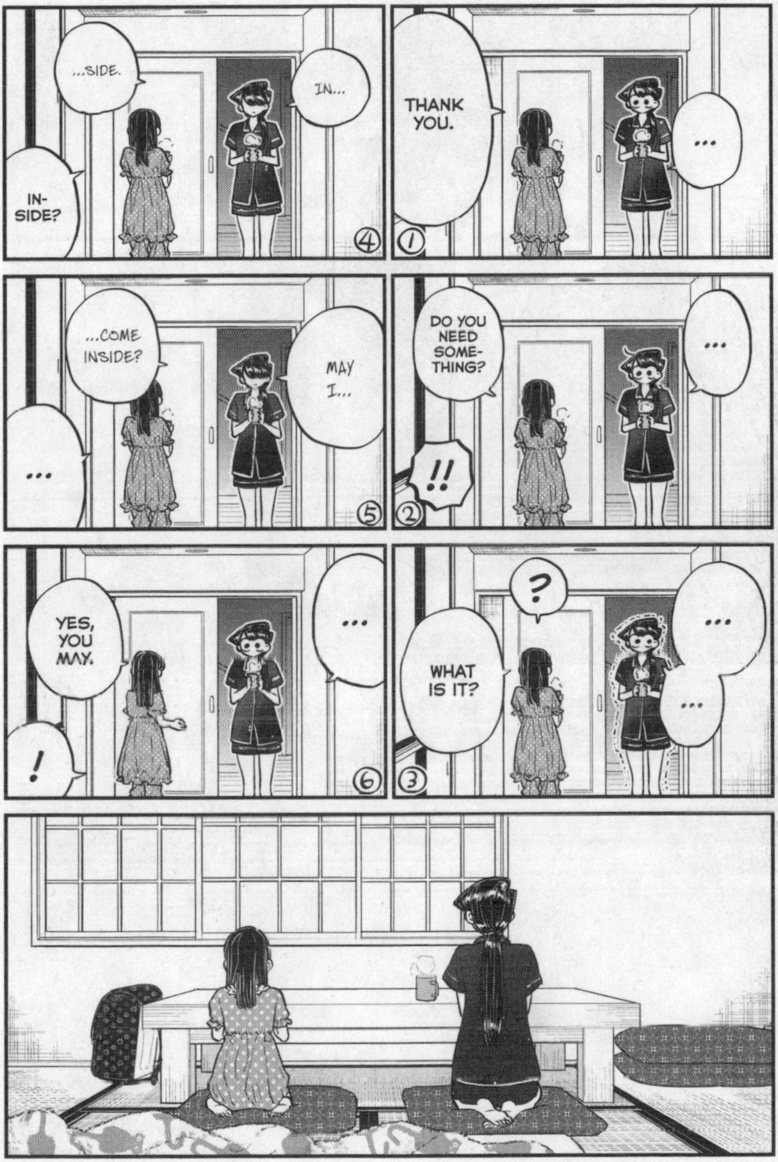
THANK YOU.
...
...
DO YOU NEED SOME-THING?
!!
...
?
WHAT IS IT?
...
IN...
...SIDE.
IN-SIDE?
MAY I...
...COME INSIDE?
...
...
YES, YOU MAY.
!

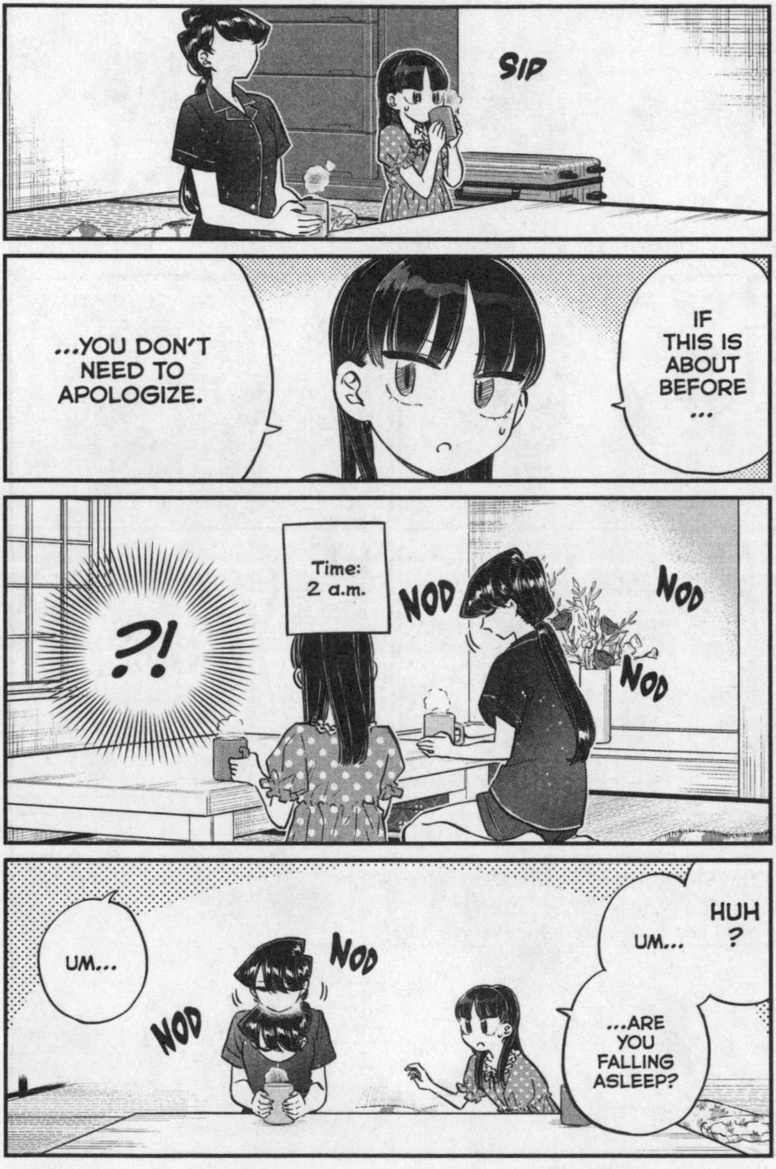
SIP
IF THIS IS ABOUT BEFORE ...
...YOU DON'T NEED TO APOLOGIZE.
NOD
NOD
NOD
Time: 2 a.m.
?!
HUH ?
UM...
...ARE YOU FALLING ASLEEP?
NOD
NOD
UM...

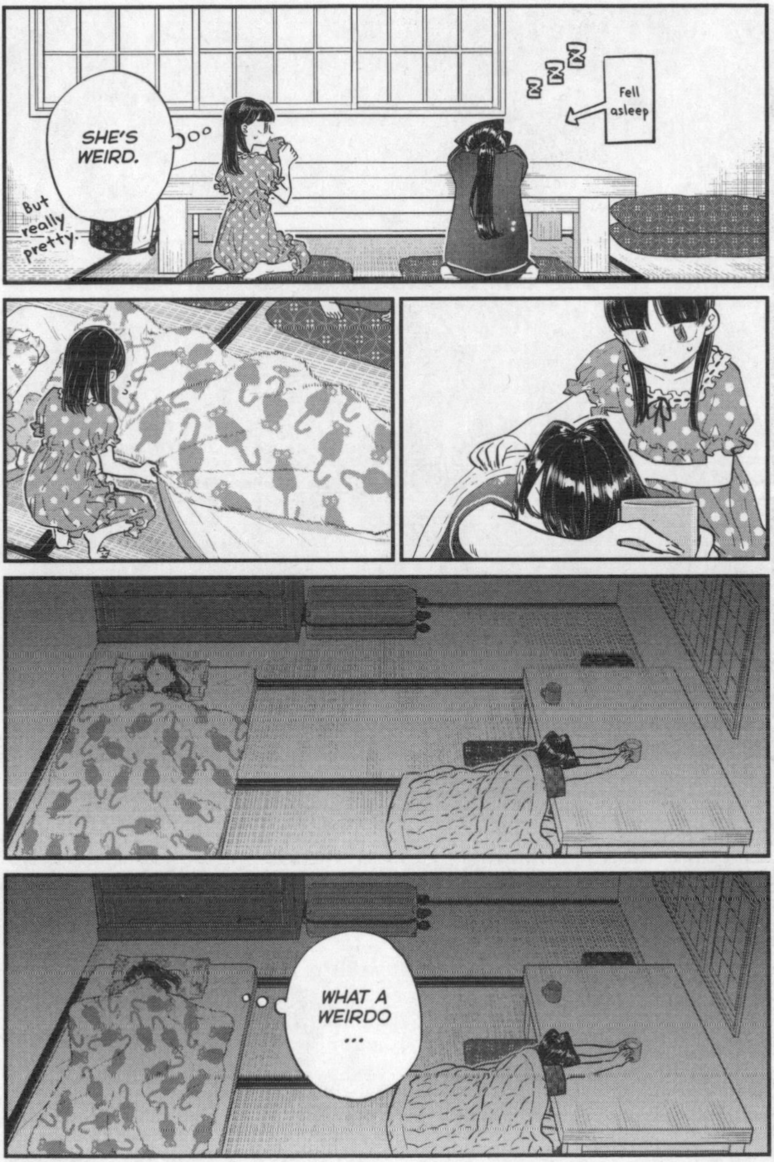
Fell asleep
SHE'S WEIRD.
But really pretty.
WHAT A WEIRDO ...

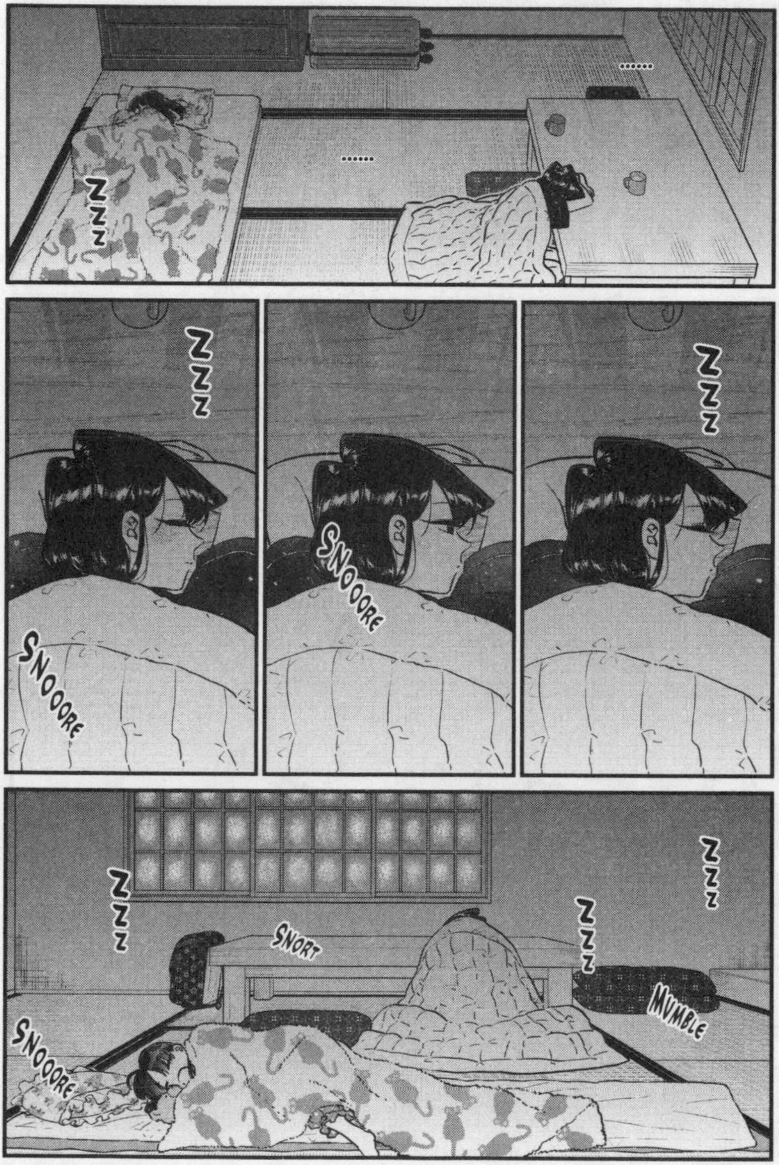
......
......
ZZZ
ZZZ
SNOOORE
ZZZ
SNOOORE
ZZZ
ZZZ
MUMBLE
SNORT
ZZZ
SNOOORE

Communication 168 — The End

Komi Can't Communicate

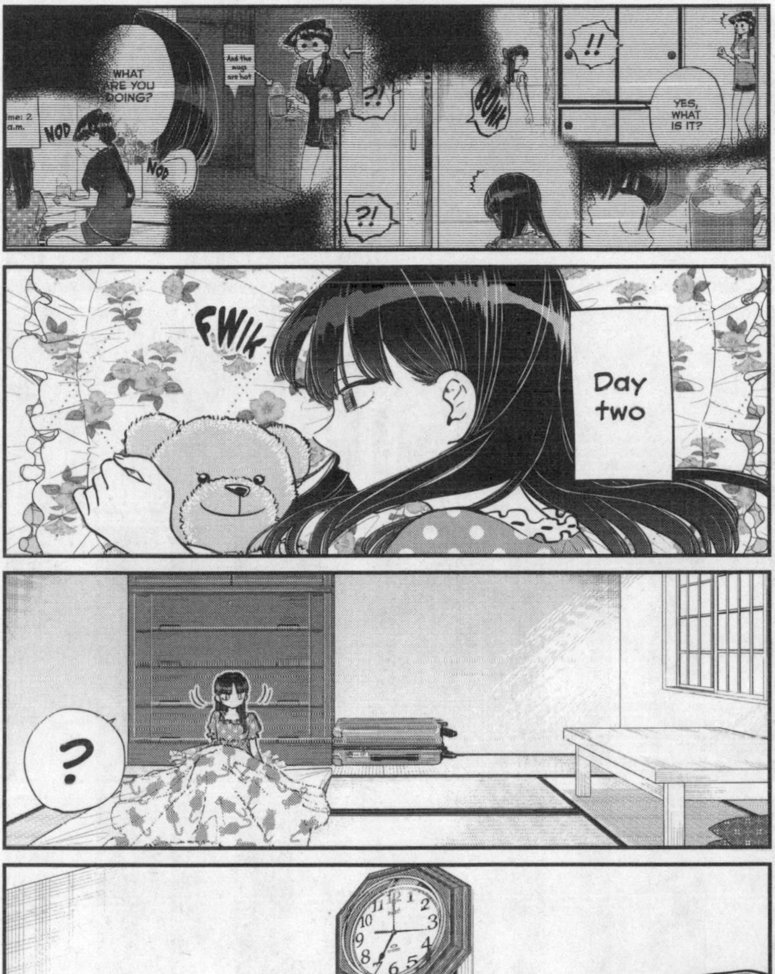
YES, WHAT IS IT?
!!
BONK
?!
?!
And the mugs are hot
WHAT ARE YOU DOING?
NOD
NOD
me: 2 a.m.
Day two
FWIK
?

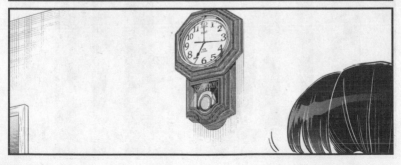

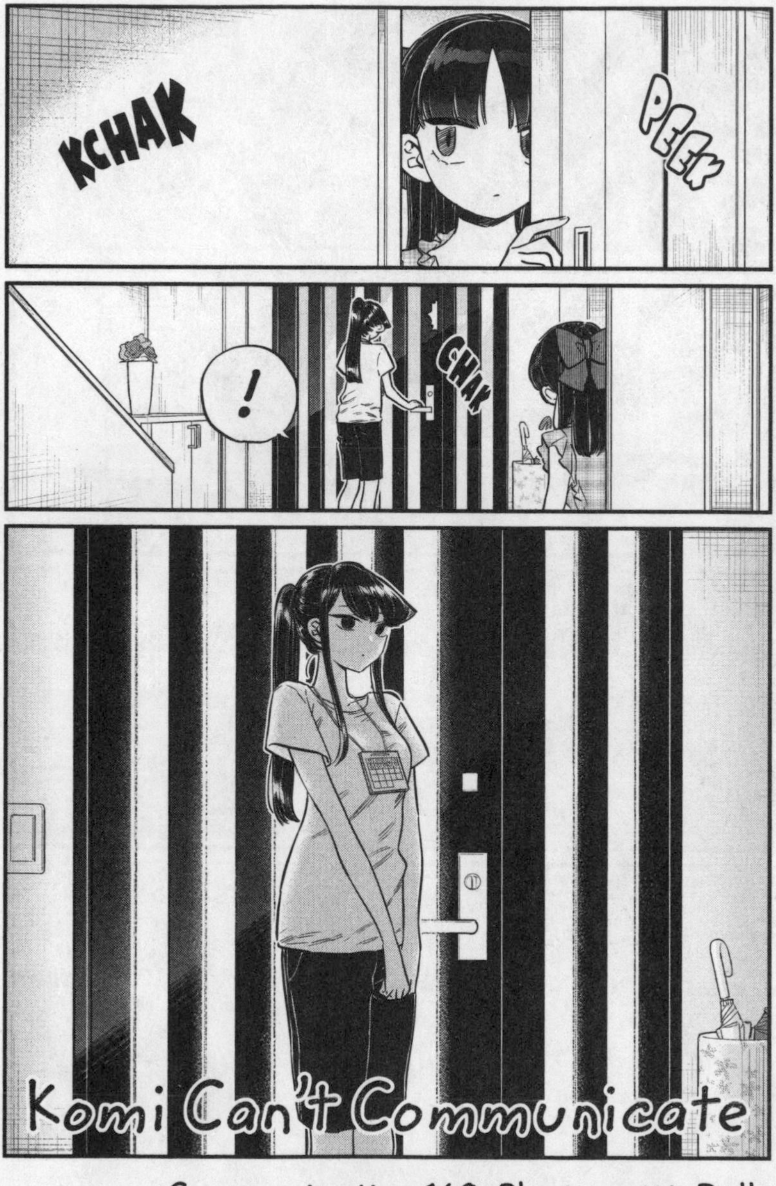
PEEK
KCHAK
CHAK
!
Komi Can't Communicate

Communication 169: Playing with Dolls

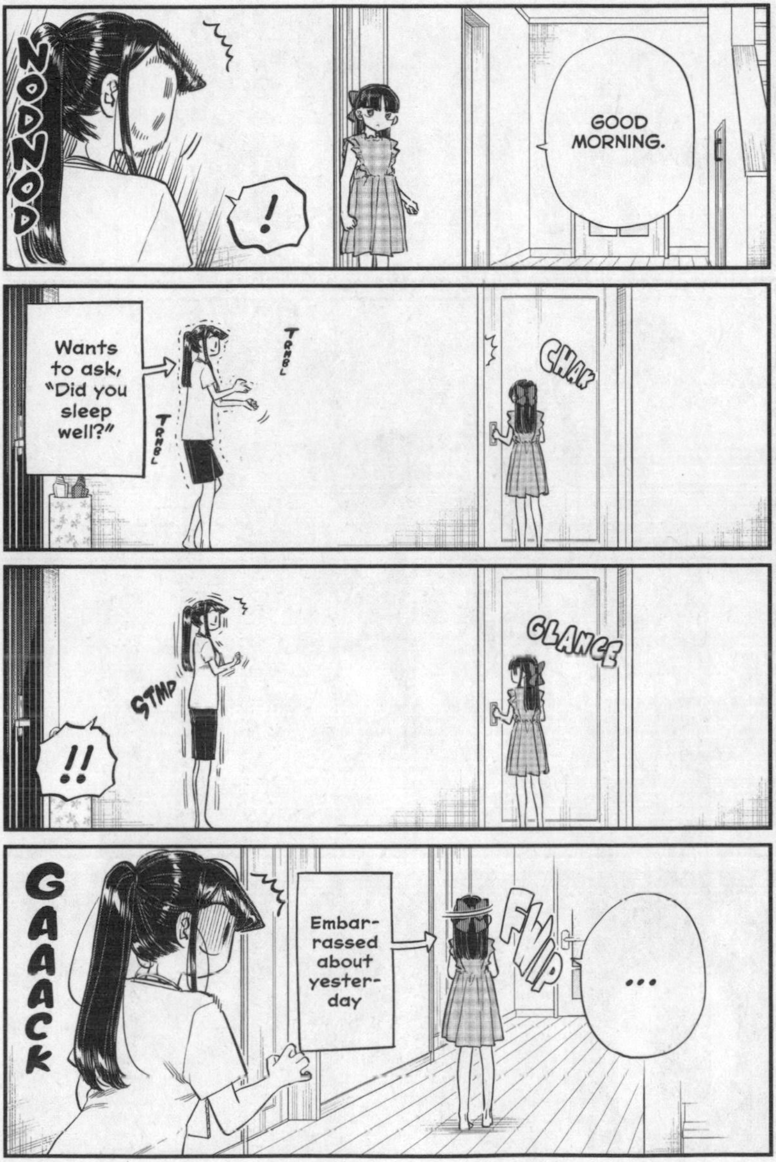
GOOD MORNING.
!
NODNOD
CHAK
TRMBL
Wants to ask, "Did you sleep well?"
TRMBL
GLANCE
STMP
!!
...
FWIP
Embar-rassed about yester-day
GAAACK

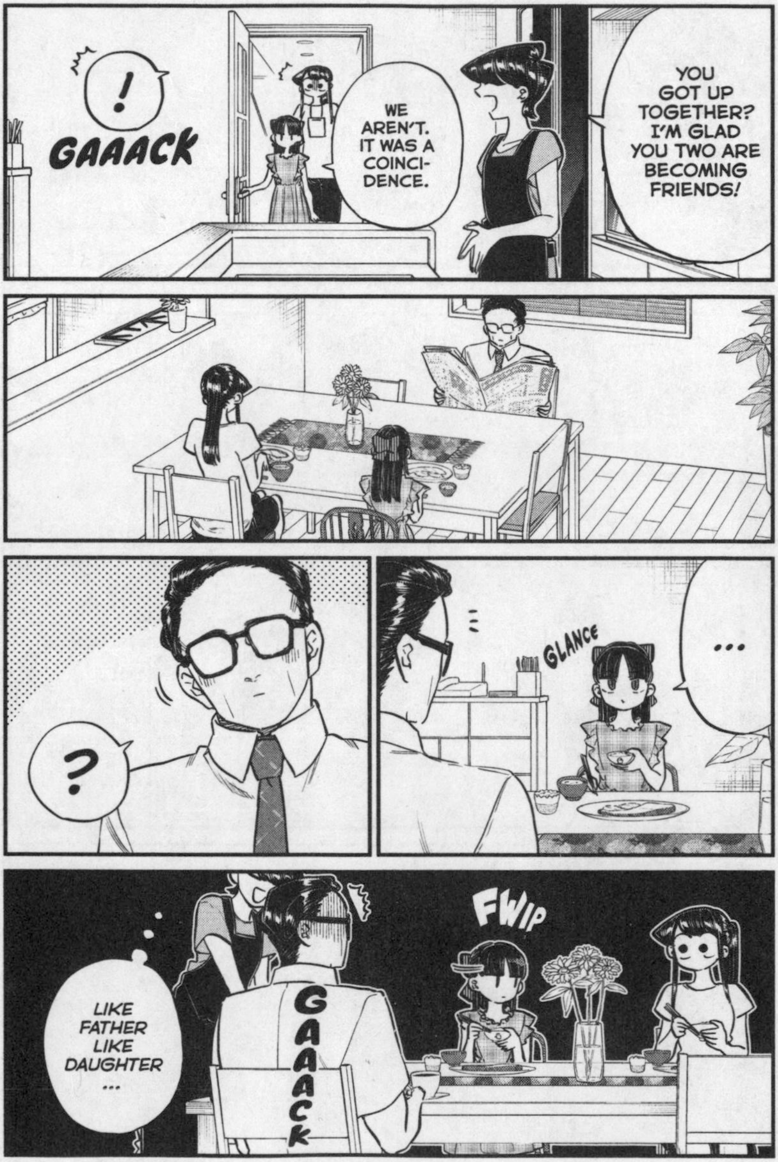
YOU GOT UP TOGETHER? I'M GLAD YOU TWO ARE BECOMING FRIENDS!
WE AREN'T. IT WAS A COINCIDENCE.
!
GAAACK
...
GLANCE
?
FWIP
GAAACK
LIKE FATHER LIKE DAUGHTER ...

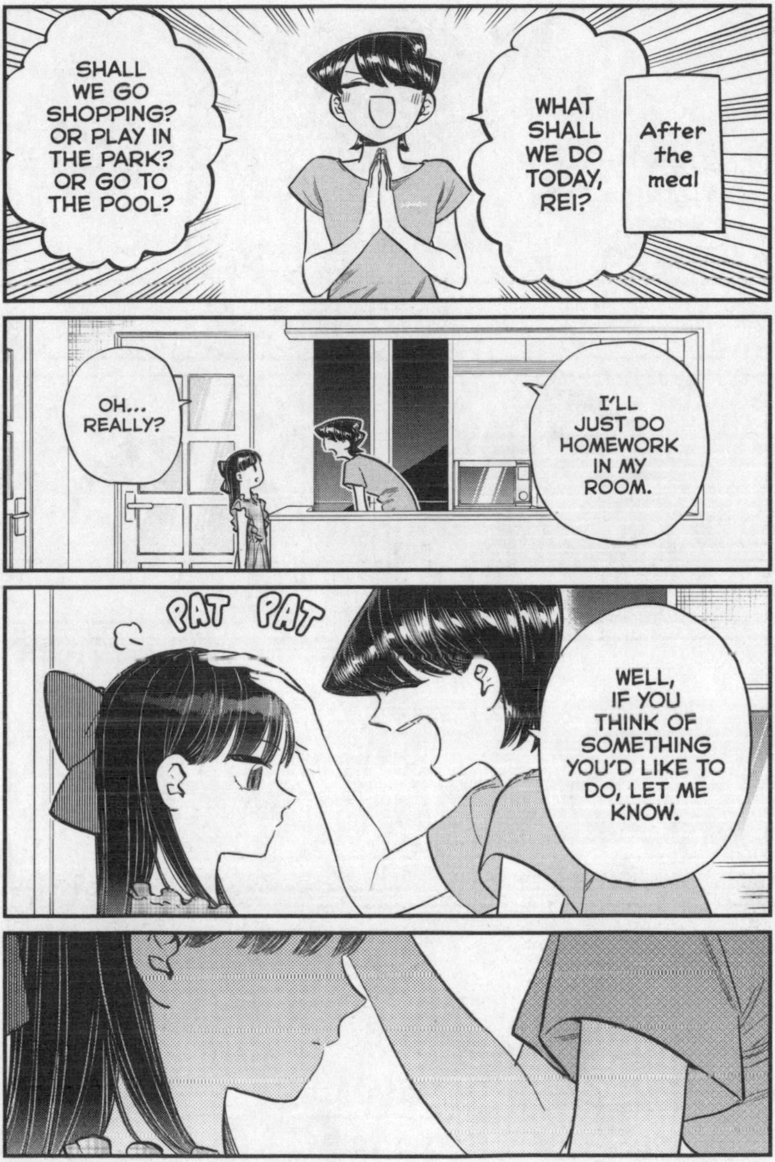
After the meal
WHAT SHALL WE DO TODAY, REI?
SHALL WE GO SHOPPING? OR PLAY IN THE PARK? OR GO TO THE POOL?
I'LL JUST DO HOMEWORK IN MY ROOM.
OH... REALLY?
WELL, IF YOU THINK OF SOMETHING YOU'D LIKE TO DO, LET ME KNOW.
PAT PAT

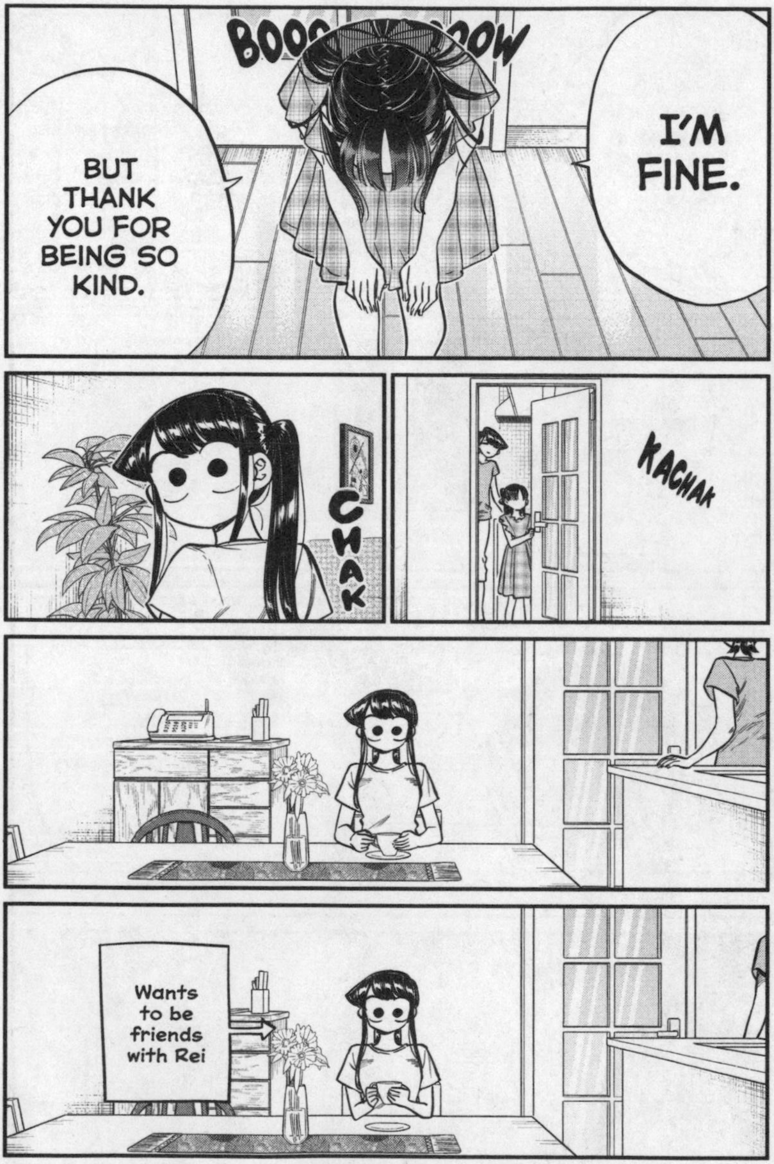
I'M FINE.
BUT THANK YOU FOR BEING SO KIND.
KACHAK
CHAK
Wants to be friends with Rei

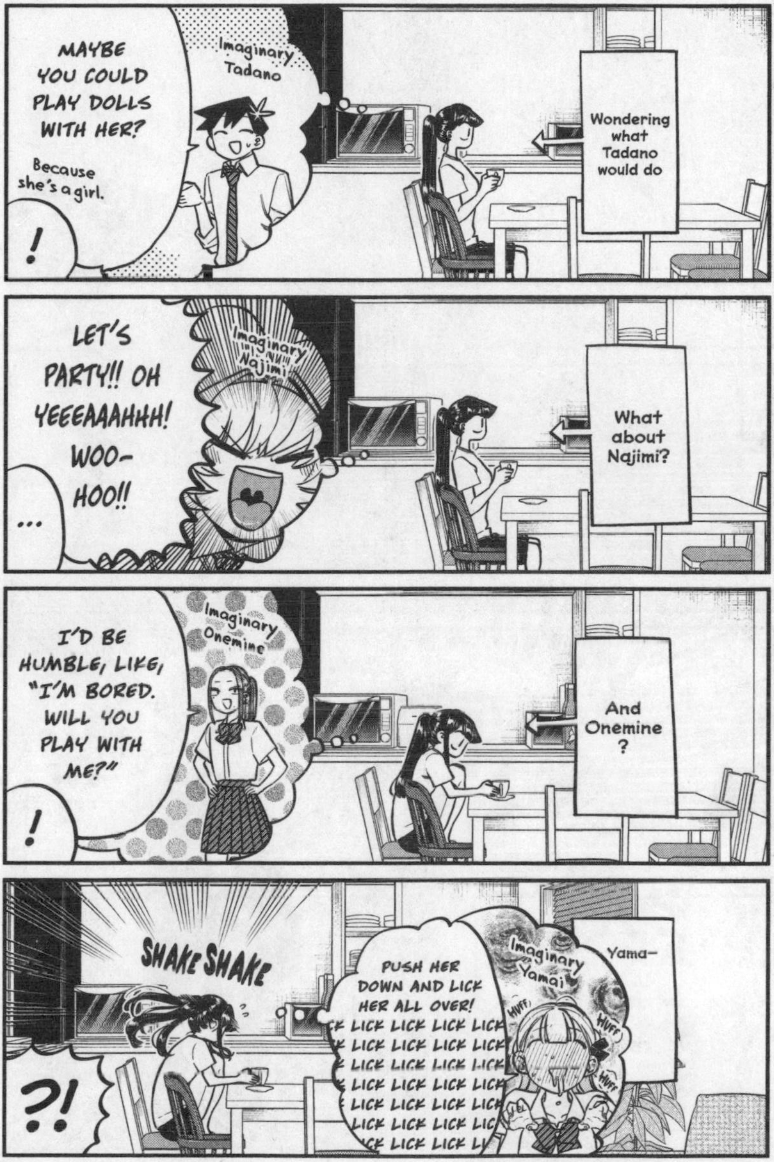
Wondering what Tadano would do
Imaginary Tadano
MAYBE YOU COULD PLAY DOLLS WITH HER?
Because she's a girl.
!
What about Najimi?
Imaginary Najimi
LET'S PARTY!! OH YEEEAAAHHH! WOO-HOO!!
...
And Onemine?
Imaginary Onemine
I'D BE HUMBLE, LIKE, "I'M BORED. WILL YOU PLAY WITH ME?"
!
Yama-
Imaginary Yamai
HUFF HUFF HUFF
PUSH HER DOWN AND LICK HER ALL OVER!
LICK LICK LICK LICK
SHAKE SHAKE
?!

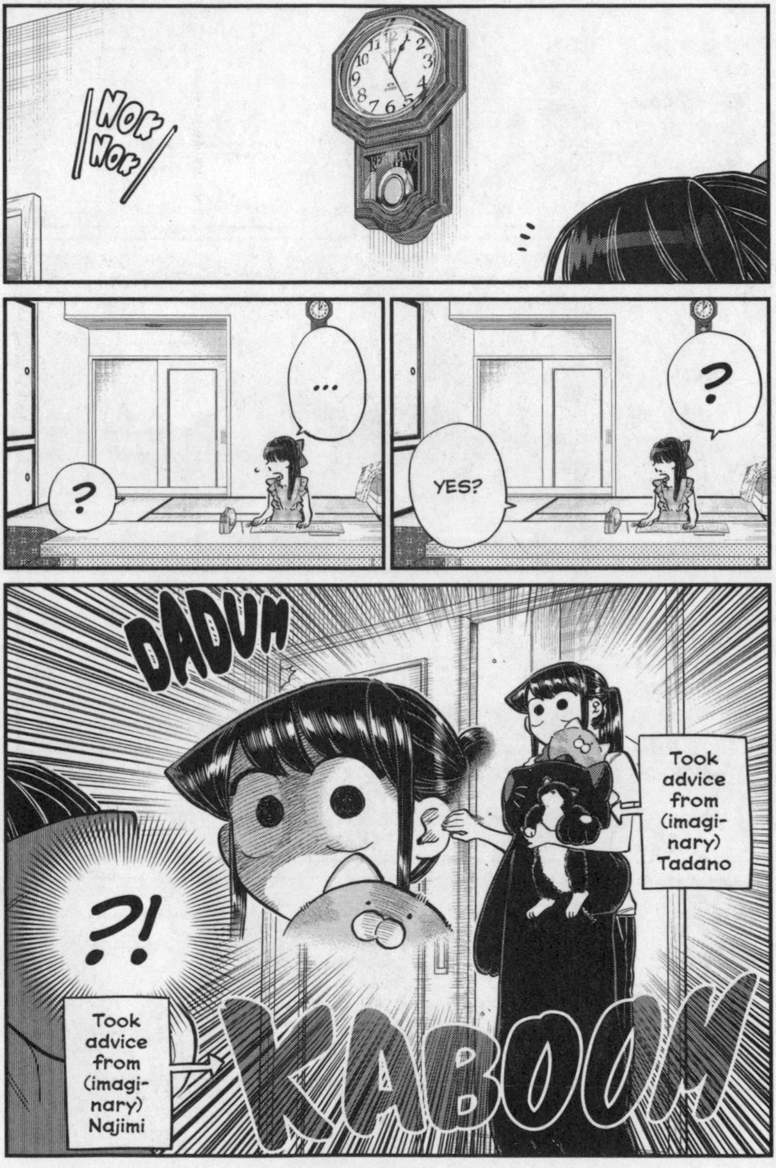
NOK NOK
?
YES?
...
?
DADUM
Took advice from (imaginary) Tadano
?!
KABOOM
Took advice from (imaginary) Najimi

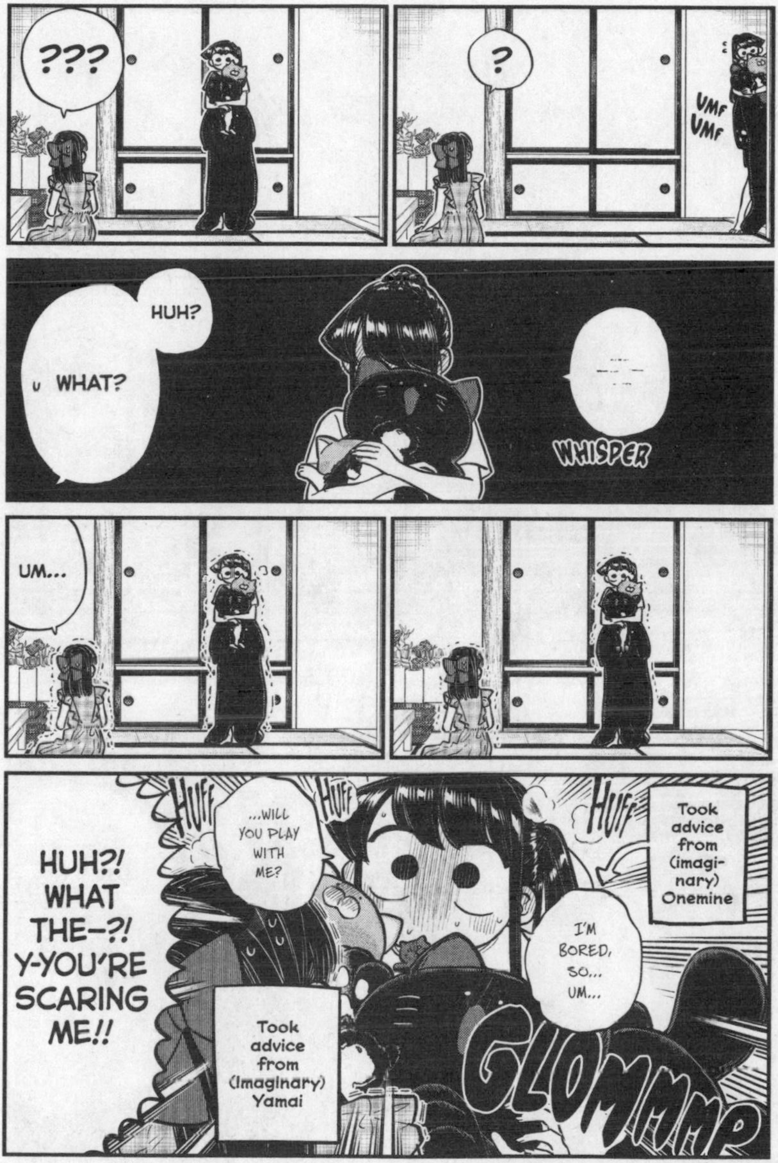
?
UMF UMF
???
WHISPER
HUH?
WHAT?
UM...
Took advice from (imagi-nary) Onemine
HUFF
I'M BORED, SO... UM...
...WILL YOU PLAY WITH ME?
HUFF
HUFF
GLOMMMP
Took advice from (Imaginary) Yamai
HUH?! WHAT THE-?! Y-YOU'RE SCARING ME!!

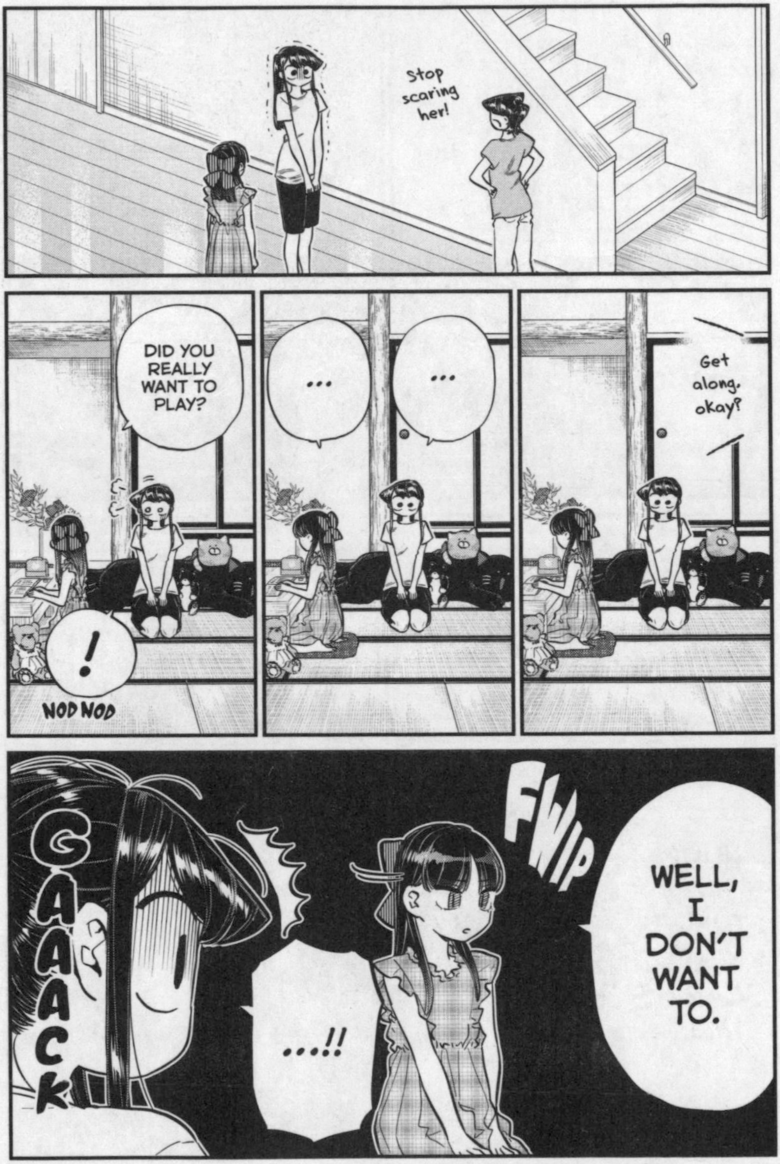
Stop scaring her!
Get along, okay?
...
...
DID YOU REALLY WANT TO PLAY?
!
NOD NOD
FWIP
WELL, I DON'T WANT TO.
...!!
GAAACK

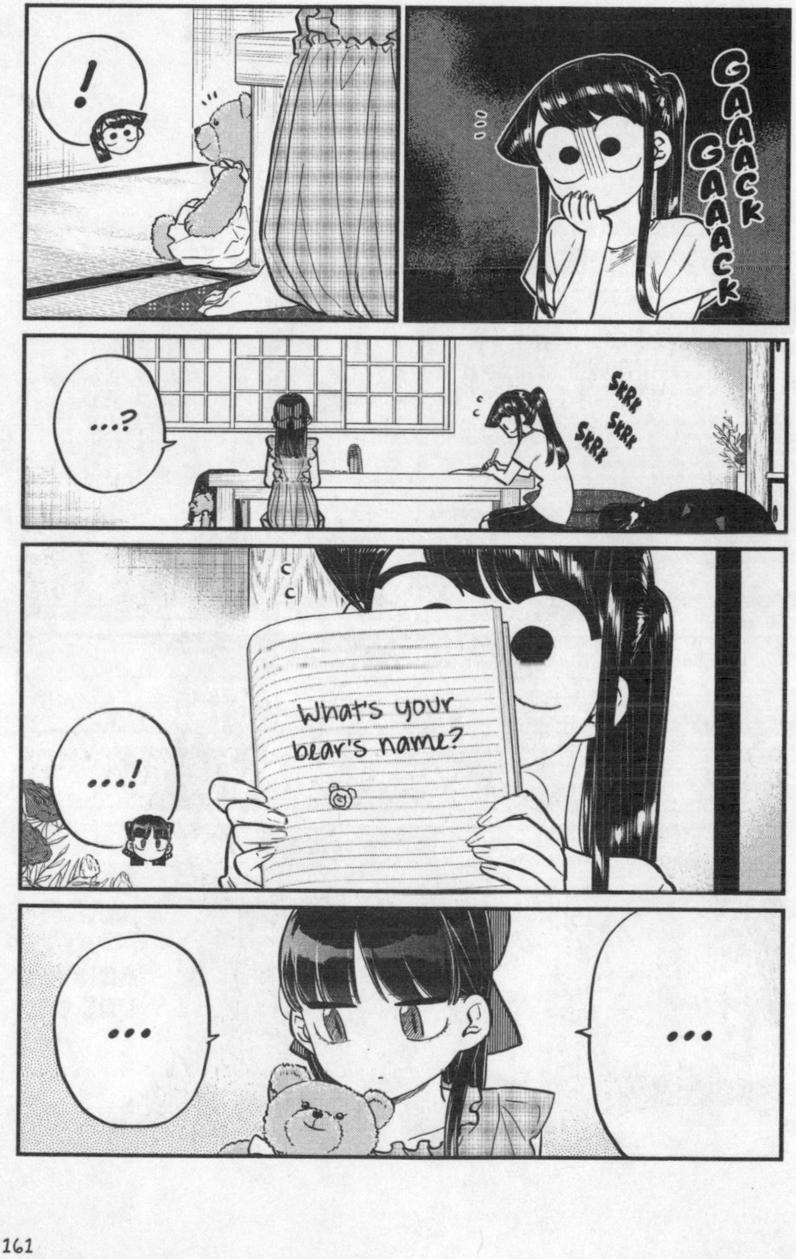
GAAACK
GAAACK
!
SKRK
SKRK
SKRK
...?
What's your bear's name?
...!
...
...

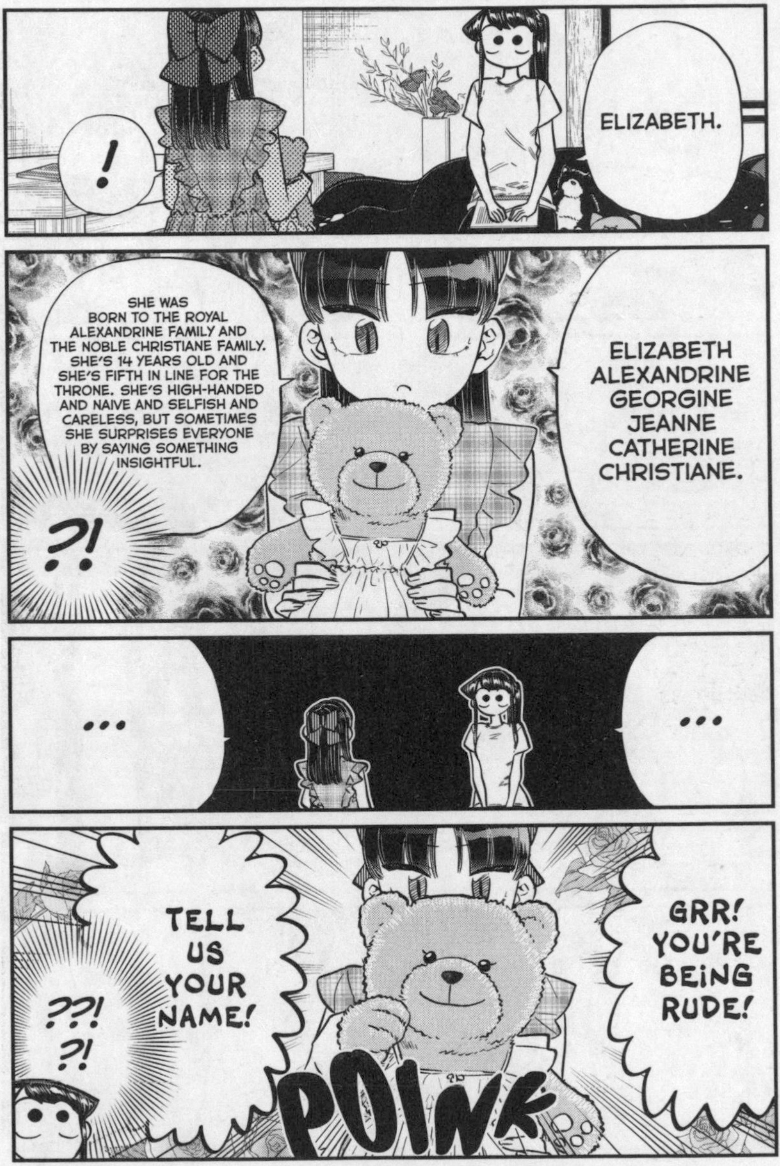
ELIZABETH.
!
ELIZABETH ALEXANDRINE GEORGINE JEANNE CATHERINE CHRISTIANE.
SHE WAS BORN TO THE ROYAL ALEXANDRINE FAMILY AND THE NOBLE CHRISTIANE FAMILY. SHE'S 14 YEARS OLD AND SHE'S FIFTH IN LINE FOR THE THRONE. SHE'S HIGH-HANDED AND NAIVE AND SELFISH AND CARELESS, BUT SOMETIMES SHE SURPRISES EVERYONE BY SAYING SOMETHING INSIGHTFUL.
?!
...
...
GRR! YOU'RE BEING RUDE!
TELL US YOUR NAME!
POINK
??! ?!

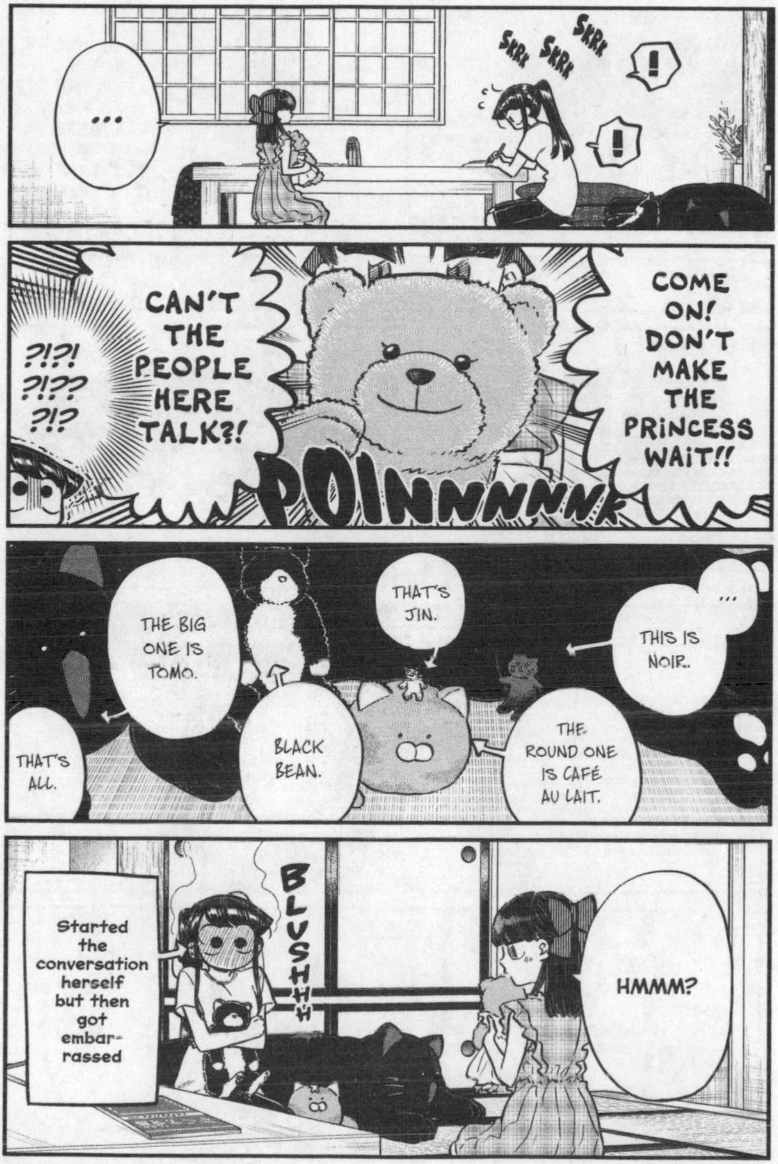
SKRK SKRK SKRK
!
!
...
COME ON! DON'T MAKE THE PRINCESS WAIT!!
CAN'T THE PEOPLE HERE TALK?!
POINNNNNNK
?!?! ?!?? ?!?
...
THIS IS NOIR.
THAT'S JIN.
THE BIG ONE IS TOMO.
THE ROUND ONE IS CAFÉ AU LAIT.
BLACK BEAN.
THAT'S ALL.
HMMM?
BLUSHHH
Started the conversation herself but then got embarrassed

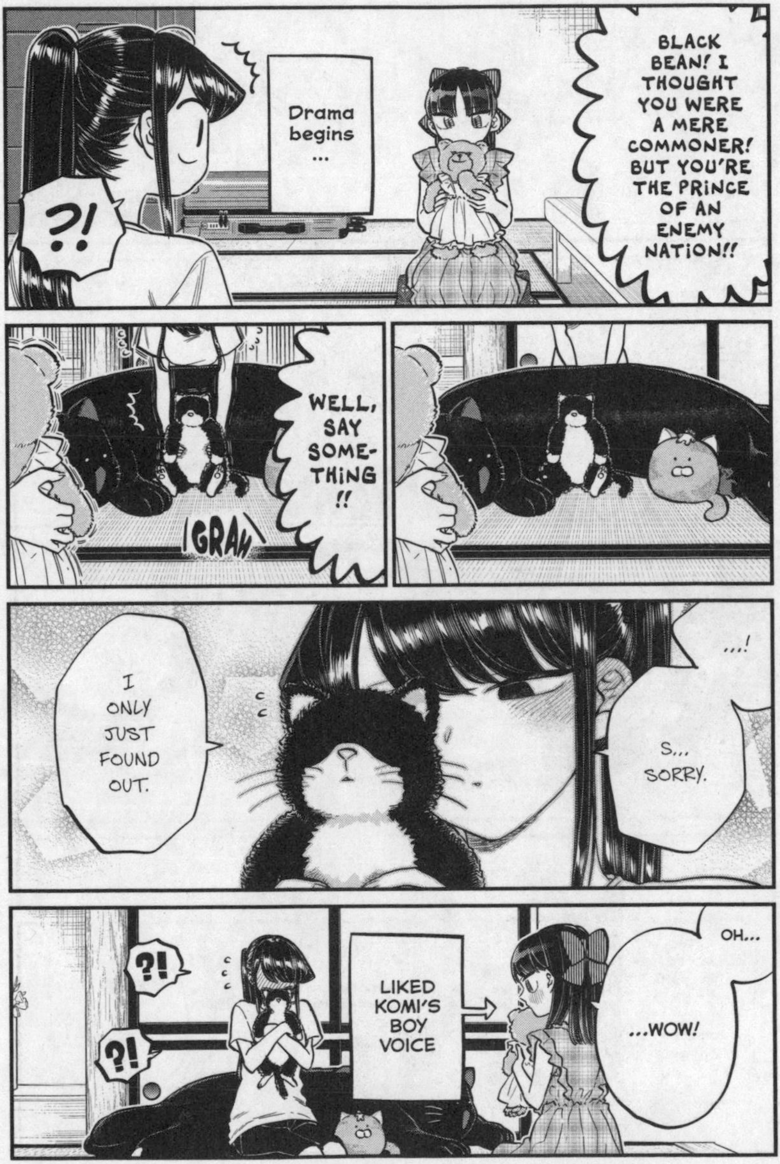
BLACK BEAN! I THOUGHT YOU WERE A MERE COMMONER! BUT YOU'RE THE PRINCE OF AN ENEMY NATION!!
Drama begins ...
?!
WELL, SAY SOME-THING !!
GRAH
...!
S... SORRY.
I ONLY JUST FOUND OUT.
OH... ...WOW!
LIKED KOMI'S BOY VOICE
?!
?!

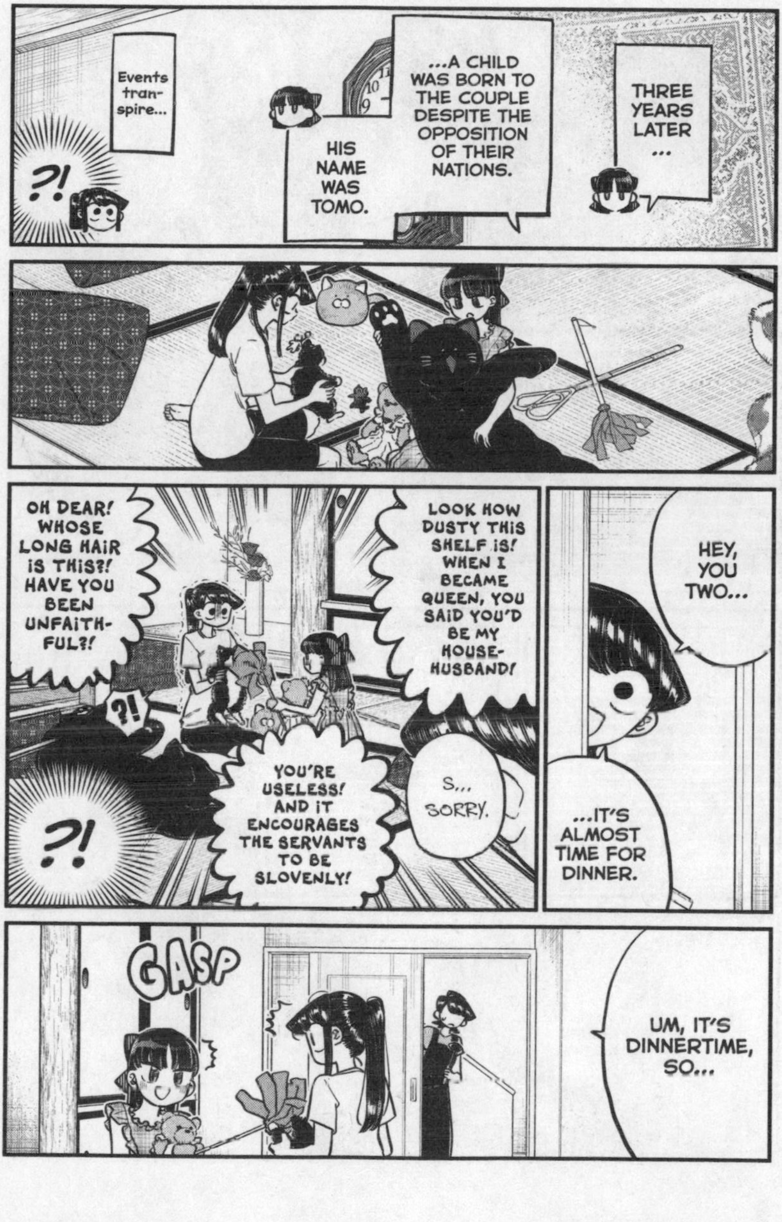
THREE YEARS LATER ...
...A CHILD WAS BORN TO THE COUPLE DESPITE THE OPPOSITION OF THEIR NATIONS.
HIS NAME WAS TOMO.
Events tran-spire...
?!
HEY, YOU TWO...
...IT'S ALMOST TIME FOR DINNER.
LOOK HOW DUSTY THIS SHELF IS! WHEN I BECAME QUEEN, YOU SAID YOU'D BE MY HOUSE-HUSBAND!
OH DEAR! WHOSE LONG HAIR IS THIS?! HAVE YOU BEEN UNFAITH-FUL?!
?!
S,... SORRY.
YOU'RE USELESS! AND IT ENCOURAGES THE SERVANTS TO BE SLOVENLY!
?!
UM, IT'S DINNERTIME, SO...
GASP

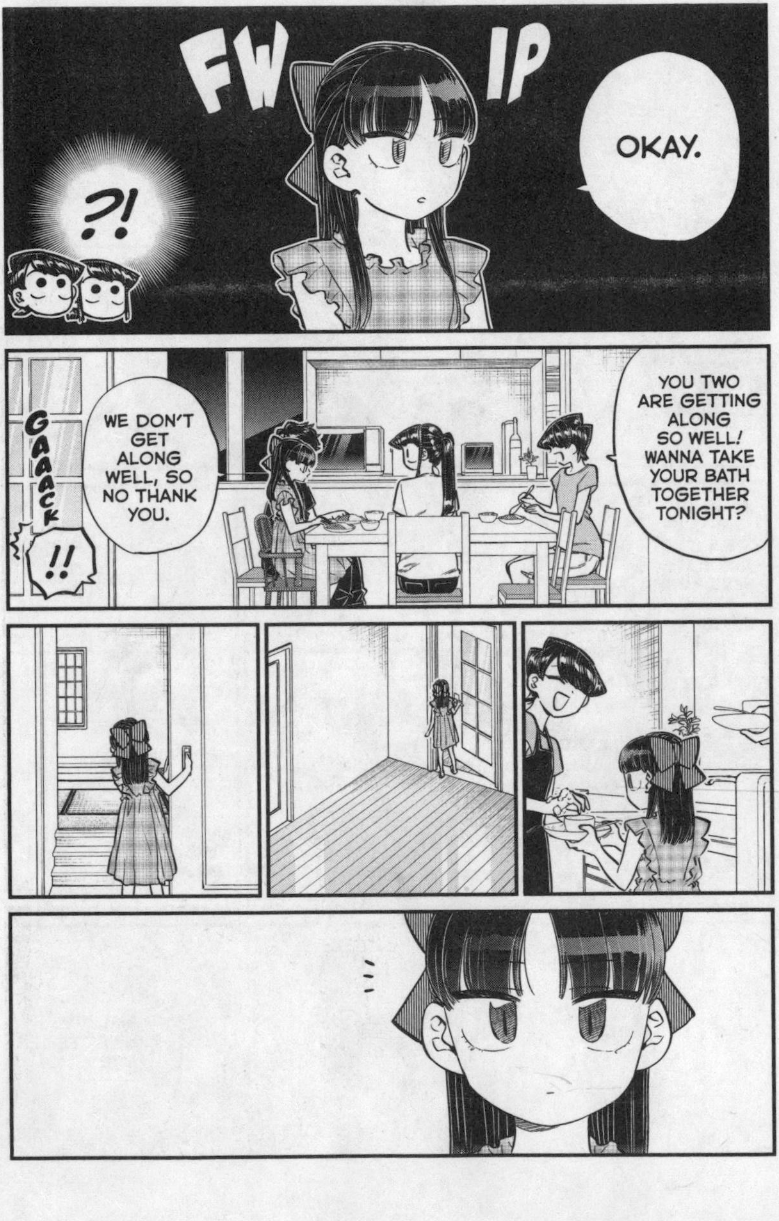
FW IP
OKAY.
?!
YOU TWO ARE GETTING ALONG SO WELL! WANNA TAKE YOUR BATH TOGETHER TONIGHT?
WE DON'T GET ALONG WELL, SO NO THANK YOU.
GAAACK
!!

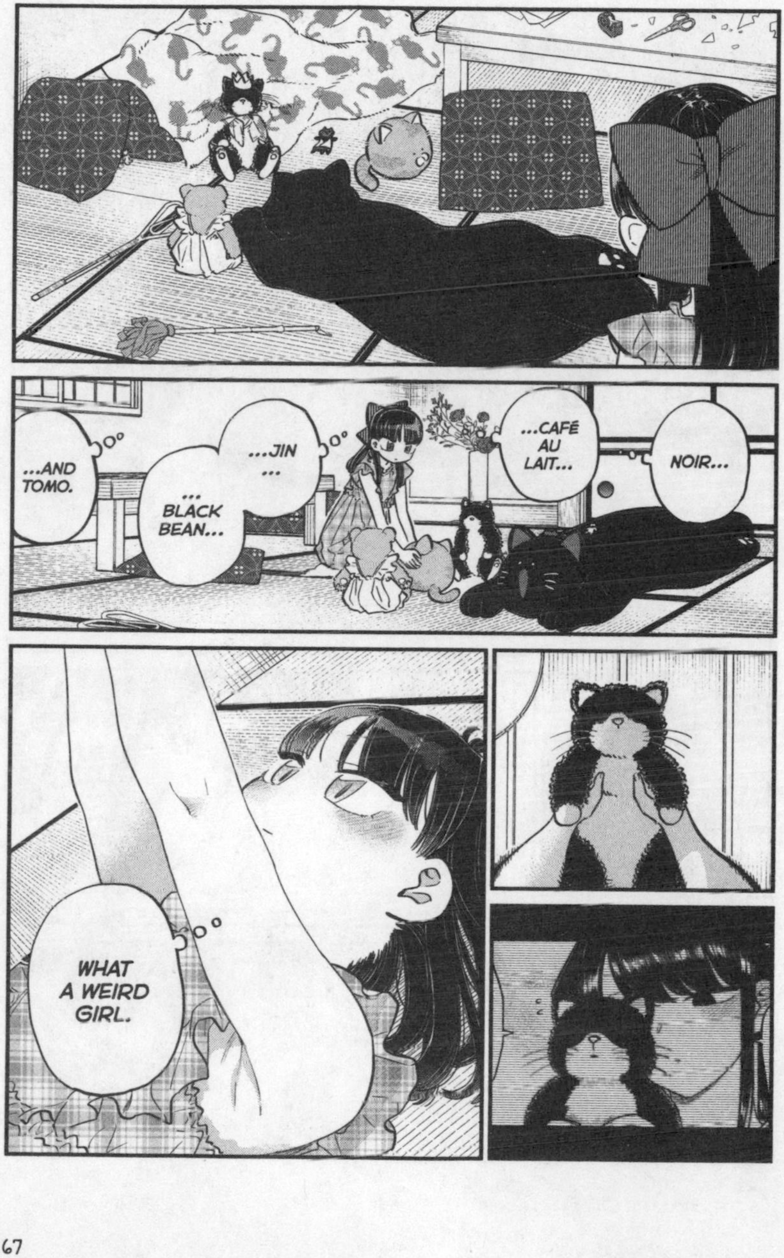
NOIR...
...CAFÉ AU LAIT...
...JIN ...
... BLACK BEAN...
...AND TOMO.
WHAT A WEIRD GIRL.

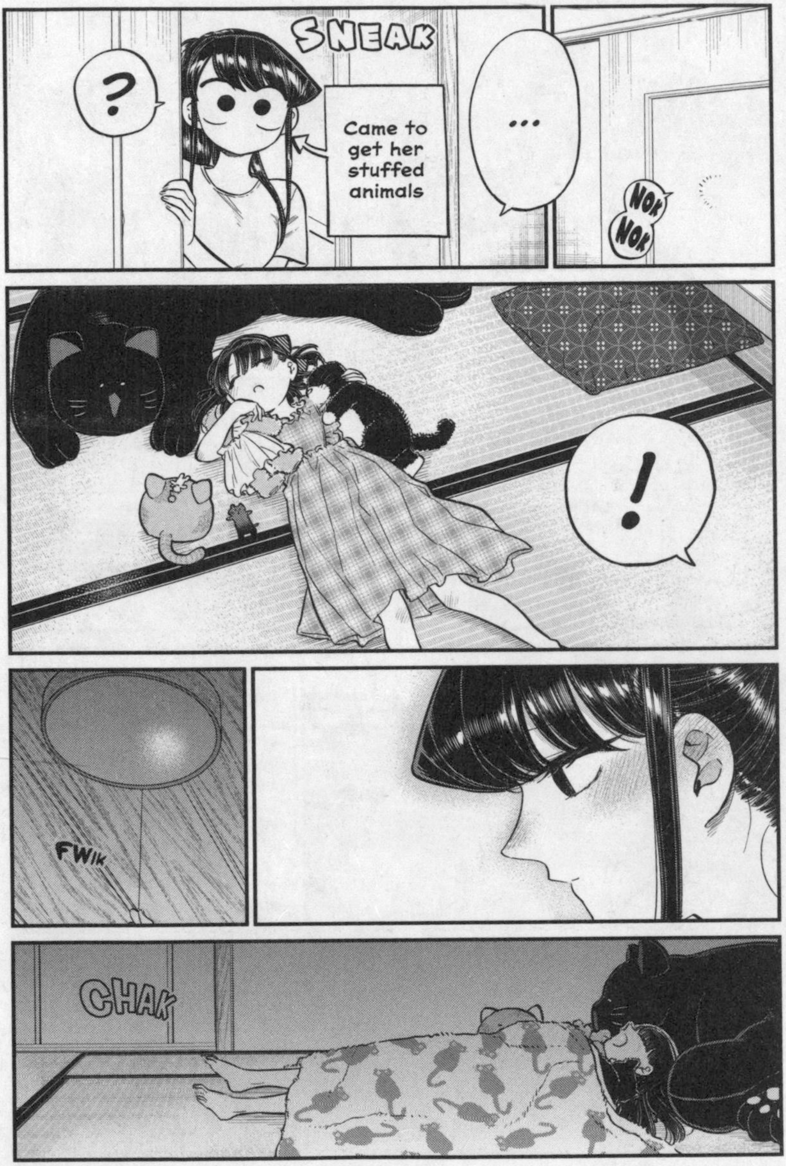
NOK
NOK
...
SNEAK
Came to get her stuffed animals
?
!
FWIK
CHAK

Communication 169 — The End

Komi Can't Communicate

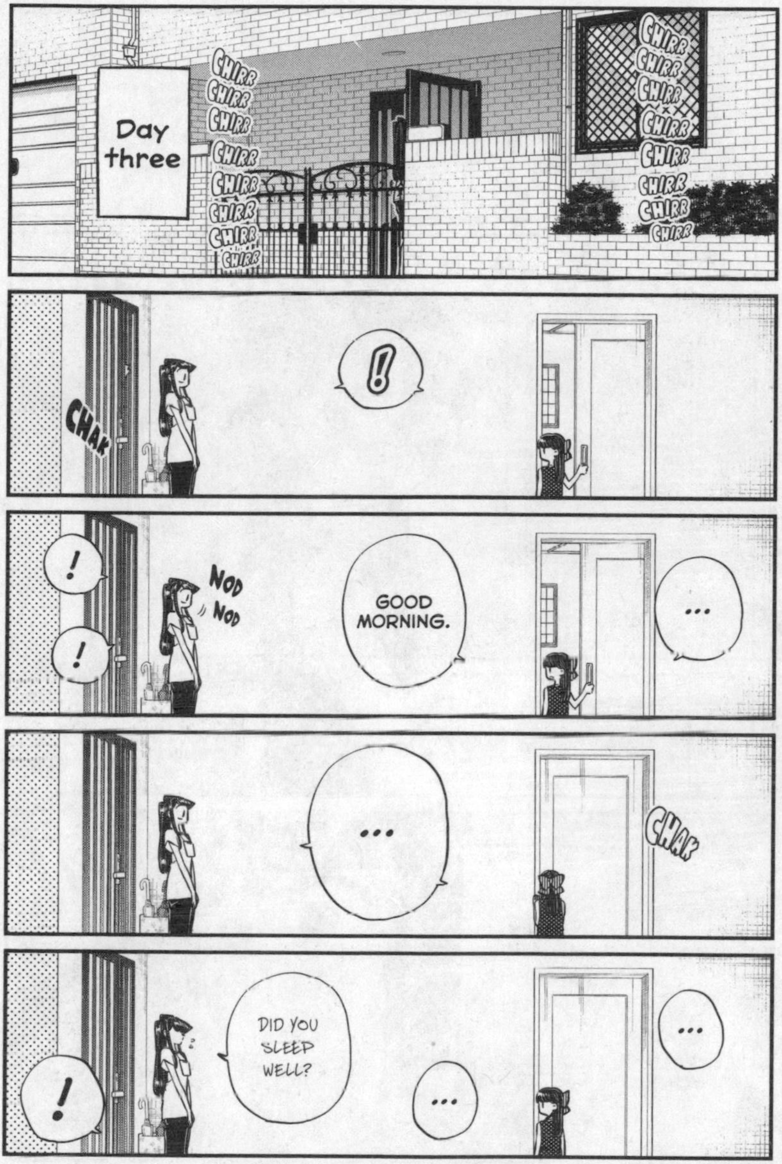
CHIRR CHIRR CHIRR CHIRR CHIRR CHIRR CHIRR CHIRR
CHIRR CHIRR CHIRR CHIRR CHIRR CHIRR CHIRR CHIRR
Day three
!
CHAK
...
GOOD MORNING.
NOD NOD
!
!
CHAK
...
...
...
DID YOU SLEEP WELL?
!

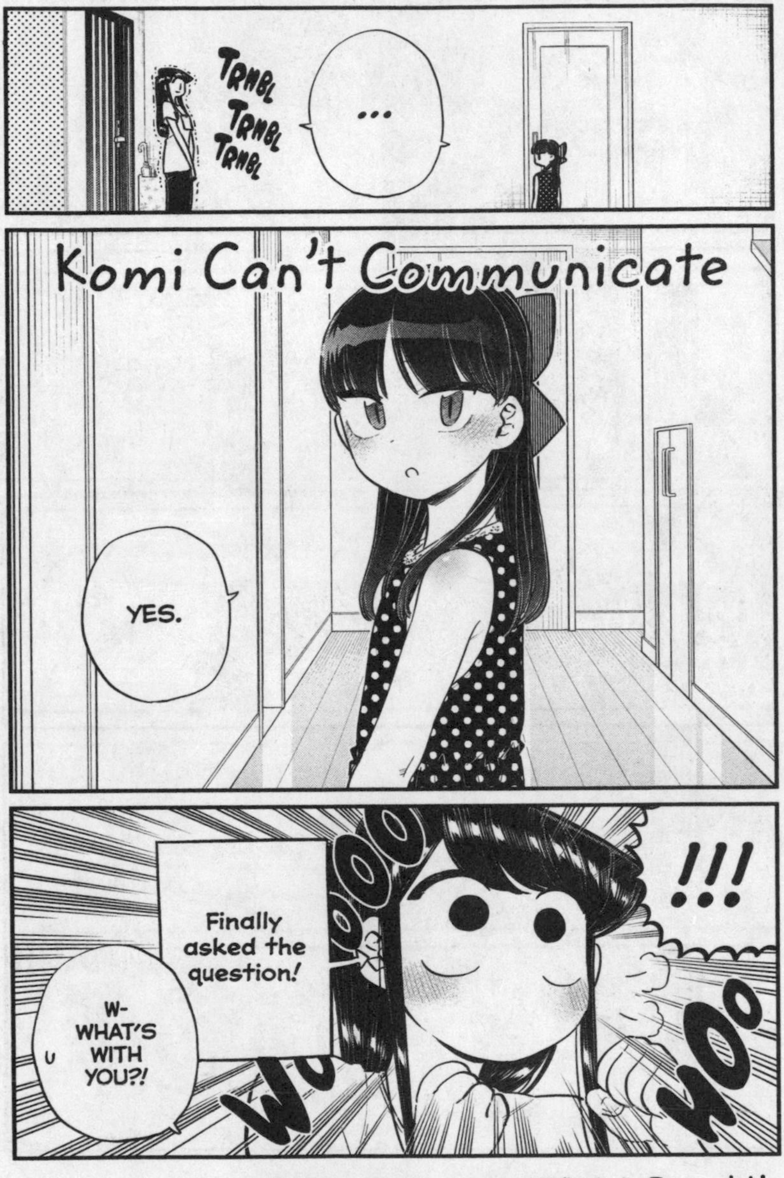
...
TRMBL TRMBL TRMBL TRMBL
Komi Can't Communicate
YES.
!!!
WOOOOOOO
Finally asked the question!
W- WHAT'S WITH YOU?!
U

Communication 170: WcDonald's

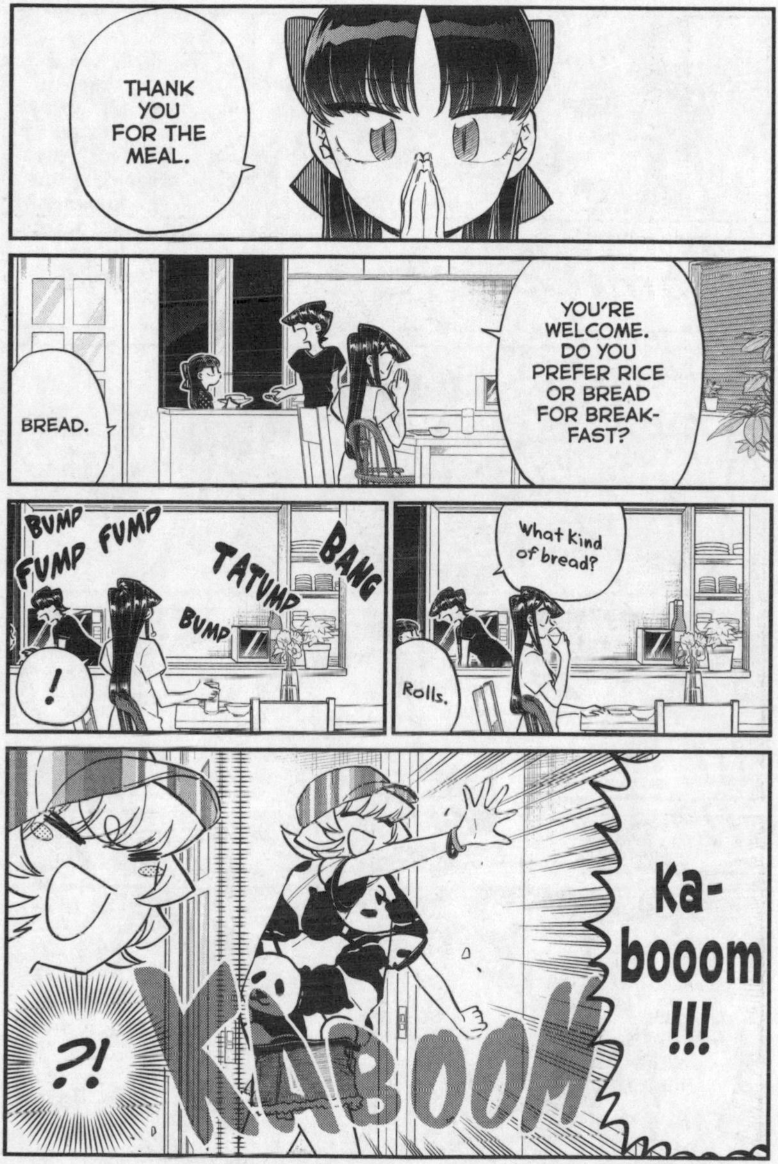
THANK YOU FOR THE MEAL.
YOU'RE WELCOME. DO YOU PREFER RICE OR BREAD FOR BREAK-FAST?
BREAD.
What kind of bread?
Rolls.
BANG
TATUMP
BUMP
BUMP
FUMP FUMP
!
Ka-booom!!!
KABOOM
?!

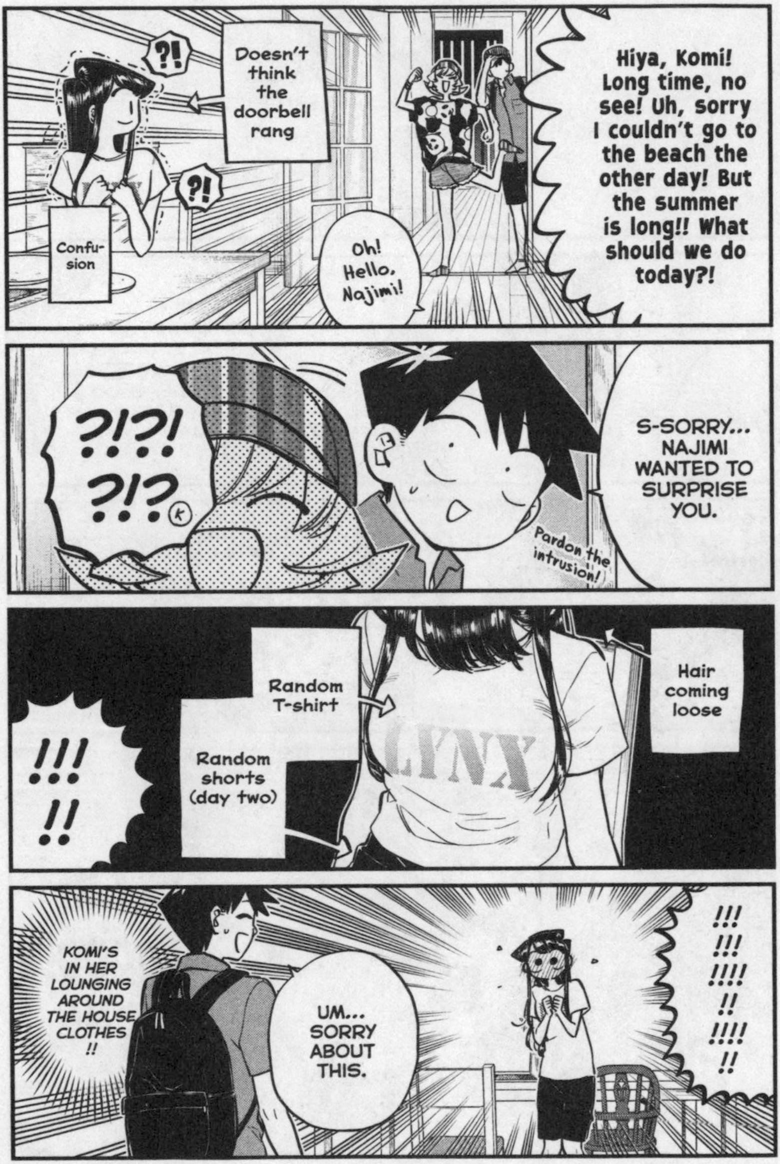
Hiya, Komi! Long time, no see! Uh, sorry I couldn't go to the beach the other day! But the summer is long!! What should we do today?!
Oh! Hello, Najimi!
Doesn't think the doorbell rang
?!
?!
Confu-sion
S-SORRY... NAJIMI WANTED TO SURPRISE YOU.
Pardon the intrusion!
?!?! ?!?
Hair coming loose
Random T-shirt
LYNX
Random shorts (day two)
!!! !!
!!! !!! !!!! !! !!!! !!
UM... SORRY ABOUT THIS.
KOMI'S IN HER LOUNGING AROUND THE HOUSE CLOTHES !!

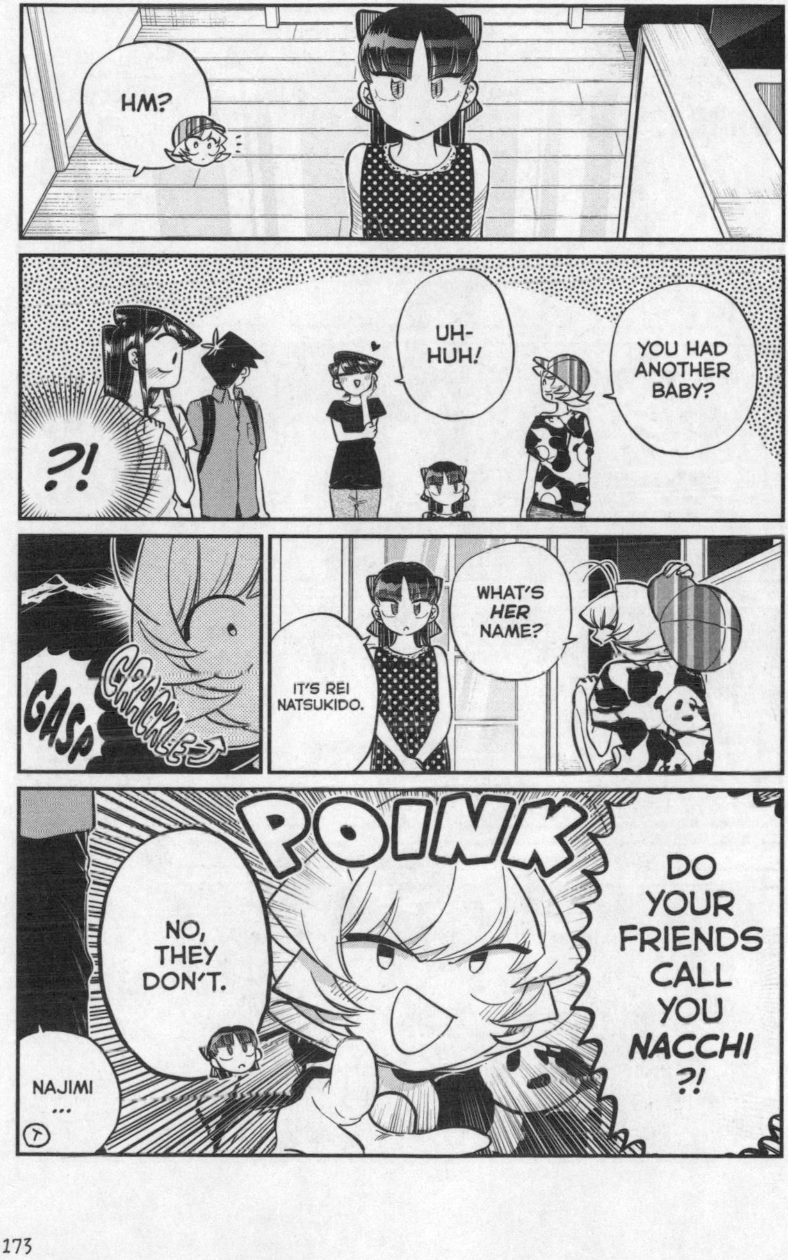
HM?
YOU HAD ANOTHER BABY?
UH-HUH!
?!
WHAT'S *HER* NAME?
IT'S REI NATSUKIDO.
CRACKLE
GASP
POINK
DO YOUR FRIENDS CALL YOU *NACCHI* ?!
NO, THEY DON'T.
NAJIMI ...

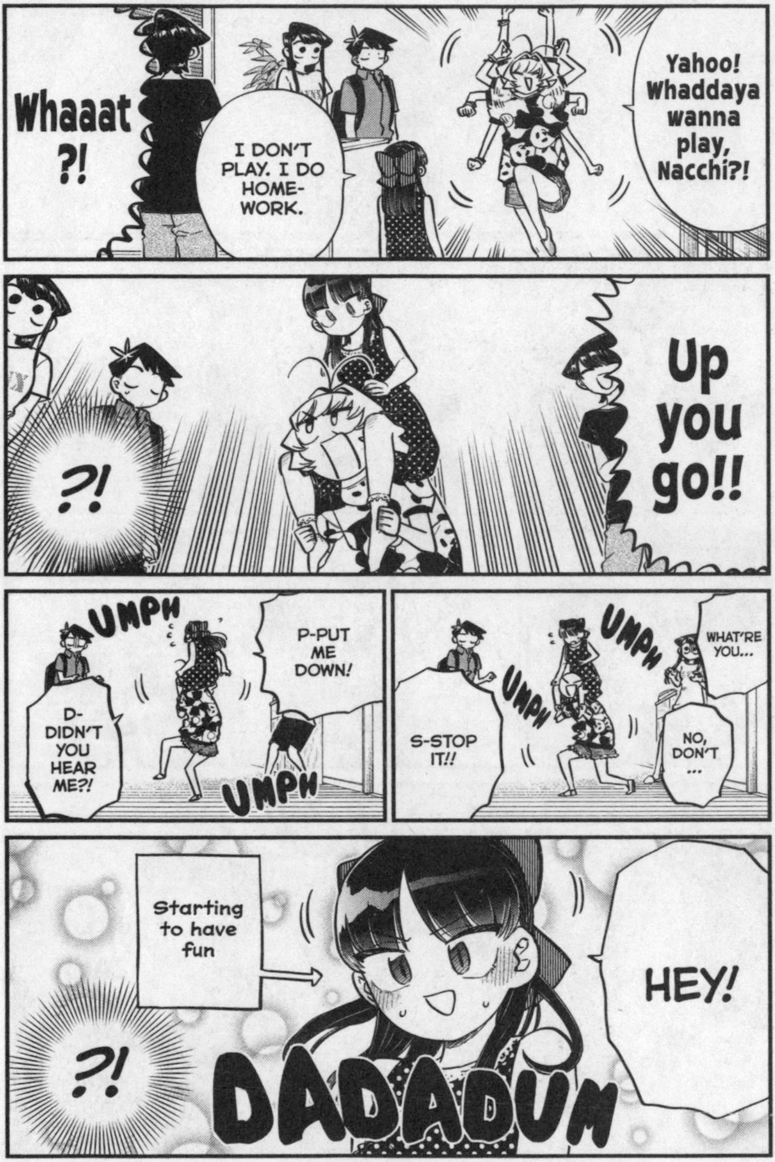
Yahoo! Whaddaya wanna play, Nacchi?!
I DON'T PLAY. I DO HOME-WORK.
Whaaat ?!
Up you go!!
?!
WHAT'RE YOU...
NO, DON'T ...
UMPH
UMPH
S-STOP IT!!
P-PUT ME DOWN!
UMPH
UMPH
D-DIDN'T YOU HEAR ME?!
HEY!
DADADUM
Starting to have fun
?!

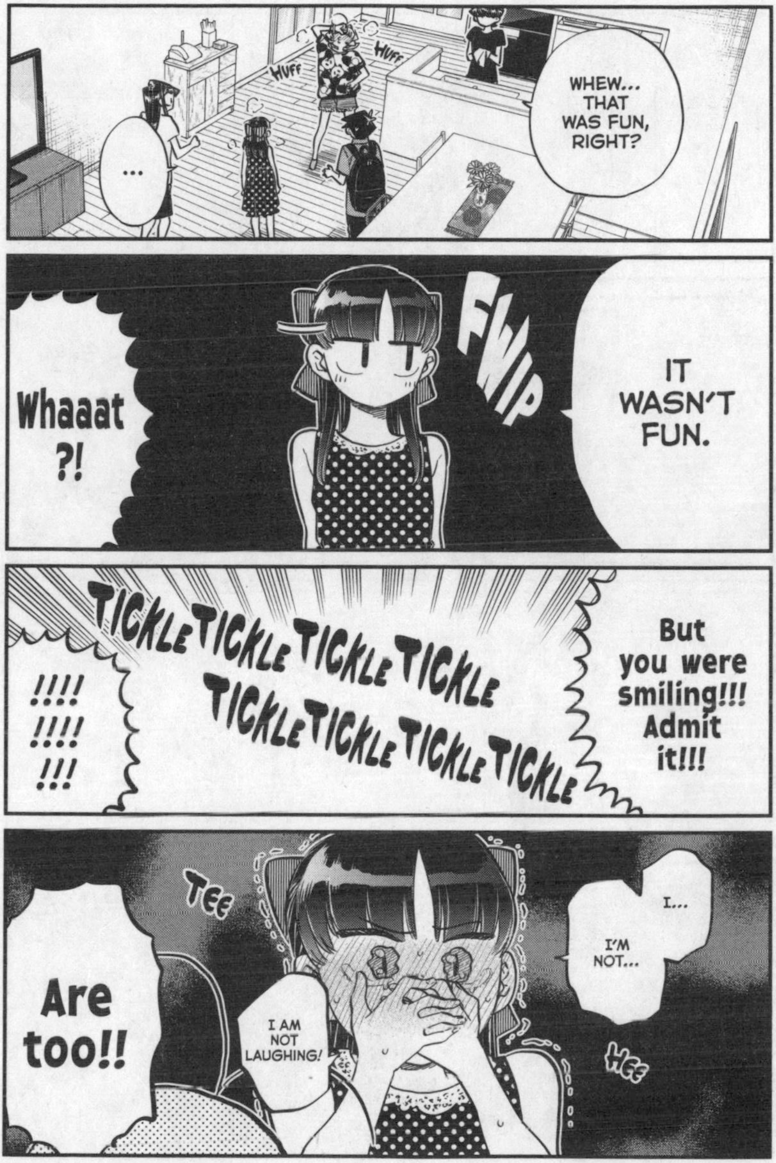
WHEW... THAT WAS FUN, RIGHT?
HUFF
HUFF
...
IT WASN'T FUN.
FWIP
Whaaat ?!
But you were smiling!!! Admit it!!!
TICKLE TICKLE TICKLE TICKLE
TICKLE TICKLE TICKLE TICKLE
!!!! !!!! !!!
I...
I'M NOT...
HEE
TEE
I AM NOT LAUGHING!
Are too!!

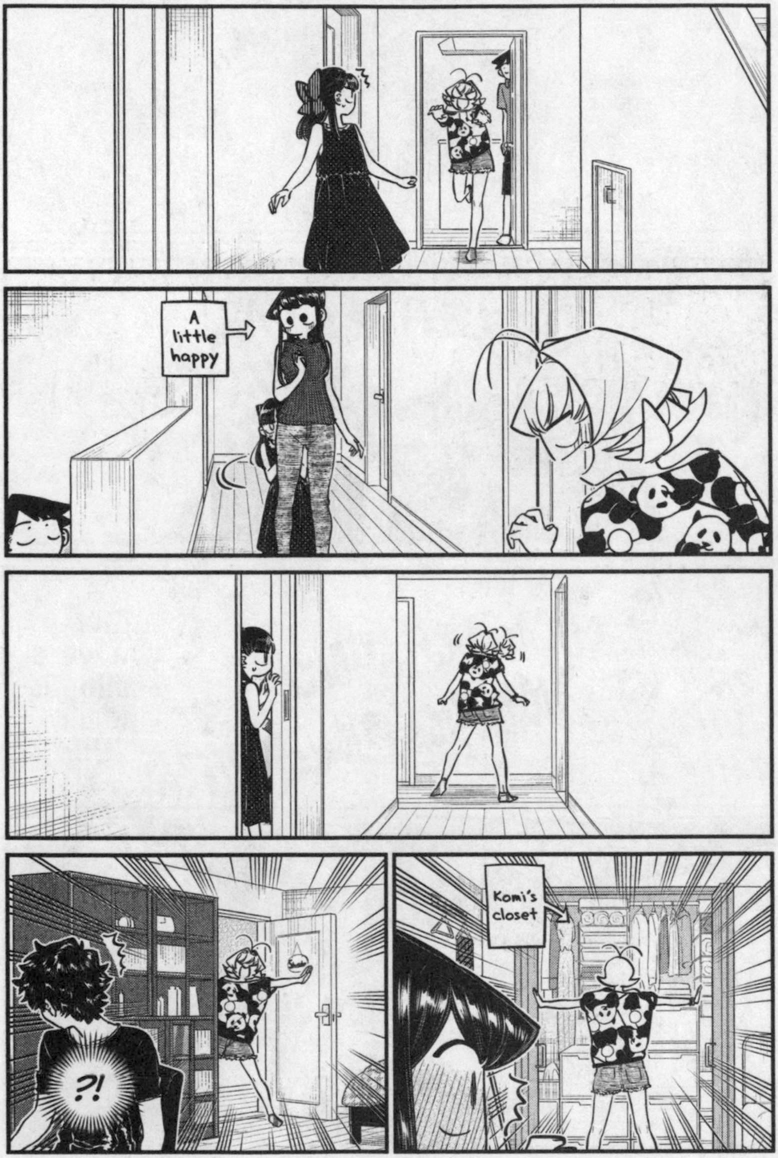
A little happy
Komi's closet
?!

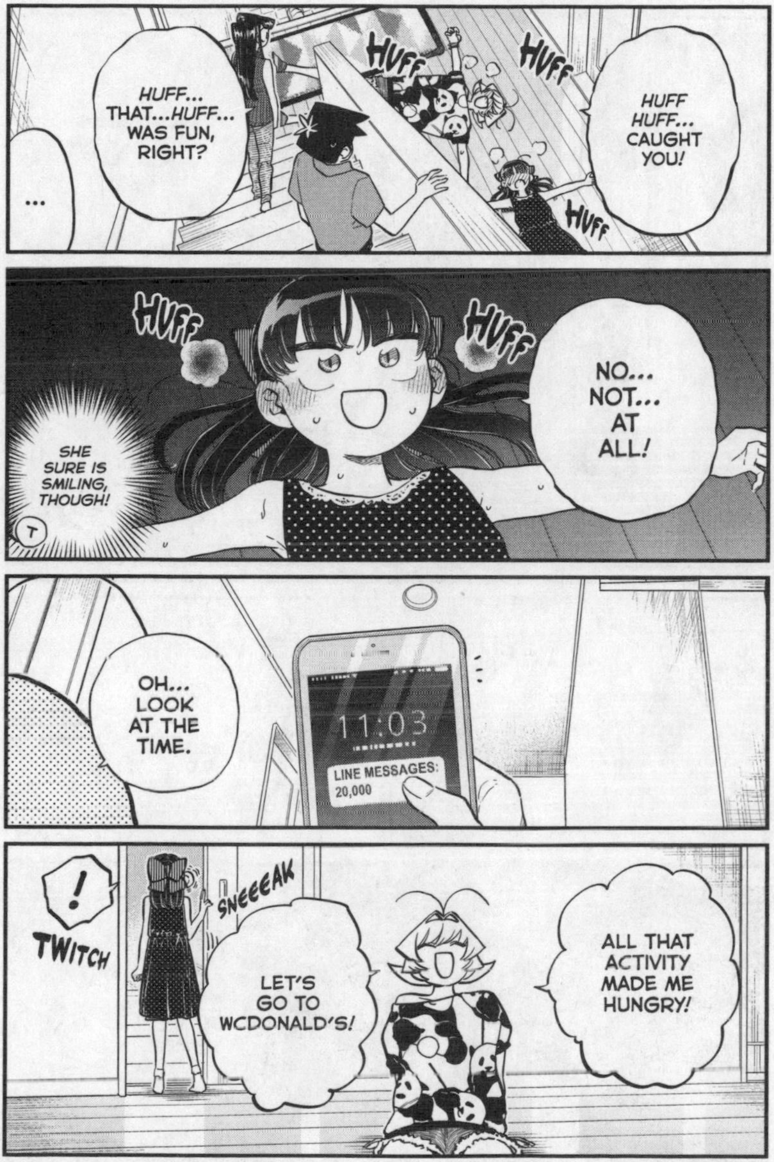
HUFF HUFF... CAUGHT YOU!
HUFF
HUFF
HUFF
HUFF... THAT...HUFF... WAS FUN, RIGHT?
...
NO... NOT... AT ALL!
HUFF
HUFF
SHE SURE IS SMILING, THOUGH!
11:03
LINE MESSAGES: 20,000
OH... LOOK AT THE TIME.
ALL THAT ACTIVITY MADE ME HUNGRY!
LET'S GO TO WCDONALD'S!
SNEEEAK
!
TWITCH

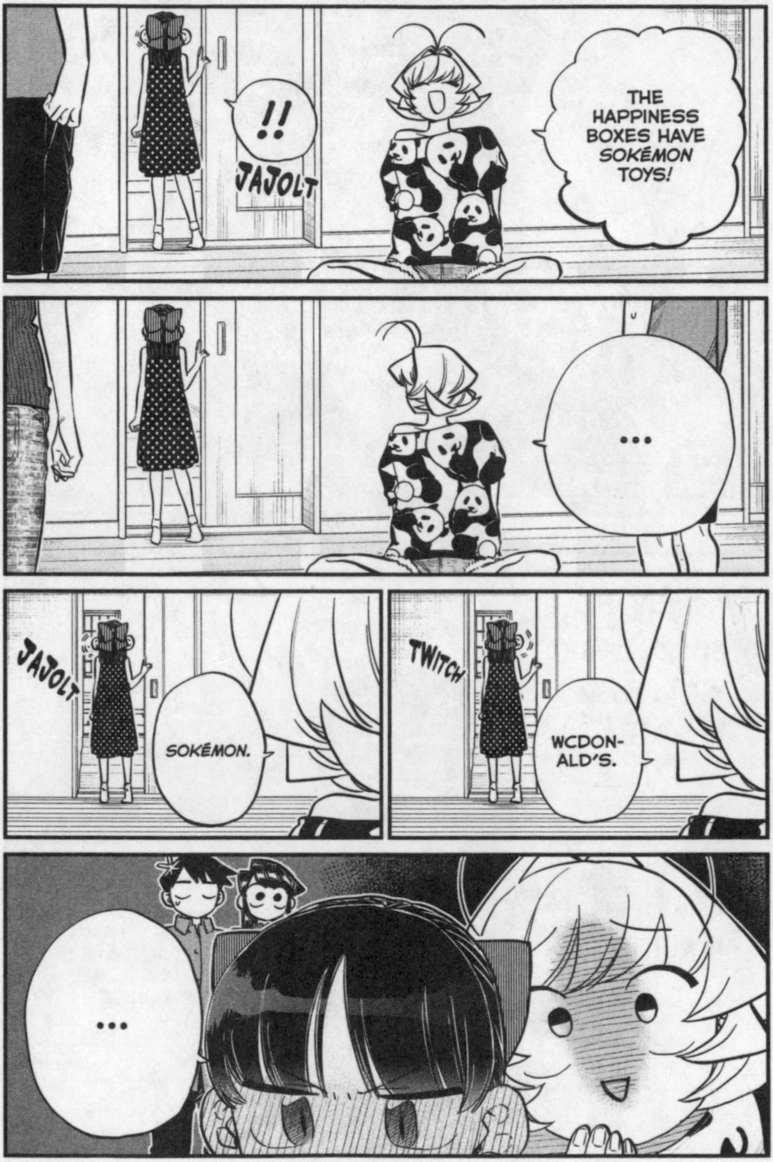
THE HAPPINESS BOXES HAVE SOKÉMON TOYS!
!!
JAJOLT
...
WCDON-ALD'S.
TWITCH
SOKÉMON.
JAJOLT
...

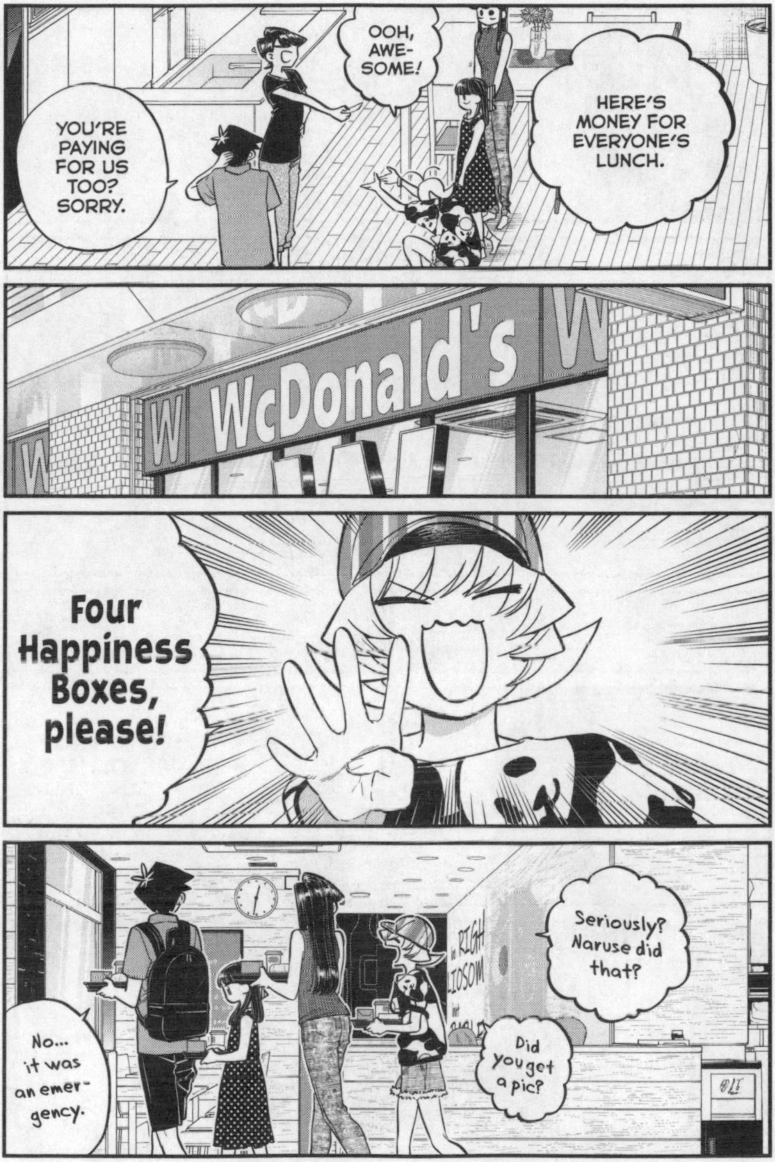
HERE'S MONEY FOR EVERYONE'S LUNCH.
OOH, AWE-SOME!
YOU'RE PAYING FOR US TOO? SORRY.
WcDonald's
Four Happiness Boxes, please!
Seriously? Naruse did that?
Did you get a pic?
No... it was an emer-gency.

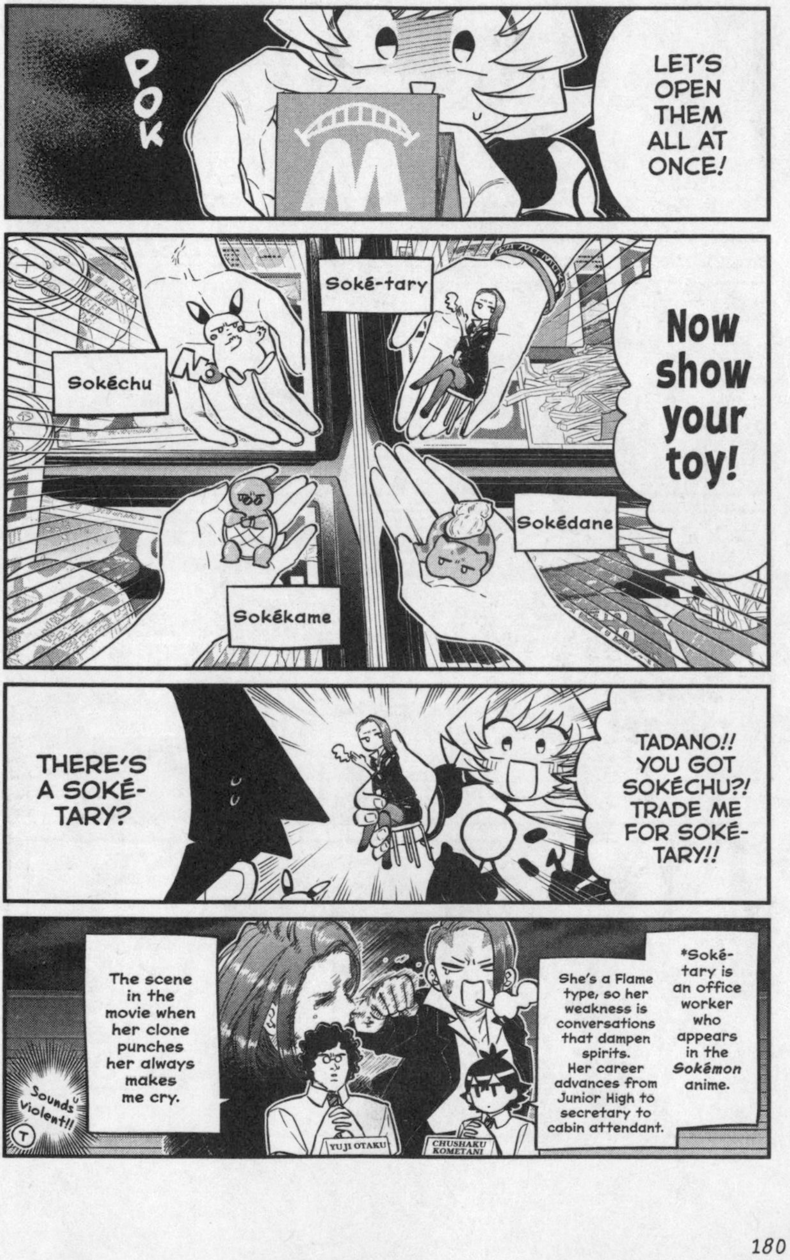

LET'S OPEN THEM ALL AT ONCE!
POK
Now show your toy!
Soké-tary
Sokéchu
Sokédane
Sokékame
TADANO!! YOU GOT SOKÉCHU?! TRADE ME FOR SOKÉ-TARY!!
THERE'S A SOKÉ-TARY?
*Soké-tary is an office worker who appears in the *Sokémon* anime.
She's a Flame type, so her weakness is conversations that dampen spirits. Her career advances from Junior High to secretary to cabin attendant.
The scene in the movie when her clone punches her always makes me cry.
Sounds violent!!
YUJI OTAKU
CHUSHAKU KOMETANI

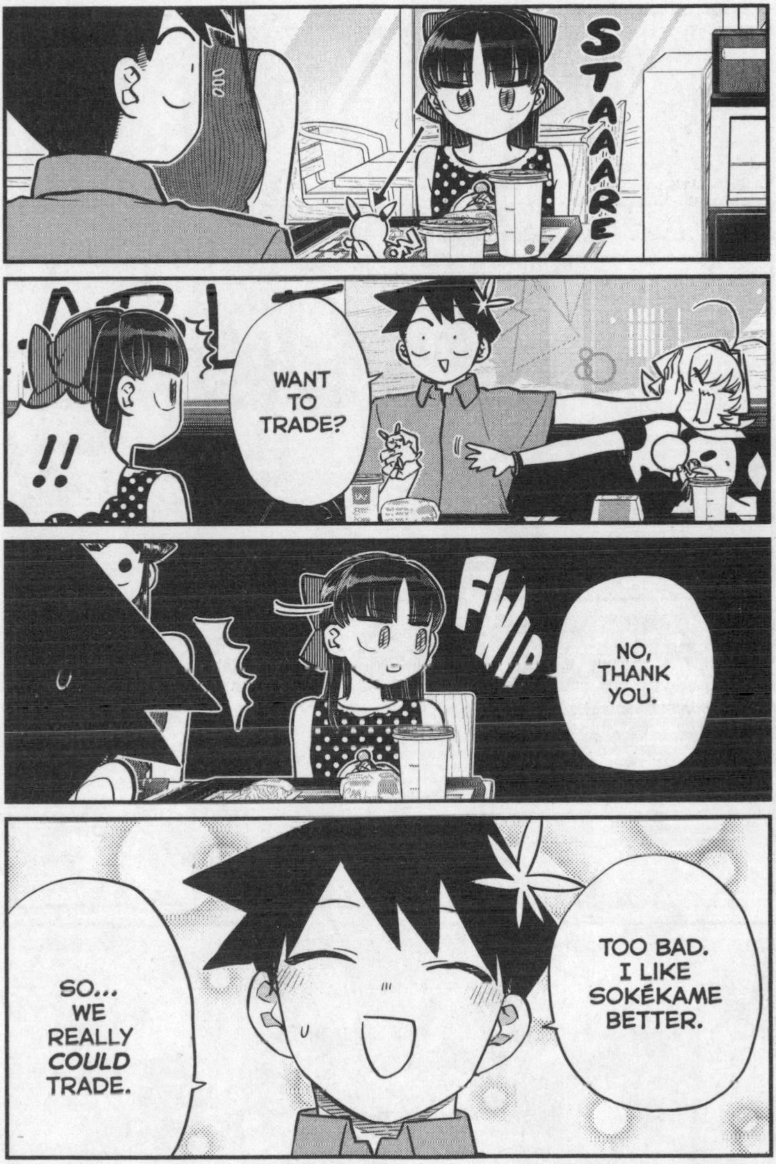
STAAARE
WANT TO TRADE?
!!
FWIP
NO, THANK YOU.
TOO BAD. I LIKE SOKÉKAME BETTER.
SO... WE REALLY *COULD* TRADE.

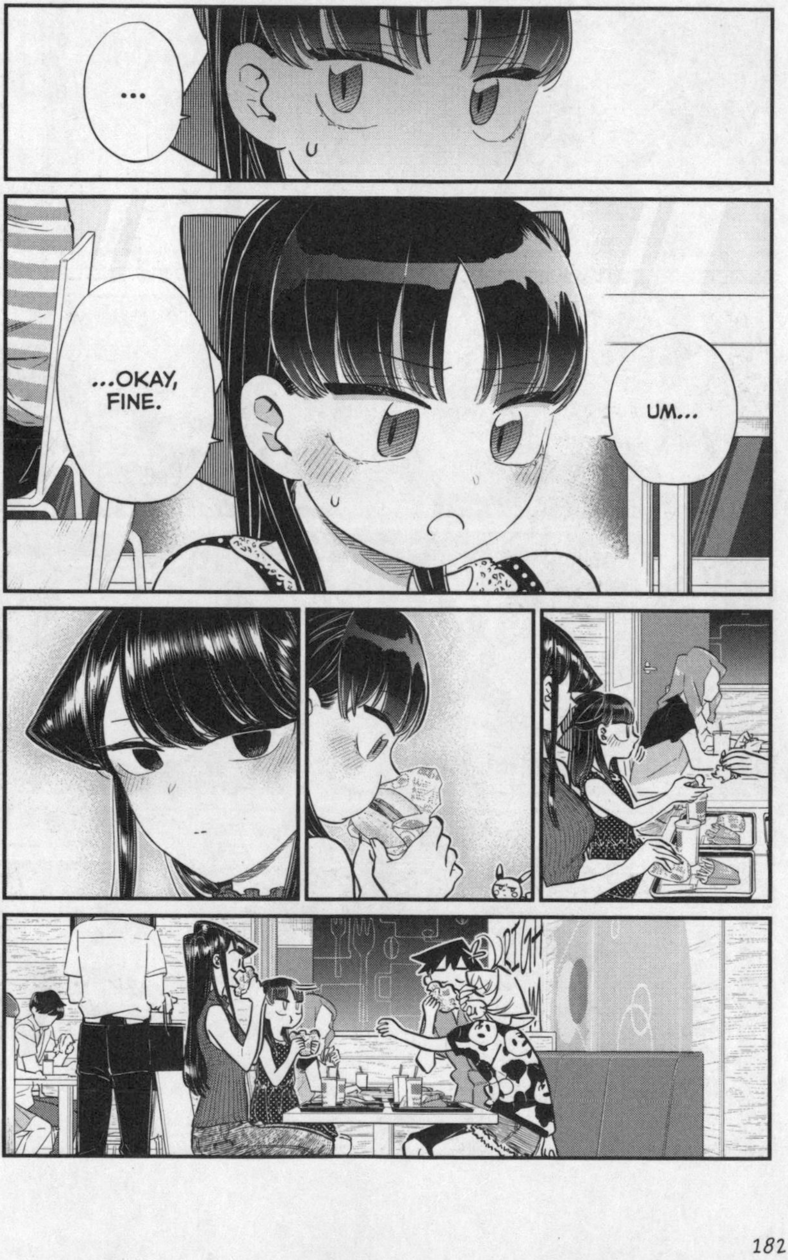
...
UM...
...OKAY, FINE.

Worried they get along better with Rei than she does →

Komi Can't Communicate

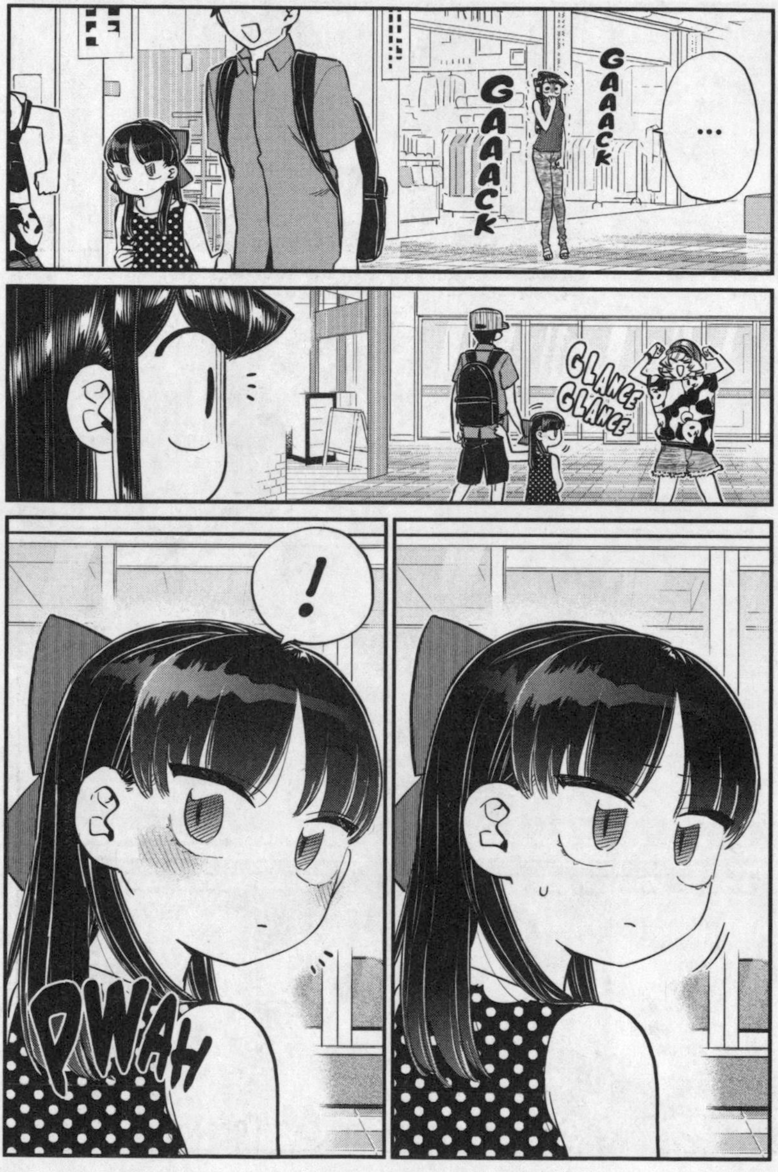
...
GAAACK
GAAACK
GLANCE GLANCE
!
PWAH

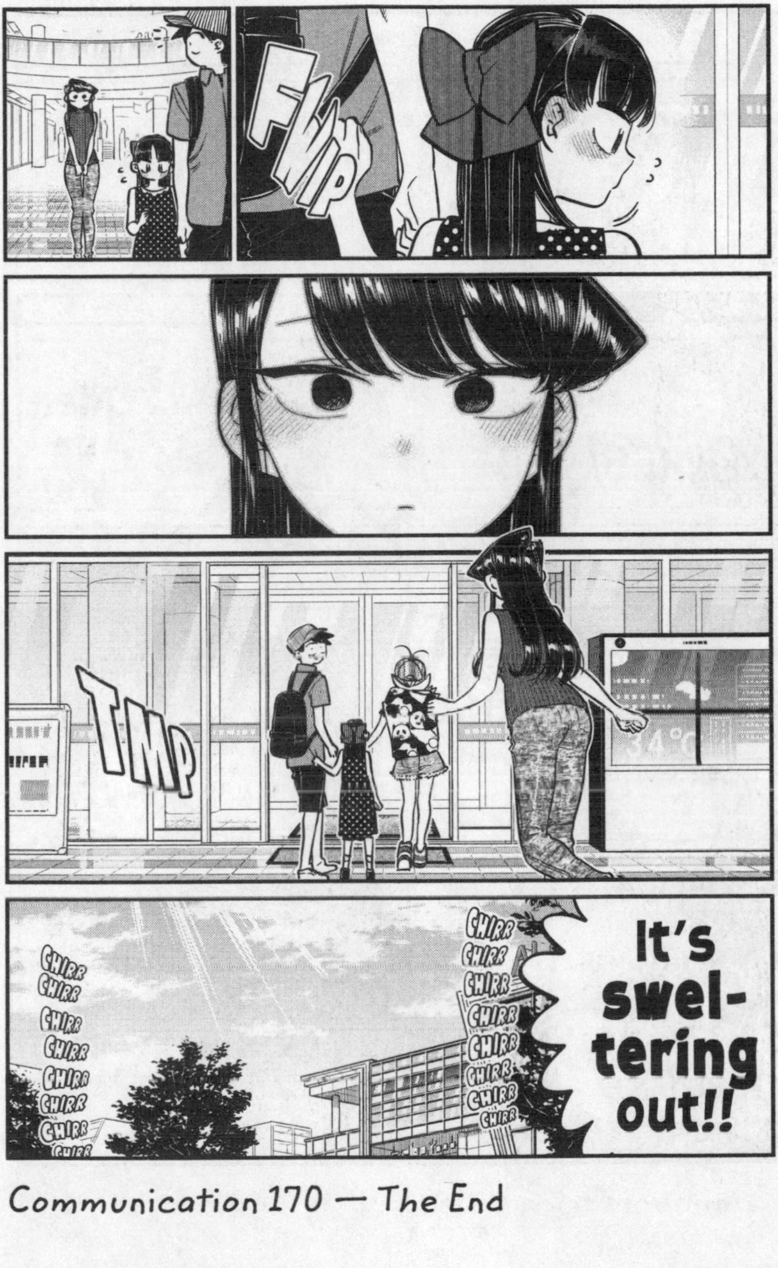
FWIP
TMP
It's swel-
tering
out!!
CHIRR
CHIRR
CHIRR
CHIRR
CHIRR
CHIRR
CHIRR
CHIRR
CHIRR
CHIRR
CHIRR
CHIRR
CHIRR
CHIRR
CHIRR
CHIRR

Communication 170 — The End

Extra

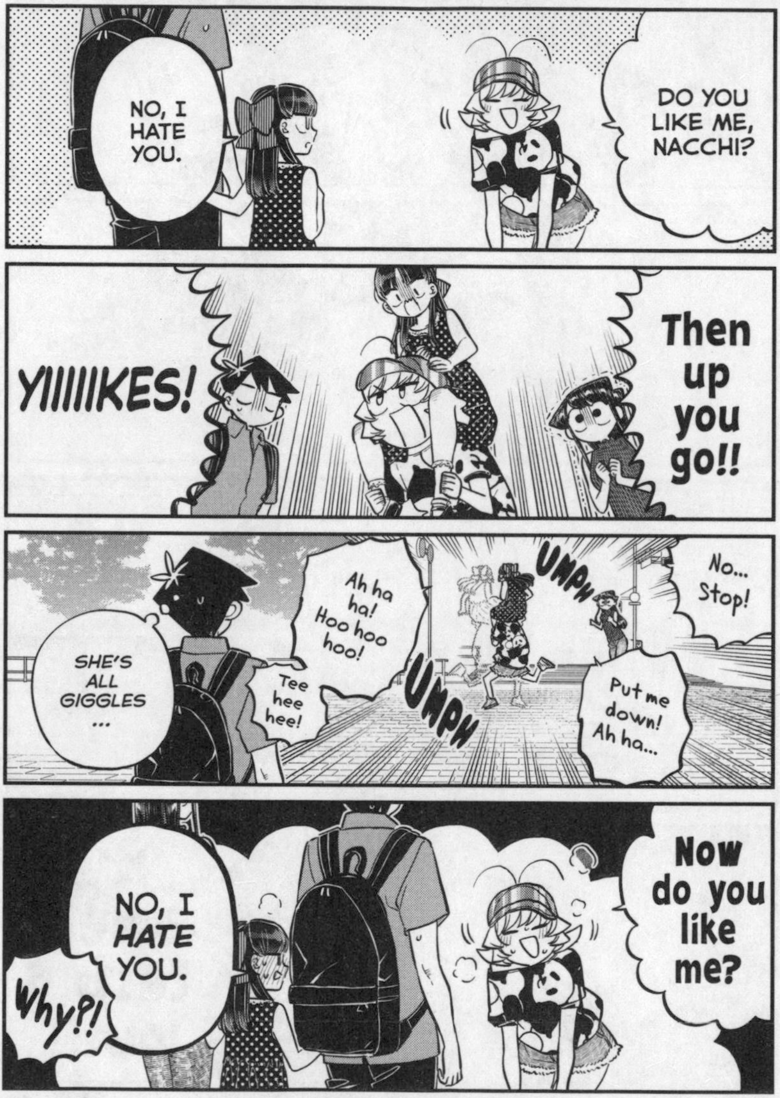
DO YOU LIKE ME, NACCHI?
NO, I HATE YOU.
Then up you go!!
YIIIIIKES!
No... Stop!
UMPH
Put me down! Ah ha...
UMPH
Ah ha ha! Hoo hoo hoo!
Tee hee hee!
SHE'S ALL GIGGLES ...
Now do you like me?
NO, I HATE YOU.
Why?!

Communication Extra — The End

Komi Can't Communicate

Komi Can't Communicate Bonus

"Najimi Rejoices After Exams" Theater

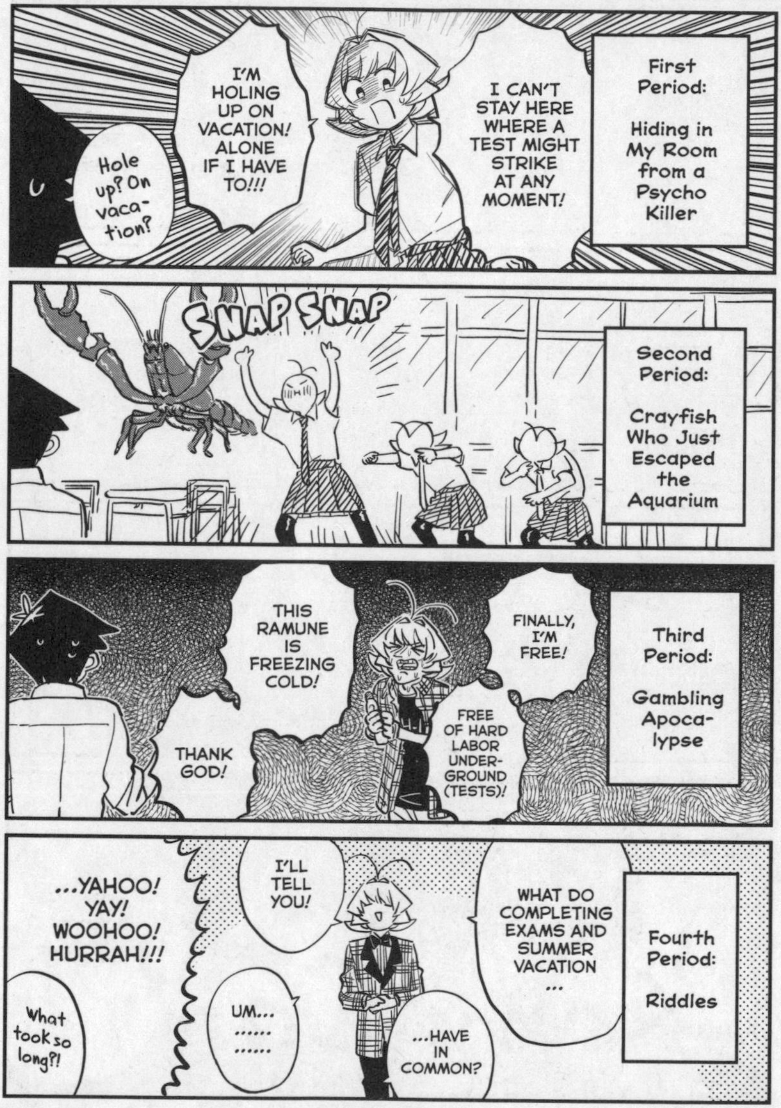
First Period: Hiding in My Room from a Psycho Killer
I CAN'T STAY HERE WHERE A TEST MIGHT STRIKE AT ANY MOMENT!
I'M HOLING UP ON VACATION! ALONE IF I HAVE TO!!!
Hole up? On vacation?
Second Period: Crayfish Who Just Escaped the Aquarium
SNAP SNAP
Third Period: Gambling Apocalypse
FINALLY, I'M FREE!
FREE OF HARD LABOR UNDERGROUND (TESTS)!
THIS RAMUNE IS FREEZING COLD!
THANK GOD!
Fourth Period: Riddles
WHAT DO COMPLETING EXAMS AND SUMMER VACATION...
...HAVE IN COMMON?
I'LL TELL YOU!
UM... ....
...YAHOO! YAY! WOOHOO! HURRAH!!!
What took so long?!

Komi Can't Communicate Bonus

Can Komi Make a Hundred Friends? Frozen Young Soul

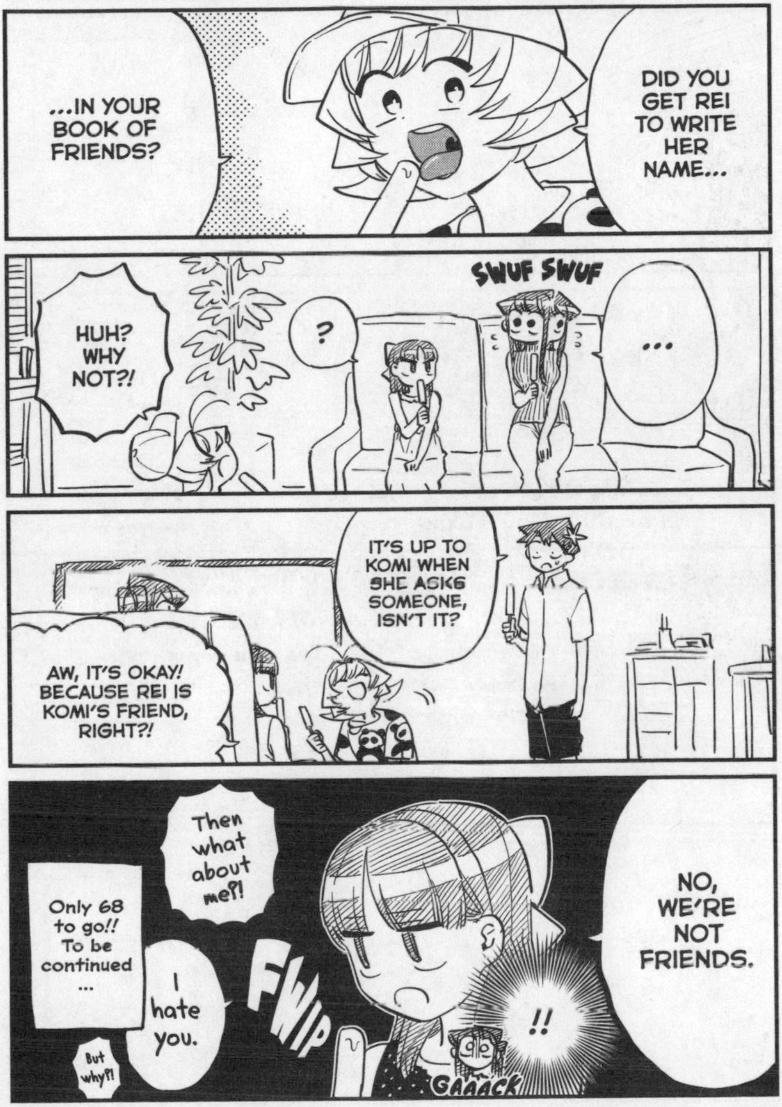
DID YOU GET REI TO WRITE HER NAME...
...IN YOUR BOOK OF FRIENDS?
...
SWUF SWUF
?
HUH? WHY NOT?!
IT'S UP TO KOMI WHEN SHE ASKS SOMEONE, ISN'T IT?
AW, IT'S OKAY! BECAUSE REI IS KOMI'S FRIEND, RIGHT?!
NO, WE'RE NOT FRIENDS.
!!
GAAACK
FWIP
Then what about me?!
I hate you.
Only 68 to go!! To be continued ...
But why?!

Tomohito Oda won the grand prize for *World Worst One* in the 70th Shogakukan New Comic Artist Awards in 2012. Oda's series *Digicon*, about a tough high school girl who finds herself in control of an alien with plans for world domination, ran from 2014 to 2015. In 2015, *Komi Can't Communicate* debuted as a one-shot in *Weekly Shonen Sunday* and was picked up as a full series by the same magazine in 2016.

Komi Can't Communicate

VOL. 12
Shonen Sunday Edition

Story and Art by Tomohito Oda

English Translation & Adaptation/John Werry
Touch-Up Art & Lettering/Eve Grandt
Design/Julian [JR] Robinson
Editor/Pancha Diaz

COMI-SAN WA, COMYUSHO DESU. Vol. 12
by Tomohito ODA
© 2016 Tomohito ODA
All rights reserved.
Original Japanese edition published by SHOGAKUKAN.
English translation rights in the United States of America, Canada, the United
Kingdom, Ireland, Australia and New Zealand arranged with SHOGAKUKAN.

Original Cover Design/Masato ISHIZAWA + Bay Bridge Studio

Printed in Canada

Published by VIZ Media, LLC
P.O. Box 77010
San Francisco, CA 94107

10 9 8 7 6 5 4 3 2 1
First printing, April 2021

viz.com

shonensunday.com

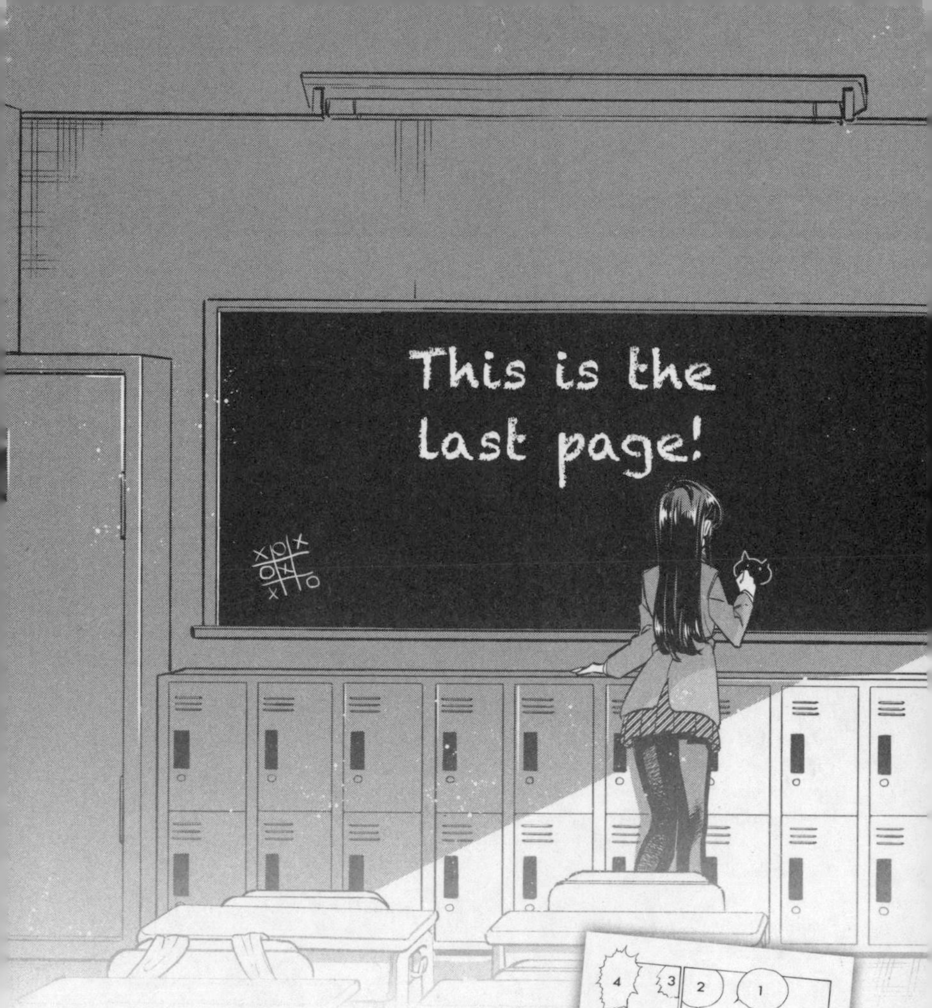
This is the last page!

Komi Can't Communicate has been printed in the original Japanese format to preserve the orientation of the artwork.

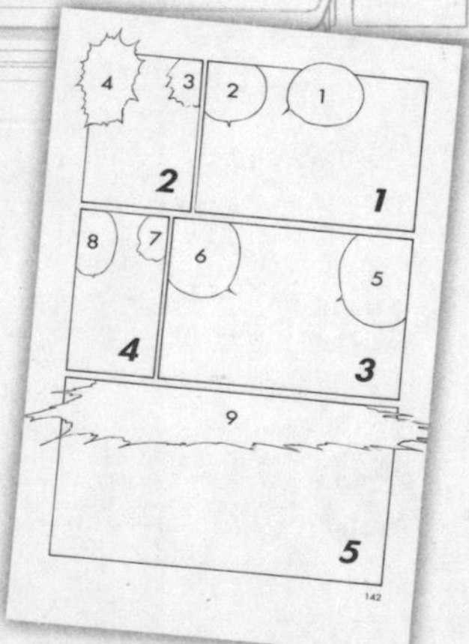
1
2
3
4
5

Follow the action this way.